ALAN LEO'S
DICTIONARY OF ASTROLOGY

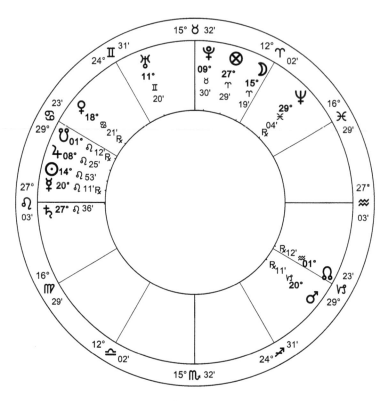

Natal chart of Alan Leo.

Born William Frederick Allen, on August 7, 1860,
5:49 am GMT (approximate), Westminister (London)

ALAN LEO'S
DICTIONARY
OF
ASTROLOGY

Edited by
VIVIAN E. ROBSON, B.Sc.

Price 7/6

Published at
"MODERN ASTROLOGY" OFFICE, IMPERIAL BUILDINGS, LUDGATE CIRCUS, E.C.4
The Trade Supplied by
L. N. FOWLER & CO., 7 Imperial Arcade, London, E.C.4
1929

On the cover: Strasbourg, December 1977

Front, clockwise from the left:
Das Münster, one of a number of 15th century cathedrals that were once
   the "second tallest" buildings in the world. (Second to the Pyramid.)
Ancien hôpital civil
Transept sud de la Münster
A portrait of Alan Leo
Messe de Minuit (midnight mass)

Back cover: Details from Notre Dame de Strasbourg:
Top, left to right: La nef ver l'ouest; les vitraux; le bas-côté sud ver l'est.
Bottom: Details from above the rose window, western façade.

Except for Alan Leo's portrait, all photos by David R. Roell

ISBN: 978 1 933303 42 0

First published in 1929.
This edition, Christmas, 2010.

Published by
Astrology Classics
the publication division of
The Astrology Center of America
207 Victory Lane, Bel Air MD 21014
on line at www.**AstroAmerica**.com

FOREWORD

By the Editor

For many years before his death, Mr. Alan Leo had contemplated the publication of an astrological dictionary, and had arranged and classified much of the material to be used in it. It was originally proposed to issue it as a supplement to *Modern Astrology*, and in this form the whole of the present work as far as the end of the article " Horoscope " appeared in Mr. Leo's lifetime, but for some reason the publication was discontinued and Mr. Leo had two or three copies bound, presumably for his own use. After his death nothing more was thought of the dictionary for over a year, until the incomplete copies were discovered behind a desk where they must have fallen and become wedged. Meanwhile I had begun the publication of a dictionary in *Modern Astrology*, and Mrs. Leo suggested that I should take over Mr. Leo's incompleted manuscript and notes, and finish off the work for publication in book form. Upon further consideration, however, this idea was found to be impracticable, for the result would have been two entirely separate works joined together in the middle, and in which the spirit of Mr. Leo's early work would have been quite lost. It was therefore finally decided that the first half should be reprinted exactly as Mr. Leo left it, and that I should complete the work from his notes and in his own words. This was felt to be the arrangement that would make the greatest appeal to Mr. Leo's countless admirers.

In its present form the book stands entirely to the credit of Mr. Leo. Up to the end of the article " Horoscope," it has had the benefit of his personal supervision, but the remainder is based entirely upon his notes, and in the case of almost every entry is put into his own words. There are barely a dozen lines in the whole book that were not written by him, and it may be looked upon as not only his own selection of material, but also his own method of presentation. The editing of the work has been a great pleasure, and the result will, I trust, afford as much satisfaction to the reader.

V. E. ROBSON.

Selected topics of interest:

See also the complete list of topics, pgs. 206-209

DICTIONARY OF ASTROLOGY

A. THE first letter in the word astrology is the first letter in nearly all the world alphabets. *Aleph*, the first word of the Hebrew alphabet, is symbolised by the bull, and indicates that Taurus is the first of the zodiacal signs, or constellations. A symbolises the one, or the I. This letter has also some affinity with the moon, whose exaltation is the sign Taurus.

AARON'S ROD. Aaron means the Enlightened, a seer, or initiate. The rod, or wand, had a serpent twined around it, and in it was the sacred fire. Aaron, as the first high priest, used the rod in all the great ceremonies of initiation. Its symbology conceals a mystery. Aaron was the brother of Moses the law-giver, and belonged to the tribe of Levi. This tribe was under the sign Sagittarius, and it is probable that the mystery of the rod or wand is concealed in the ninth sign of the Zodiac, which governs religion, prophecy, the Guide or Guru, or new birth.

ABSCISSION OF LIGHT. See FRUSTRATION.

ABERRATION. This word is used in Astronomy. The aberration of a star is that alteration in the apparent position of the star which is produced by the motion of the earth in its orbit and the effect of that motion on the time taken for the light from the star to reach the earth. The motion of the earth across the ray of light causes a slight apparent change in the direction of the latter, and this change of angle is called the aberration of light, to which is due the aberration of the star. The effect of this aberration is to make each star appear annually to describe a minute circle of about $40\frac{1}{2}''$ diameter parallel to the earth's diameter.

ACCIDENTAL DIGNITY. See DIGNITIES.

ACRONICAL. Pertaining to the rising of a star at the time when the sun is setting, or the setting of a star when the sun is rising.

ACTINOLOBA. A ray.

ADEPT. The word means one who has attained. An Astrologer who has completed the science of Astrology is an adept. Properly speaking, an adept is one who, through the development of his spirit, has attained to transcendental knowledge and powers.

ÆON. A vast cycle of time. Valentinus, in the second century taught that in the pleroma (the Gnostic name for the habitation of God) there were thirty æons, fifteen male and fifteen female, and four unmarried : Horus ; Christ ; the Holy Spirit ; and Jesus.

AFFINITY. A binding by mutual attraction. The Sun may be said to have affinity with all the planets. Mars has affinity with Venus in a magnetic or physical sense, but Venus and Jupiter are affinities in the highest sense, also Venus and Mercury.

AFFLICTION. Inharmonious aspects are called afflictions. The angle containing ninety degrees formed by the division of the circle of three hundred and sixty degrees into four, and named a quartile or square aspect, is always considered as evil or an affliction. Saturn, when in discordant aspect, is the primary afflictor, and then Mars. Venus or Jupiter cannot afflict, being benefic planets. The afflicting aspects are the Semi-square, 45° ; Square, 90° ; Sesquiquadrate, 135° ; and the conjunction of a malefic planet. See MALEFICS.

AGNI. The God of Fire. He is one of the three great deities : Agni, Vâyu, and Sûrya. In Agni we have the triple aspect of fire— the fire of the sun, the lightning of the air, and the ordinary fire on earth.

AIR. The gaseous substance which surrounds our globe— the atmosphere.

AIRY SIGNS. These are Gemini, ♊ ; Libra, ♎ ; and Aquarius, ♒. They are the mental or humane signs of the Zodiac, and they form the triangle of harmony, peace, and equilibrium. Many planets or the ruler placed in these signs give humane, refined, and artistic tendencies.

ALCHEMIST. A name given to those who originally sought for hidden spirit concealed in matter. They were the Rosicrucians of the Middle Ages. Their secrets consisted of the transmutation of the gross into the fine, or the animal consciousness into the human, and finally into the spiritual.

ALCHEMY. The Chemistry of Nature. Modern Chemistry bears the same relation to Alchemy as Astronomy to Astrology. The alchemical properties were Sulphur, Mercury, and Salt ; each of which was related to the three great departments of evolution, the cosmic, human, and terrestrial. They rightly believed that there is one universal solvent, and their teachings would be similar to those of the Theosophist of to-day, which assert that there is but One Life, and that we are bathed eternally in that life.

ALCYONE. A fixed star of the third magnitude. It has been said that this is the central Sun of our universe.

ALDEBARAN. A star of the first magnitude. It is remarkable for its brilliancy. It is of the nature of Mars, and shines with a bright red colour. It may easily be found by drawing a line through the three bright stars in the belt of Orion.

ALMANAC. The origin of almanacs goes back to the time of the Alexandrian Greeks. All almanacs were prophetic until the year 1828, and until 1834 the stamp duty upon almanacs was 1s. 3d. per copy. The earliest record dates from the twelfth century, when Solomon Jarchus published his almanac in 1150. Purbach published one from 1450–61, and his pupil Regiomontanus brought out the first printed almanac in 1475, but by far the most wonderful almanac maker of the Middle Ages was the well-known Nostradamus. Astrologers are indebted to the celebrated Astronomer Royal, Neville Maskelyne, D.D., F.R.S., who was born in London, October 6th, 1732, for the Nautical Almanac, which he began in 1767. This most important almanac has been published by the Government every year since that date, and may now be obtained three or four years in advance.

The chief Astrological Almanacs in our modern times are " Raphael's " and " Zadkiel's." " Raphael's " almanac was first published in 1820, and enjoys a circulation of upwards of 200,000, and next in the list is " Zadkiel's," published in 1830, with a sale of upwards of 90,000. Both these almanacs claim to be prophetic, and each year they publish the fulfilled predictions of the former year. See also EPHEMERIS.

ALPHABET OF ASTROLOGY. The alphabet of Astrology is made out of certain symbols, or hieroglyphics, which stand as Ideographs, each conveying the whole meaning of the symbol in itself. With the exception of the five planets, the sun, and the moon, we have but few of the real symbols left to us from the original ideographs, but the whole of the symbols seem to have originated out of the circle, half circle, and cross. See SYMBOLS.

The symbols represent the planets, signs of the Zodiac, and aspects—three distinct groups, which may be termed the letters, words, and sentences. The symbols are as follows :—

Sun, Moon, and Planets.

⊙ Sun	♀ Venus	♄ Saturn
☽ Moon	♂ Mars	♅ Uranus
☿ Mercury	♃ Jupiter	♆ Neptune

To these may be added Vulcan and two other planets yet to be astronomically discovered.

Signs of the Zodiac.

♈ Aries	♋ Cancer	♎ Libra	♑ Capricorn
♉ Taurus	♌ Leo	♏ Scorpio	♒ Aquarius
♊ Gemini	♍ Virgo	♐ Sagittarius	♓ Pisces

Aspects.

⚺ Semi-sextile	✶ Sextile	△ Trine	☍ Opposition
∠ Semi-square	☐ Square	⚼ Sesquiquadrate	☌ Conjunction

Minor Symbols.

⊕ Part of Fortune   ☊ Dragon's head   ☋ Dragon's tail

ALMUTEN. See LORD.

ALTITUDE. The elevation of a heavenly body above the horizon. Meridian altitude is the passing of a planet or star over the Meridian, this being the highest point it can reach.

AMBIENT. Surrounding or encompassing on all sides.

AMPLITUDE. The angular distance from the last point of the heavenly body at the moment of its rising, or from the west point at the instant of its setting.

ANARETA. A term used for description of the planet which destroys form. The killing planet in a nativity, if such a term may be used.

ANAXAGORAS. A famous Ionian philosopher who lived 500 years B.C. He was most learned in astronomy, and was one of the first to explain openly that which was taught by Pythagoras secretly concerning astrology.

ANAXIMANDER. An ancient Astrologer.

ANGELS. The angels of the planets are as follows : Sun, Michael ; Moon, Gabriel ; Mercury, Raphael ; Venus, Anael ; Mars, Samael ; Jupiter, Zadkiel ; Saturn, Cassiel.

ANGLES. The four cardinal points. Also the first, fourth, seventh and tenth houses in the map erected. They are called the Ascendant, the Meridian, Western Angle, and Nadir. They are the most powerful and important houses in Astrology.

ANSATED CROSS. (Crux Ansata.) The handled tau cross, found in the hands of the old Egyptian deities, and always regarded as the symbol of life.

ANTIPATHY. Disharmony of two bodies, which attract or repel by the nature of their different magnetism.

APHELION. The point in a planet's orbit which is most distant from the sun. The nearest point is called the perihelion.

APHETA. The giver or disposer of life in a nativity.

APHORISMS. Short, pithy truths, based upon experience ; sayings of wise men.

APOGEE. The point in a planet's or in the moon's orbit which is most distant from the earth. The nearest point is called the perigee.

APPLYING. A term used to express the formation of an aspect by application. See ASPECTS.

APRIL. The opening month of the year astrologically.

APSIDES. The point of greatest and least distance of a heavenly body from its centre of attraction.

AQUARIUS. The water-carrier. This is the eleventh sign of the zodiac. Its qualities are hot, moist, rational, fixed, humane, diurnal, sanguine, and masculine, of the airy triplicity. This is the day house of Saturn. It is at present thought that Uranus has his greatest influence in this sign, if he is not actually the ruler of it. The Sun appears to enter this about the 22nd of January each year. It is an important and somewhat mystical sign. It governs all things which are artistic and essentially pure and refined. In the human system it governs the legs, ankles, and the blood. It represents that division in the circle which is measured from 300° to 330° out of the 360°. See also SIGNS OF THE ZODIAC.

ARC. Part of a circle.

ARES. The Greek name for Mars, the God of War.

ARIES. The portion of the ecliptic, between 0° and 30° longitude, which the sun enters on the 21st of March (the vernal equinox). It is an equinoctial, cardinal, diurnal, movable, fiery, choleric, hot, dry, and violent sign of the fiery triplicity. It governs the head and face.

ASCENDANT. The eastern angle, or the first house of the nativity or horoscope. The whole of this is considered as the ascendant, but, correctly speaking, it is the degree upon the cusp of the first house, or the portion of the earth that is rising at the time for which a map of the heavens is erected. The ascendant of the horoscope is the vital point, and the sign rising contains the dominant features of the life that is to be expressed, or the question that is to be answered. See RISING SIGN.

ASCENDING. Planets between the fourth house rising eastward to the M.C. are ascending.

ASCENSIONAL DIFFERENCE. The difference between the right and oblique ascensions.

ASCENSION, OBLIQUE. See OBLIQUE ASCENSION.

ASCENSION, RIGHT. The right ascension of a star or point of the sphere is that arc of the equator intercepted between its circle of declination and the vernal equinox or first point of Aries, reckoned towards the east. See RIGHT ASCENSION.

ASPECTS. These are certain numbers of degrees having special natures, each having a quality of its own and known by certain symbols. The circle, or belt of zodiac, contains 360 degrees. If we take any point of this circle and measure off a certain portion we shall obtain what is astrologically known as an aspect. If we start from the first point of Aries and measure to the first point of Taurus we shall obtain a semi-sextile aspect, the symbol for which is made thus ⚺.

The following is the value of each part of the circle of 360°.

30° Thirty degrees   Semi-Sextile Aspect ⚺ ⚹

45°	Forty-five degrees	Semi-Square Aspect	∠
60°	Sixty degrees	Sextile ,,	✶
90°	Ninety ,,	Square ,,	☐
120°	One hundred and twenty degrees	Trine ,,	△
135°	One hundred and thirty-five ,,	Sesquiquadrate ,,	⬓
150°	One hundred and fifty ,,	In conjunct ,,	⊼
180°	One hundred and eighty ,,	Opposition ,,	☍

The quality of the aspects may be judged from the nature of the signs which form the aspect, for instance the trine aspect, △, is formed by signs that are always in harmony, but the square aspect ☐ by signs that are of a different nature, into which all the elements commingle, such as fire, earth, air and water. The term good has been applied to the semi-sextile, sextile, and trine aspects, and evil to the semi-square, square, sesquiquadrate, and opposition.

The conjunction is a position or aspect of two planets in or near the same degree, evil with the malefics and good with the benefics. The planets apply or separate from the complete aspects according to the orbs, etc.

ASTEROIDS. There are over 1,000 small bodies termed planetoids, or minor planets, placed together between Mars and Jupiter. There are many theories in connection with the origin of the asteroids, but nothing is definitely known concerning them so far as the scientific world is concerned.

ASTRAL. A starry luminous ether-like substance, a higher form of matter than that composing the physical earth. In it are reflected the counterparts of the earth, the astral world interpenetrating the physical world.

ASTRAL BODY. The vehicle or luminous body containing the astral soul. It is the seat of the emotions and the desires, as governed by the watery signs.

ASTRAL LIGHT. The invisible region which surrounds our globe. In the astral light is reflected the emotional and mental vibration of the physical man, which eventually precipitates itself upon the earth as fate, etc.

ASTRAL PLANE. The next plane to that of the earth, into which all men pass at what is called death ; it is the home of spirits. On this plane is manifested the desire nature of humanity. When man is free from desire he passes out of the astral plane into higher regions.

ASTROLABE.   An instrument for taking the altitude of a star.

ASTROLATRY.   Worship of the stars.

ASTROLOGY. The science which defines the action of celestial bodies upon human character, and its expression in the physical world. It is the soul of astronomy, and by it the inequalities of humanity are explained.   It shows the working of a definite law by which we may realise that as we sow, we also reap.   Its antiquity is such as to place it among the very earliest records of human learning.   It remained for long ages a secret science in the East, and its final expression remains so to this day.

The science is divided into seven branches. Esoteric, natal, medical, horary, national, astro-meteorological and spiritual, each of which is a special study in itself.   See different headings as enumerated. It is impossible at present to obtain the date when Astrology was first introduced to the world.   It probably reached its zenith two hundred thousand years ago, and it is feasible to suppose that it was first taught by the Manu who had charge of the fourth root-race.

The abuse of the science, by those who practised it solely for personal gain, has introduced so much corruption, that, in the nineteenth century, it may be said that the key to the true Astrology has been lost by all save the Initiate.

ASTRONOMER.   One who classifies the stars.

ASTRONOMOS. The title given to the Initiate in the seventh degree of the reception of the mysteries. The great Astrological Initiation took place in Egypt at Thebes, where the priests thoroughly understood the chemistry of the stars.

ASTRONOMY. Originally Astrology and Astronomy were one science, but the latter now treats of the distances, magnitudes, masses, composition, motions, and all that is discoverable regarding the heavenly bodies. It is founded upon observations made with elaborately-constructed instruments. Astronomy is a purely objective science, concerned as it is with the form or body ; while Astrology may be considered as subjective, dealing with the life within the form. To deny the truth of Astrology is to ignore the existence of the Soul in humanity.

ASTROTHEOLOGY.   Theology founded on what is known of the heavenly bodies and the laws which regulate their movements.

B. The second letter in almost all the alphabets. Its symbol is a *house*, to which it has some faint resemblance.

BAAL. The chief male divinity among the Phœnicians, as Ashtoreth was the leading female one. Baal appears to have symbolised the Sun. In reality the word means simply "Lord," and it has therefore been used by various subdivisions of the race to indicate different deities at the successive periods of their history.

BABYLONIAN. The Babylonians were past masters in Astrology, this being their religion. See CHALDÆANS.

BACON, ROGER. A Franciscan monk, famous as an adept in alchemy and magic arts. His name is often mentioned in connection with Astrology, and he may be said to have been a sincere and firm believer in philosophical Astrology.

BARDESANES. A great astrologer who followed the Eastern Occult system. Porphyry called him the Babylonian. He connected the Soul with the seven stars, deriving its origin from the higher beings (the divine Ego) ; and therefore "admitted spiritual resurrection but denied the resurrection of the body," as charged with by the Church Fathers. Ephraim shows him preaching the signs of the zodiac, the importance of the birth hours, and "proclaiming the seven." Calling the Sun "Father of life" and the Moon the "Mother of life," he shows the latter "laying aside her garments of light (principles) for the renewal of the earth."

BARREN SIGNS. Gemini ♊, Leo ♌, and Virgo ♍, are said to be barren signs.

BASSANTIN, JAMES. A Scotch astrologer. He lived in the 16th century, and is said to have predicted to Sir Robert Melville, in 1562, the death of Mary, the unfortunate Queen of Scots, and all the events connected therewith.

BEL. The oldest and mightiest God of Babylonia—in reality another form of Baal.

BESTIAL SIGNS. Aries ♈, Taurus ♉, Leo ♌, Sagittarius ♐, and Capricorn ♑.

BELTS, JUPITER'S. A varying number of dusky belt-like bands or zones encircling the planet Jupiter parallel to his equator, as if the clouds of his atmosphere had been forced into a series of parallels through the rapidity of his rotation, and the dark body of the planet was seen through the comparatively clear spaces between.

BENEFICS. The two benefic planets are Venus and Jupiter.

BENEFIC ASPECTS. These are the trine, sextile, and semi-sextile.

BENEFIC INFLUENCES. These are produced by the benefic planets and aspects in the nativity, or by transits, etc.

BESIEGED. A planet between two malefics is besieged; it is always considered a very evil position. A planet between Mars and Saturn is evilly besieged, but when between Venus and Jupiter it is extremely good.

BI-CORPORAL SIGNS. These are Gemini ♊, Sagittarius ♐ and Pisces ♓; the term now generally used is double-bodied signs.

BIRTH-MARK. All birth-marks and blemishes upon the body at birth are supposed to correspond with the planetary position at the birth-time.

BIRTH-TIME. The moment the first breath is drawn at an infant's birth into the physical world. Every student or believer in Astrology should make it a rule to tabulate the birth-time of all the members of the family.

BI-QUINTILE. An aspect of the planets first noted by Kepler. This occurs when two planets are distant from each other 144°. It is generally considered a weak aspect, but benefic in its influence.

BITTER SIGNS. The fiery signs are said to be hot and *bitter*.

BLACK-DEATH. The name given to a deadly epidemic which broke out in Dublin, in March, 1866. The name arose from the dark blotches which came out upon the skin of the sufferers. It is worth putting this fact upon record, owing to the positions of the planets at that time; Mars was in the sign Aquarius, which rules the blood, and passed from the square aspect of Saturn, who was retrograde in Scorpio, the opposite side to that governing Ireland, to the parallel of this major malefic. This name also applied to an epidemic which ravaged England in the fourteenth century.

BOÖTES. The northern constellation which contains the splendid star Arcturus; the handle of the Plough points toward it.

BOREAL SIGNS. The six northern signs, ♈,♉, ♊, ♋, ♌, ♍.

BRAHMA. The first person in the Hindu triad, the others being Vishnu and Shiva. The first has been spoken of as the Creator, the second as the Preserver, and the third as the Destroyer.

BRAHMAN. The impersonal, supreme, and uncognisable Principle of the Universe, from the essence of which all emanates, and into which all returns.

BRAHMANASPATI. The planet Jupiter ; a deity in the *Rig-Veda*, known exoterically as Brihaspati, whose wife Târâ was carried away by Soma (the Moon).

BUDDHA. Esoterically connected with the planet Mercury, meaning the enlightened and wise ; one who has attained perfect wisdom. Gautama, the " Buddha," was one. He is a perfect example of a divine godly man. His is the only *absolutely bloodless* religion, tolerant and liberal, teaching universal compassion and charity, love and self-sacrifice, poverty and contentment with one's lot, whatever it may be. No persecutions, and enforcement of faith by fire and sword, have ever disgraced it ; should the simple, humane and philosophical code of daily life left to us by the greatest Man-Reformer ever known, come to be adopted by mankind at large, then indeed an era of bliss and peace would dawn on Humanity.

BULL. The constellation Taurus.

BULL-WORSHIP. A form of worship connected with generative creation. It ceased over 3,000 years ago, but the worship of the lamb and ram still continues. The worship of the Bull was connected with Osiris, the Sun-God.

C. CACODEMON. The word signifies an evil spirit, or elemental. It has been used in connection with the twelfth house, because it was considered to correspond with the nature of this house, but in modern Astrology the word is no longer used. Although it is true that the twelfth may be considered an evil house, it is not because this house is possessed with evil elementals, but owing to the fact that in natal Astrology this is the house of self-undoing. The apex of occultism is represented in Astrology by the fourth house, and the twelfth and eight houses are at its base.

CADENT. Those houses which fall from the angles are called cadent houses ; they are the third, sixth, ninth, and twelfth. These positions are said to be weak. In horary Astrology planets in these positions cause delays, etc.

CADUCEUS. This is a cosmical, sidereal, or astronomical, as well as a spiritual and even physiological symbol, its significance changing with its application. Originally it was a triple-headed serpent, but now it is a rod with two serpents twined round it, the rod of Mercury.

It represents the fall of primary matter into the grosser terrestrial. Astronomically, the head and tail represent the points of the ecliptic, where the planets and even the Sun and Moon meet in close embrace. See AARON'S ROD.

CALENDAR. The register of the days, weeks, and months of the year.

CANCER. The fourth sign of the zodiac. The Sun enters this sign on June 21st ; it occupies a place in the ecliptic between 90 and 120 from the vernal equinox. The constellation Cancer is situated between the Twins and the Lion ; it contains no star brighter than the third magnitude. Cancer is a watery and cardinal sign, and governs the breast (magnitude).

CAPELLA. A star remarkable for its brilliancy, in the constellation Auriga. It may be found nearly midway between Orion and the Pole-star, but nearer the latter.

CAPRICORN. The tenth sign of the zodiac, by nature earthy and cardinal. It is the sign of the winter solstice into which the Sun enters about December 21st.

> " And, what was ominous, that very morn
> The Sun was entered into Capricorn."—DRYDEN.

Capricornus, or Makara, was considered on account of its hidden meaning the most important of the constellations, but its mysteries are known to none save the adept.

CAPUT DRACONIS. The dragon's head, ♌.

CARDAN, JÉROME. An astrologer, alchemist, mystic, and kabbalist. He was born at Pavia, September 24th, 1501, and died at Rome, on September 21st, 1576.

CARDINAL POINTS. The east, west, north, and south. Also the 1st, 4th, 7th, and 10th houses, called the angles.

CARDINAL SIGNS. These are Aries, ♈ ; Cancer, ♋ ; Libra, ♎ ; and Capricorn, ♑.

CASTING THE HOROSCOPE. The term used by astrologers to imply that the necessary calculations are to be made previous to judgment, or the delineations. See HOROSCOPE.

CASTOR AND POLLUX. The two bright and conspicuous stars in the constellation Gemini.

CAUDA DRACONIS. The dragon's tail, ☋.

CAZIMI. A term used to describe a planet that may be placed within seventeen minutes (17′) of the Sun's body ; it is then said to be in the heart of the Sun, and well fortified.

CAZOTTE, JACQUES. The astrologer who predicted the beheading of several royal personages, and also his own decapitation, at a gay supper some time before the first Revolution in France.

CECCO D'ASCOLÎ. Surnamed "Francesco Stabili." The most famous astrologer of the 13th century. He was burnt alive by the Inquisition in 1327. A work of his, published at Basle in 1485, and called *Commentarii in Spheram Joannis de Sacrabosco*, is still extant.

CENTAURUS. One of the constellations in the southern hemisphere.

CEPHEUS. A constellation lying between Cassiopeia and Draco.

CERES. The first discovered of the Asteroids.

CHALDÆANS. The Chaldæans were first a tribe, but later they were magians of Babylonia, astrologers and diviners. We know very little of the Chaldæan astrology to-day, but we may gather some idea of their teachings from the Chaldæan Oracles. Astrology with them was a religion, but it was Astrology of a type far different from that which has come down to modern times. The Chaldæan priests were especially famous in Astrology. They held that the world was eternal, having neither beginning nor end ; they maintained however, that all things were ordered, and the fabric of the universe was supported by Divine providence. They called the Sun, Mars, Venus, Mercury, and Jupiter "interpreters," as being principally concerned in making known the will of God to man. From the motions and regularity of the heavenly bodies, they inferred that they were either themselves intelligent beings, or each under a presiding intelligence. Hence arose Sabianism, or the worship of the host of heaven. The highest object of their worship was the Sun, called Belus, and to him was erected the tower of Belus, and the image of Belus. But they did not worship the stars as God, they thought of Him as too great to be concerned with mundane affairs ; but they worshipped those whom they believed He had appointed as governors in the starry host, looking on them as mediators between God and man. Their true religion was a belief in the one impersonal, universal, deific Principle, which they never mentioned by any name. They erected huge temples of peculiar construction, specially adapted for star worship, etc.,

B

in which they healed the sick, and performed certain magical ceremonies.

Another of their gods was named Nebo, to whom were erected temples and statues. The following is one of the inscriptions that was found on the pedestals of two of the colossal statues :

" To the god Nebo, guardian of the mysteries, the director of the stars, the supreme chief . . . . the protector, the director of the shining works, the surveyor of the legions of the heavens and of the earth ; the teacher of those who bless his name, and who listen attentively to him ; he who holds the table of destinies ; he who presides at the rising and the setting of the sun ; he who marks time ; the glorifier of Nel ; the lord of lords ; whose power is immutable, and for whom the heaven was created, the conqueror, the august one, the guardian, whose guardianship is good. Whoever thou mayest be, thou who wilt live after me, have confidence in Nebo, and in no other God."

The Chaldæans alleged in the time of Alexander the Great, B.C. 356, that their Astrology had existed 473,040 years.

CHALDÆAN ORACLES. The Chaldæans had an Oracle which they venerated as highly as the Greeks did that at Delphi. The Oracles urged men to devote themselves to things divine, and not to give way to the promptings of the irrational soul. " Although destiny, our destiny, may be written in the stars, yet it was the mission of the divine soul to raise the human soul above the circle of necessity, and the Oracles gave victory to that masterly will."

Much, if not all, of the true Chaldæan teaching may be found in Theosophy to-day, its teachings with regard to karma and re-incarnation being identical ; all astrologers who are desirous of understanding the Chaldæan mysteries will find their time profitably employed in a thorough study of Theosophy.

CHANCE. Nothing happens by chance according to astrological rules, all being governed by a law so perfect that chance can have no place in it ; that which appears to happen by chance can be traced to this law by all astrologers who know the inner meaning of planetary conditions, for they are students of the evolution of the life as well as the form.

CHANGEABLE SIGNS. The cardinal signs are also considered changeable.

CHARACTER. The most important feature of Astrology is its description of the character, and as character is destiny, no definite or correct prediction can be made as to the future of the life under consideration until the character of the nativity is fully understood. Character in itself is the accumulated result of aggregated experiences in the past, and there are no two characters alike, the experiences of the past being different. All the planets contribute their share in forming, or to use a better term, in representing the character. Mars gives strength, energy, and courage. Saturn indicates stability, patience, perseverance, and industry, giving seriousness, contemplation, and meditation. Venus describes the love nature, giving mirthfulness and harmlessness. Mercury governs the intellectual side of the character. Jupiter rules over the benevolent and compassionate side, bringing out the religious and social qualities. The Sun governs the moral side and indicates the amount of firmness and dignity, and the Moon governs the animal and instinctual side of the character. The sign that is rising at birth will describe the general tendency of the character, also the signs that the majority of the planets occupy at the time.

CHAVIGNY. A disciple of the famous Nostradamus. He left a precious manuscript on the pre-natal and post-natal influence of the stars on certain individuals, a secret revealed to him by his teacher.

CHEMISTRY. Each of the chemical elements is governed by its planet, and the examination of this forms a separate study known as occult chemistry, or alchemy.

CHRISTIAN ASTROLOGY. The name given to a book written by Wm. Lilly.

CHRONOCRATORS. The markers of time. It is supposed that the Moon rules the first four years of life, Mercury the next ten, and so on, according to the following table ;

Planet.	Period	Motion per year	per month.
Moon	4 years	90°	7° 30'
Mercury	10 ,,	36°	3°
Venus	8 ,,	45°	3° 45'
Sun	19 ,,	19°	1° 35'
Mars	15 ,,	24°	2°
Jupiter	12 ,,	30°	2° 30'
Saturn	30 ,,	12°	1° 0'
Uranus	90 ,,	4°	20'
Neptune	184 ,,	2°	10'

There is also the following :

Table for calculating the duration
of the life according to the
position of the planets in the Radix

P.	HOUSES OF ANGLES	SUCCEED-ENT HOUSES	CADENT HOUSES
♄	57	43½	30
♃	79	57	10
♂	62	40	13
☉	120	69½	19
♀	80	44	7
☿	70	48	20
☽	108	63	24

which may be used as follows : Saturn in an angle, the period of year will generally be fifty-seven years ; if cadent then only thirty years ; but the Hyleg should be first studied. See also HYLEG.

CIRCLE. The circumference of the zodiac, containing 360 degrees.

CLAIRAUDIENCE. A faculty, or higher sense, coming under the rule of Saturn, whereby the hearing is extended to whatever distance it is desired.

CLAIRVOYANCE. Extended vision, or the faculty of seeing with the inner eye, through and beyond the densest matter, irrespective of time. As the sight is governed by Mercury it may be considered as a future sense, or what may be termed a soul sense.

CLIMACTERICAL PERIODS. Every seventh and ninth year is considered a climacterial period in Astrology, owing to the Moon's position in the radix ; every 7th day, or year, she squares her own place, and every 9th day, or year, forms the trine aspect, and from this the following become the climaterical years : the 7th, 9th, 14th, 18th, 21st, 27th, 28th, 35th, 36th, 42nd, 45th, 49th, 51th, 56th, and 63rd years.

COLD PLANETS AND SIGNS. These are Saturn and the Moon, Capricorn and Cancer.

COLLECTION OF LIGHT. A term used in Horary Astrology with regard to a planet receiving the aspects of any two planets that are not in aspect themselves.

COLOURS OF THE PLANETS. The latest tabulation is as follows :—
Sun, gold. Moon, silver, or shot violet. Mercury, orange and shot lemon. Mars, scarlet red and shot crimson. Venus, sky blue to green. Jupiter, violet with white splashes. Saturn, green to grey. Uranus, deep rich blue. Neptune, indigo blue. It will of course be understood that these are simply the symbolical colours assigned to the various planets and signs, and in no way correspond with the colours of the physical planets as seen in the sky.

COLOURS OF THE SIGNS. Aries, white and red. Taurus, red mixed with citron. Gemini, red and white mixed. Cancer, green. Leo, red and gold. Virgo, brown spotted with blue. Libra, blue and dark crimson. Scorpio, dark brown. Sagittarius, light green and blue. Capricorn, very dark brown and dark grey. Aquarius, sky blue. Pisces, glistening white.

COMBUST. Within 8° 30′ of the Sun. It is said that a planet so placed is burnt up, and that its influence is nil, or destroyed. In all horary considerations combustion should be taken to imply that the planet so placed is unusually weak.

COMETS. Luminous bodies, either wandering through space from Sun to Sun, or circulating around our Sun in a very elongated orbit. They are visible to us only when they approach the Sun, and usually consist of three elements, nucleus, envelope, and tail. When seen they have been considered as omens of evil by those who were not conversant with their nature.

COMMON SIGNS. Gemini, Virgo, Sagittarius, and Pisces. These are also the dual, or as they have been called, double-bodied signs.

They are also the active signs of the zodiac, particularly Gemini and Sagittarius.

CONCEPTIVE SIGNS.   Taurus, Leo, Scorpio, and Aquarius.

CONCEPTION.   See PRE-NATAL EPOCH.

CONFIGURATION.   The relative positions of the planets, a term used in connection with the horoscope, as indicating the planetary positions at birth, or at the time of taking the figure.

CONJUNCTION.   When two planets are in the same degree of longitude they are in exact conjunction.   It is usual to allow a distance of five degrees on either side, some astrologers taking the orbs of the planets, and when one planet is within the orb of another then they are said to be in conjunction ; the nearer they are together the stronger the effect of the conjunction.

CONJUNCTION PARTILE.   When two planets are in the same degree and minute.   PLATIC.   When two planets are within half orbs.

CONSTELLATIONS.   The ancient twelve constellations were the now twelve signs of the zodiac, but are in no way connected with these signs excepting by name.   There were originally forty-eight constellations, but many have since been added, making in all eighty-three.   There is much confusion in the minds of many students as to the real difference between the signs and the constellations.   See SIGNS OF THE ZODIAC.

CONVERSE.   A term used in connection with the direction of the planets and the M.C., meaning from east to west astrologically. Instead of moving the mid-heaven forward from west to east, it is directed backward toward the west, and this is called converse motion. This term is also used, when, owing to the earth's diurnal motion, a planet appears to move from east to west.

CO-SIGNIFICATOR.   A term used in horary astrology.

COPERNICAN SYSTEM.   A system attributed to Copernicus, based on the conception that the Sun was the centre of the solar system ; it was anticipated, however, by Pythagoras, who taught the helio-centric system of astronomy.   It has been the practice of those imperfectly informed to contend that the present system of astrology is false owing to this fact, but this is not the case ; if we were mani-festing our consciousness upon the sun, then a heliocentric system of Astrology would probably be needed, if required at all ; but we are here upon this earth incased in matter, and dependent upon our physical vehicle for experience, hence we must study the influences as they play upon the earth, and believing, as we do, that the planets have some correspondence with our vehicles and states of consciousness, we cannot do better than deal with the earth as our centre of observation, while we still remember that it is not the centre of the solar system any more than that our real centre of consciousness belongs to matter.

CORRECTIONS. Correction has always to be made between sidereal and mean time, so that the correct right ascension of the midheaven may be obtained ; the following is a table of corrections :

TABLE OF CORRECTION BETWEEN MEAN AND SIDEREAL TIME.

HOURS.		MINUTES.				SECONDS.				
Meantime.	Correction.	Meantime	Correction.	Meantime.	Correction.	Meantime.	Correction.	Meantime.	Correction.	Example.
H.	M. S.	M.	S.	M.	S.	S.	S.	S.	S.	
1	0 9.86	1	0.16	31	5.09	1	.00	31	.09	
2	0 19.71	2	0.33	32	5.26	2	.00	32	.09	
3	0 29.57	3	0.49	33	5.42	3	.01	33	.09	To the sidereal time given for noon
4	0 39.43	4	0.66	34	5.58	4	.01	34	.09	in the nautical almanac, or Ephemeris for the year required ; add or deduct the
5	0 49.28	5	0.82	35	5.75	5	.01	35	.10	difference between mean and sidereal
6	0 59.14	6	0.99	36	5.91	6	.02	36	.10	times as follows :—
7	1 9.00	7	1.15	37	6.08	7	.02	37	.10	Napoleon III. was born in Paris at
8	1 18.85	8	1.31	38	6.24	8	.02	38	.10	0hr. 44min. a.m. April 20th, 1808. The birth time being before noon the sidereal
9	1 28.71	9	1.48	39	6.41	9	.02	39	.11	time should be taken for the previous
10	1 38.57	10	1.64	40	6.57	10	.03	40	.11	noon.
11	1 48.42	11	1.81	41	6.73	11	.03	41	.11	H. M. S.
12	1 58.28	12	1.97	42	6.90	12	.03	42	.11	s. T. April 19, 1808 . . . . Add time elapsed . . . 12 44 0
13	2 8.13	13	2.14	43	7.06	13	.04	43	.12	Correction for 12hrs. . . 1 58.28
14	2 17.99	14	2.30	44	7.23	14	.04	44	.12	,, ,, 44min. . . 7.23
15	2 27.85	15	2.46	45	7.39	15	.04	45	.12	Corrected s.t. . . . 14 35 44.51
16	2 37.70	16	2.63	46	7.56	16	.04	46	.13	
17	2 47.56	17	2.79	47	7.72	17	.05	47	.13	Now, there is a correction to be made for longitude. Paris is 2° 20′ east of
18	2 57.42	18	2.96	48	7.88	18	.05	48	.13	Greenwich, which turned into time is
19	3 7.27	19	3.12	49	8.05	19	.05	49	.13	9 mins. 20secs. The correction for 9′ 20″
20	3 17.13	20	3.28	50	8.21	20	.05	50	.14	is 1.53″, and time being east of Green-
21	3 26.99	21	3.45	51	8.38	21	.06	51	.14	wich, this must be deducted from the
22	3 36.84	22	3.61	52	8.54	22	.06	52	.14	s.t. as follows :—
23	3 46.70	23	3.78	53	8.71	23	.06	53	.15	H. M. S.
		24	3.94	54	8.87	24	.07	54	.15	s.t. . . . . . 14 35 44.51 Corr. for Long. . 1.53
		25	4.11	55	9.03	25	.07	55	.15	
N.B.—If making		26	4.27	56	9.20	26	.07	56	.15	True Dis. Time . 14 35 42.98
the correction be-fore noon deduct,		27	4.43	57	9.36	27	.07	57	.16	
and if after noon add. If the time is		28	4.60	58	9.53	28	.08	58	.16	N.B.—When the longitude is west the
a.m. always add to the sidereal time		29	4.76	59	9.69	29	.08	59	.16	correction for longitude must be added to the sidereal time, but when east sub-
at previous noon. See example.		30	4.93	60	9.86	30	.08	60	.16	tracted.

CRITICAL DAY. See CLIMACTERICAL PERIODS.

CULMINATION. The arrival of a planet at the mid-heaven.

CUSP. The beginning of the house ; the degrees upon the house mark the commencement of the cusp. All planets in the same sign of a less number of degrees than that upon the cusp of the house are not in that particular house until they have passed this number of degrees. If at the time of birth or the erection of a map of the heavens ten degrees of Aries was rising, then this would mark the cusp of the ascendant.

CYCLE. An imaginary orb, or circle in the heaven. A cycle marks the return of the planets to their own places, each of the planets having a cycle or revolution of its own. The cycle of the Moon is nineteen years, of the Sun twenty-eight years. The following from *Kabalistic Astrology* is useful :

CYCLE OF SATURN.

Saturn	-	-	1765	1772	1779	1786	1793	1800
Jupiter	-	-	1766	1773	1780	1787	1794	
Mars	-	-	1767	1774	1781	1788	1795	
Sun	-	-	1768	1775	1782	1789	1796	
Venus	-	-	1769	1776	1783	1790	1797	
Mercury	-	-	1770	1777	1784	1791	1798	
Moon	-	-	1771	1778	1785	1792	1799	

CYCLE OF VENUS.

Venus	-	-	1801	1808	1815	1822	1829	1836
Mercury	-	-	1802	1809	1816	1823	1830	
Moon	-	-	1803	1810	1817	1824	1831	
Saturn	-	-	1804	1811	1818	1825	1832	
Jupiter	-	-	1805	1812	1819	1826	1833	
Mars	-	-	1806	1813	1820	1827	1834	
Sun	-	-	1807	1814	1821	1828	1835	

CYCLE OF JUPITER.

Jupiter	-	-	1837	1844	1851	1858	1865	1872
Mars	-	-	1838	1845	1852	1859	1866	
Sun	-	-	1839	1846	1853	1860	1867	
Venus	-	-	1840	1847	1854	1861	1868	
Mercury	-	-	1841	1848	1855	1862	1869	
Moon	-	-	1842	1849	1856	1863	1870	
Saturn	-	-	1843	1850	1857	1864	1871	

CYCLE OF MERCURY.

Mercury	-	-	1873	1880	1887	1894	1901	1908
Moon	-	-	1874	1881	1888	1895	1902	
Saturn	-	-	1875	1882	1889	1896	1903	
Jupiter	-	-	1876	1883	1890	1897	1904	
Mars	-	-	1877	1884	1891	1898	1905	
Sun	-	-	1878	1885	1892	1899	1906	
Venus	-	-	1879	1886	1893	1900	1907	

D. DAY HOUSES. The positive signs of the zodiac are the day houses of the planets, as follows : Aries, day house of Mars ; Gemini, of Mercury ; Libra, of Venus ; Sagittarius, of Jupiter ; and Aquarius, of Saturn. The external expression of the planets is stronger in these houses ; for instance, the force of Mars in Aries is more mental, being expressed externally through the mind, but Mars expressed through generation, taking time for maturity.

DAILY MOTION. The planets have an average daily motion as follows : Saturn 2'. Jupiter 5'. Mars 32'. The Moon 13°. The Sun, Venus, and Mercury 1°. The exact daily motion of the Sun, Moon, and planets may be found by subtracting their longitude on the day required, using the ephemeris for that date, from the positions at the previous noon. When found, the hourly motion may be obtained from the following table :

Day Per Hr. Degrees or Minutes ″ ‴	Day Hour ° ′ ″ ′ ″ ‴	Day Hour ° ′ ″ ′ ″ ‴	Day Hour ° ′ ″ ′ ″ ‴
1 2.30	16 40. 0	31 77.30	46 115. 0
2 5. 0	17 42.30	32 80. 0	47 117.30
3 7.30	18 45. 0	33 82.30	48 120. 0
4 10. 0	19 47.30	34 85. 0	49 122.30
5 12.30	20 50. 0	35 87.30	50 125. 0
6 15. 0	21 52.30	36 90. 0	51 127.30
7 17.30	22 55. 0	37 92.30	52 130. 0
8 20. 0	23 57.30	38 95. 0	53 132.30
9 22.30	24 60. 0	39 97.30	54 135. 0
10 25. 0	25 62.30	40 100. 0	55 137.30
11 27.30	26 65. 0	41 102.30	56 140. 0
12 30. 0	27 67.30	42 105. 0	57 142.30
13 32.30	28 70. 0	43 107.30	58 145. 0
14 35. 0	29 72.30	44 110. 0	59 147.30
15 37.30	30 75. 0	45 112.30	60 150. 0

Example.—If we find the Sun moving 1° per day, and the time for which we want to find the Sun's position is 6 p.m., we refer to the figure 6, and opposite we find 15, which is 15' per 6 hours, and should be added to the longitude at noon. Again, if Mars be moving 28' per day, and the time for which his true longitude is required be 6 a.m., then look in the column for 28' and we find 70″, which is 1' 10″ per hour multiplied by 6, gives 7', which is to be deducted from noon longitude.

DEATH. See TERMINUS VITÆ.

DEBILITIES. A planet in a weak or afflicted position is termed debilitated.

DECANATES. Each sign of thirty degrees is divided into three separate portions of ten degrees each, which are then called decanates.

The following is the substance of the symbology of the decanates published in the *Brihat Jataka*, a work on Hindu Astrology :

First decanate of Aries, 0° to 10°.—Mars is its lord. It represents a man having a white cloth tied round his loins, facing a person, as if able to protect him, holding an axe in his hand. His eyes are red, and he is of fearful appearance ; his countenance is black.

Second decanate ♈, 10° to 20°.—Sun. A female fond of sweetmeats and ornaments ; she is very corpulent, rests upon one foot, and her features resemble those of a horse.

Third decanate ♈, 20° to 30°.—Jupiter. A wicked man, learned in arts, holding a stick in his hand, raised. He fails to carry out the objects of his work. He is in red attire, and looks very angry.

First decanate of Taurus, 0° 10°.—Venus. A female with hair cut short and curled. She is corpulent, her clothes are burnt, and she is very thirsty, fond of food and ornaments.

Second decanate ♉, 10° to 20°.—Mercury. A man with the face of a ram, and the full Taurus neck ; he is skilful in connection with agriculture, also in various arts. He is dressed in dirty garments, and has full bibacity.

Third decanate ♉, 20° to 30°.—Saturn. A man with a body resembling that of an elephant ; he has large, white teeth.

First decanate of Gemini, 0° to 10°.—Mercury. A beautiful woman fond of needlework and decorations. She is childless, and very amorous with her arms.

Second decanate ♊, 10° to 20°.—Venus. A man with the face of a *Garuda* (eagle or vulture). He wears a coat of mail, and is standing in a flower-garden armed with bow and arrows. His meditations are directed to sport, children, ornaments and wealth.

Third decanate ♊, 20° to 30°.—Saturn. A man decorated with many ornaments, and possessing many gems ; he is clad in armour, and is learned in all the various arts ; is also a writer.

First decanate of Cancer, 0° to 10°.—The Moon. An animal

with the body of an elephant and huge feet, a boar's head and a horse's neck, upholding leaves, roots, and fruit.

Second decanate ♋, 10° to 20°—Mars. A female in the prime of youth, wearing lotus flowers upon her head. She is standing in a forest, against the branch of a tree, with a serpent by her side.

Third decanate ♋, 20° to 30°.—Jupiter. A man in a sailing boat. He is decorated with ornaments, and has serpents entwined about him. He is sailing in search of ornaments for his wife.

First decanate of Leo, 0° to 10°. The Sun. A vulture and jackal seated on a cotton tree ; a dog is near, and a man in poor attire lamenting for his parents.

Second decanate ♌, 10° to 20°.—Jupiter. A man formed like a horse ; a garland of white flowers is borne upon the head, and he is covered with a deer-skin. He is unconquerable like the lion, and is armed with a bow ; he has a hook nose.

Third decanate ♌, 20° to 30°.—Mars. A man with the head of a bear, with a long curled beard, in disposition like the monkey ; he is armed with a club, and is carrying fruits and flesh.

First decanate of Virgo, 0° to 10°.—Mercury. A virgin carrying a vase filled with flowers ; her garments are soiled. She is fond of dress and wealth ; she goes towards her teacher.

Second decanate ♍, 10° to 20°.—Saturn. A dark man with a cloth round his head, who holds a pen in his hand, and is casting up accounts and expenditure ; beside him is a bow ; he is covered with hair.

Third decanate ♍, 20° to 30°.—Venus. A fair woman dressed in white silk ; she is pure, and is devoutly going toward the temple carrying in her hands a jar and ladle.

First decanate of Libra, 0° to 10°.—Venus. A man holding a balance in one hand. He is skilled in weighing and measurements, and his mind is fixed upon the value of articles which he is carrying.

Second decanate ♎, 10° to 20°.—Saturn. A man with the head of a vulture ; he is carrying a water-pot ; he is hungry and thirsty. His thoughts are directed towards his wife and children.

Third decanate ♎, 20° to 30°.—Mercury. A man like an ape carrying a golden bow and arrow ; he is wearing a coat of mail, and is adorned with gems. He stands in the forest scaring animals.

First decanate of Scorpio, 0° to 10°.—Mars. A beautiful woman who is nude and without ornaments. She has fallen from her place, and is quitting the ocean, and around her feet are serpents.

Second decanate ♏, 10° to 20°.—Jupiter. A woman of rotund body, her form entwined with serpents ; preparing comforts for her husband.

Third decanate ♏, 20° to 30°.—The Moon. A lion guarding a country abounding with sandal trees. He is terrifying animals.

First decanate of Sagittarius, 0° to 10°.—Jupiter. A man with the body of a horse, holding a bow, and guarding articles of sacrifice.

Second decanate ♐, 10° to 20°.—Mars. A beautiful woman, with golden complexion, sitting on a throne picking up gems.

Third decanate ♐, 20° to 30°.—The Sun. A man with long whiskers and a beard of golden colour ; he is seated upon a throne, holding a staff in his hand, and is dressed in white silk and deer-skin.

First decanate of Capricorn, 0° to 10°.—Saturn. A man with a deformed face and terrible aspect ; he has the hairy body of a hog, having huge tusks ; he holds a yoke and fetters.

Second decanate ♑, 10° to 20°.—Venus. A woman skilled in the fine arts ; has large dark eyes ; she is decorated with metallic ornament.

Third decanate ♑, 20° to 30°.—Mercury. A human figure with the head of a horse ; clothed in woollen cloth, carries a quiver, bow and armour, and bears upon his shoulder a jar adorned with gems.

First decanate of Aquarius, 0° to 10°.—Saturn. A man with the face of a vulture ; he is clothed in silk and deer-skin ; his mind is engaged in seeking oil, spirits, water, and food.

Second decanate ♒, 10° to 20°.—Mercury. A woman clad in soiled apparel, seated in a burnt car, bearing vessels upon her head.

Third decanate ♒, 20° to 30°.—Venus. A man of dark complexion and hairy ears, wearing a crown. He carries from one place to another, metal, bark, leaves, gum and fruit.

First decanate of Pisces.—Jupiter. A man bearing the vessels of sacrifice. He navigates the sea in search of ornaments for his wife ; he is laden with pearls, gems, and shells.

Second decanate ♓, 10° to 20°.—The Moon. A pretty woman of splendid complexion ; she is in a ship decorated with flags ; she approaches the shore, accompanied by her friends.

Third decanate ♓, 20° to 30°.—Mars. A naked man with a serpent coiled around him ; he is on the brink of a cavern in a forest, tormented by thieves, fire, and hunger. See also FACES OF THE ZODIAC.

DECEMBER. The month in which, about the 21st, the sun reaches the sign Capricorn.

DECLINATIONS. The angular distance of a star, or planet, north or south of the equator. The sun is never more than 23° 28' of declin., which occurs when passing through Cancer or Capricorn. The following are the tables of declination :—

DEGREES OF NORTH LATITUDE. (VIRGO / ARIES)

VIRGO D.	0° D.	M.	1° D.	M.	2° D.	M.	3° D.	M.	4° D.	M.	5° D.	M.	6° D.	M.	7° D.	M.	ARIES °
0	11	29	12	24	13	20	14	16	15	12	16	8	17	4	18	0	30
1	11	8	12	4	13	0	13	56	14	51	15	47	16	43	17	39	29
2	10	46	11	42	12	38	13	33	14	29	15	25	16	21	17	17	28
3	10	25	11	21	12	17	13	12	14	8	15	4	16	0	16	56	27
4	10	3	10	59	11	55	12	51	13	47	14	43	16	39	16	35	26
5	9	41	10	39	11	35	12	30	13	26	14	22	15	18	16	14	25
6	9	19	10	15	11	11	12	6	13	2	13	58	14	54	15	50	24
7	8	57	9	53	10	49	11	44	12	40	13	35	14	31	15	26	23
8	8	35	9	31	10	27	11	22	12	18	13	13	14	9	15	4	22
9	8	12	9	8	10	4	10	59	11	54	12	49	13	44	14	39	21
10	7	50	8	46	9	41	10	36	11	31	12	26	13	21	14	16	20
11	7	27	8	22	9	17	10	12	11	7	12	2	12	57	13	52	19
12	7	5	8	0	8	55	9	50	10	45	11	40	12	35	13	30	18
13	6	41	7	36	8	31	9	26	10	21	11	16	12	11	13	6	17
14	6	18	7	13	8	8	9	3	9	58	10	53	11	48	12	43	16
15	5	55	6	51	7	46	8	41	9	36	10	31	11	26	12	21	15
16	5	32	6	28	7	23	8	18	9	13	10	8	11	3	11	58	13
17	5	8	6	4	6	59	7	54	8	49	9	44	10	39	11	34	13
18	4	45	5	41	6	36	7	31	8	26	9	21	10	16	11	11	12
19	4	21	5	17	6	12	7	7	8	2	8	57	9	32	10	47	11
20	3	58	4	54	5	49	6	44	7	39	8	34	9	29	10	24	10
21	3	34	4	30	5	25	6	20	7	15	8	10	9	5	10	0	9
22	3	11	4	7	5	2	5	57	6	52	7	47	8	42	9	37	8
23	2	47	3	43	4	38	5	33	6	28	7	23	8	18	9	13	7
24	2	23	3	19	4	14	5	9	6	4	6	59	7	54	8	49	6
25	2	0	2	55	3	50	4	45	5	40	6	35	7	30	8	25	5
26	1	36	2	31	3	26	4	21	5	16	6	11	7	6	8	1	4
27	1	12	2	7	3	2	3	57	4	52	5	47	6	42	7	37	3
28	0	48	1	48	2	43	3	38	4	33	5	23	6	18	7	13	2
29	0	24	1	19	2	14	3	9	4	4	4	59	5	54	6	49	1
30	0	0	0	55	1	50	2	45	3	40	4	35	5	30	6	25	0

SOUTH.

DEGREES OF NORTH LATITUDE. (LIBRA / PISCES)

LIBRA D.	0° D.	M.	1° D.	M.	2° D.	M.	3° D.	M.	4° D.	M.	5° D.	M.	6° D.	M.	7° D.	M.	PISCES D.
0	0	0	0	55	1	50	2	45	3	40	4	35	5	30	6	25	30
1	0	24	0	31	1	27	2	21	3	16	4	11	5	6	6	1	29
2	0	48	0	7	1	3	1	57	2	52	3	47	4	42	5	37	28
3	1	12	0	17	0	39	1	34	2	29	3	24	4	19	5	14	27
4	1	36	0	41	0	15	1	10	2	5	3	0	3	55	4	50	26
5	2	0	1	5	0	10	0	46	1	41	2	36	3	31	4	26	25
6	2	23	1	28	0	33	0	22	1	17	2	12	3	7	4	2	24
7	2	47	1	52	0	57	0	2	0	53	1	48	2	43	3	34	23
8	3	11	2	15	1	21	0	26	0	29	1	25	2	20	3	15	22
9	3	34	2	36	1	44	0	49	0	6	1	2	1	57	2	52	21
10	3	58	3	3	2	8	1	13	0	18	0	38	1	33	2	28	20
11	4	21	3	26	2	31	1	36	0	41	0	14	1	9	2	4	19
12	4	45	3	50	2	55	2	0	1	5	0	10	0	46	1	41	18
13	5	8	4	13	3	18	2	23	1	28	0	33	0	24	1	18	17
14	5	32	4	37	3	42	2	46	1	51	0	56	0	0	0	55	16
15	5	55	5	0	4	5	3	9	2	14	1	18	0	23	0	32	15
16	6	18	5	23	4	27	3	31	2	36	1	40	0	45	0	9	14
17	6	41	5	45	4	50	3	43	2	59	2	3	1	8	0	13	13
18	7	5	6	9	5	14	4	18	3	23	2	27	1	32	0	36	12
19	7	27	6	31	5	36	4	40	3	45	2	49	1	54	0	58	11
20	7	50	6	54	5	58	5	2	4	6	3	10	2	15	1	19	10
21	8	12	7	16	6	20	5	24	4	28	3	32	2	36	1	41	9
22	8	35	7	39	6	43	5	47	4	51	3	56	3	0	2	4	8
23	8	57	8	1	7	5	6	9	5	13	4	18	3	22	2	27	7
24	9	19	8	23	7	27	6	31	5	35	4	40	3	45	2	49	6
25	9	41	8	45	7	49	6	53	5	58	5	2	4	6	3	10	5
26	10	3	9	7	8	11	7	15	6	19	5	24	4	28	3	32	4
27	10	25	9	30	8	34	7	38	6	42	5	46	4	50	3	54	3
28	10	46	9	51	8	55	8	1	7	7	4	8	5	12	4	16	2
29	11	8	10	13	9	17	8	21	7	24	6	29	5	32	4	36	1
30	11	29	10	33	9	37	8	41	7	44	6	48	5	52	4	56	0

NORTH. SOUTH.

Declinations

DECLINATION.

Top table — CAPRICORN / SAGITTARY

CAPRICORN M.D. 1830	7° M.D. 1713	6° M.D. 1614	5° M.D. 1515	4° M.D. 1516	3° M.D. 1217	2° M.D. 1118	1° M.D. 1019	0° D.D. 020 (SAGITTARY)
3129	3013	2914	2715	2616	2517	2418	2319	120
4328	4213	4114	3915	3816	3717	3618	3519	220
5527	5413	5314	5215	5016	4917	4818	4719	320
626	514	315	216	117	018	5919	5819	420
1625	1514	1415	1416	1217	1118	1019	920	521
2624	2514	2515	2516	2317	2218	2119	2020	621
3623	3514	3515	3416	3317	3218	3119	3020	721
4422	4414	4315	4416	4317	4218	4119	4020	821
5421	5414	5315	5316	5217	5118	5019	4920	921
320	215	216	117	118	019	5920	5820	1021
1219	1115	1116	1117	1018	919	820	721	1122
2018	1915	1916	1917	1818	1619	1620	1521	1222
2817	2615	2616	2617	2518	2519	2420	2321	1322
3416	3315	3316	3317	3218	3219	3120	3021	1422
3915	3815	3816	3817	3718	37	37	3721	1522
4614	4515	4516	4517	4018	4419	4420	4421	1622
5213	5115	5116	5117	5018	5019	5020	5021	1722
5812	5715	5716	5717	5618	5619	5620	5621	1822
211	216	217	218	119	120	121	122	1923
510	516	517	518	519	520	521	522	2023
99	916	917	918	919	920	1921	1922	2123
87	1316	1317	1318	1319	1320	1620	1620	2223
76	1616	1617	1618	1619	1620	1717	1717	2323
65	1916	1918	1919	1919	1920	2022	2022	2443
5	2216	2217	2218	2219	2220	2221	2222	2523
254	2516	2517	2518	2518	2519	2520	2622	2623
263	2616	2616	2617	2618	2619	2620	2622	2723
272	2716	2717	2718	2718	2719	2720	2822	2823
281	2816	2817	2818	2818	2819	2820	2822	2923
28	2816	2817	2818	2818	2819	2820	2822	3023

Bottom table — AQUARIUS / SCORPIO

SCORPIO D.D. 011	0° M.D. 2910	1° M.D. 33	2° M.D. 37	3° M.D. 41	4° M.D. 45	5° M.D. 49	6° M.D. 53	7° M. 5730 (AQUARIUS)
111	5010	5410	58 18	2	67	105	144	1829
211	1111	1510	1819	22	269	297	325	3628
311	3211	4511	4818	43	477	508	544	5827
411	5211	5610	5810	1	5	87	126	1626
512	1212	1611	1910	22	267	297	336	3625
613	3212	3611	3910	42	469	498	526	5524
713	5212	5611	5911	210	68	117	117	1423
814	1113	1412	1711	2010	238	268	297	3222
914	3113	3412	3711	4010	438	469	498	5221
1014	5013	5312	5611	5911	29	510	37	1120
1115	914	1213	1512	1811	2110	2310	2611	2919
1215	2714	3013	3312	3611	3910	419	449	4718
1315	4517	4713	5012	5311	5610	5810	5811	417
1416	315	514	813	1112	1411	1611	1911	2216
1516	2115	2314	2613	2912	3211	3411	3710	4015
1616	3915	4414	4413	4612	4911	5110	5410	5714
1716	5615	5815	312	613	612	811	1111	1413
1817	1316	1515	1814	2013	2212	2411	2710	3012
1917	2916	3116	3614	3514	3713	3912	4210	4511
2017	4616	4815	5414	5414	5713	5612	5911	110
2118	217	416	615	814	1013	1212	1511	179
2218	1717	1916	2315	2514	2614	2613	2311	308
2318	3317	3316	3615	3814	4013	4113	4311	457
2418	4817	5216	5414	5614	5714	5713	5912	66
2519	21	616	815	1015	1114	1113	1512	55
2619	1718	1917	2016	2215	2414	2513	2713	2912
2719	3118	3317	3616	3715	3714	3913	4012	4212
2819	4418	4517	4716	4915	5114	5113	5213	5412
2919	5718	5817	5917	215	116	414	5	518
3020	1019	1118	1217	1417	1616	1515	1614	1813

DECLINATION.

Top table (LEO / TAURUS)

TAURUS

DEGREES OF SOUTH LATITUDE.

	0°	1°	2°	3°	4°	5°	6°	7°	

LEO

Bottom table (CANCER / GEMINI)

GEMINI

DEGREES OF SOUTH LATITUDE.

	0°	1°	2°	3°	4°	5°	6°	7°	

CANCER

DECLINATION.

Top table — Signs Libra / Pisces (South)

Degrees of South Latitude.

Piscis M.D.	7° M.D.	7° D.	6° M.D.	6° D.	5° M.D.	5° D.	4° M.D.	4° D.	3° M.D.	3° D.	2° M.D.	2° D.	1° M.D.	1° D.	0° M.D.	0° D.	Libra D.
25 30	30	6	30	5	35	4	40	3	45	2	50	1	55	1	0	0	0
49 29	55	6	55	6	59	4	4	4	9	3	14	2	19	1	24	0	1
13 28	18	7	18	6	23	5	33	4	38	3	43	3	48	1	48	1	2
37 27	42	7	42	7	47	5	52	5	57	4	3	4	7	2	12	1	3
1 26	6	8	6	7	11	6	16	5	21	4	26	4	31	2	36	2	4
25 25	30	8	30	8	35	6	40	6	45	5	50	5	55	3	0	2	5
49 24	54	8	54	8	59	6	28	6	38	5	14	5	19	3	23	2	6
13 23	18	9	18	9	23	7	52	6	57	5	38	5	43	3	47	2	7
37 22	42	9	42	9	47	7	15	7	25	6	57	5	7	4	11	3	8
0 21	5	10	5	10	10	8	39	7	49	6	25	6	30	4	34	3	9
24 20	29	10	29	10	34	8	2	8	44	6	49	6	54	4	58	3	10
47 19	52	10	52	10	57	8	26	8	12	7	12	7	17	5	21	4	11
11 18	16	11	16	11	21	9	49	8	36	7	36	7	41	5	45	4	12
34 17	39	11	39	11	44	9	13	9	0	8	59	7	4	6	8	5	13
58 16	3	12	3	12	8	10	36	9	23	8	23	8	28	6	32	5	14
21 15	26	12	26	12	31	10	0	9	46	8	46	8	51	6	55	5	15
43 14	48	12	49	12	54	10	58	10	9	9	10	8	13	7	18	6	16
6 13	11	13	11	13	16	11	21	10	22	9	27	8	36	7	41	6	17
30 12	35	13	35	13	40	11	45	11	49	9	49	9	0	8	4	7	18
52 11	57	13	57	13	2	12	6	11	13	10	23	9	22	8	27	7	19
16 10	21	14	21	14	26	12	31	11	36	10	46	9	46	8	50	7	20
39 9	44	14	44	14	49	13	54	12	59	11	55	10	8	9	12	8	21
4 8	9	15	9	15	13	14	18	13	22	11	17	10	31	9	35	8	22
26 7	54	15	54	15	35	14	40	13	44	12	38	11	53	9	57	8	23
50 6	18	16	18	16	58	14	3	14	6	13	0	12	15	10	19	9	24
14 5	16	16	15	16	14	15	26	14	30	13	20	13	39	10	41	9	25
35 4	39	16	39	16	13	16	13	15	14	14	13	13	59	11	3	10	26
56 3	0	17	0	17	35	16	40	15	34	14	38	13	21	11	25	11	27
17 2	26	17	26	17	14	16	5	16	33	13	0	13	42	12	46	11	28
39 1	50	17	50	17	54	16	12	16	56	14	20	14	4	13	8	12	29
0 0	14	18	14	17	8	17	16	16	16	15	14	14	24	13	29	12	30

NORTH   SOUTH

Bottom table — Signs Aries / Virgo (North)

Degrees of South Latitude.

Aries M.D.	7° M.D.	7° D.	6° M.D.	6° D.	5° M.D.	5° D.	4° M.D.	4° D.	3° M.D.	3° D.	2° M.D.	2° D.	1° M.D.	1° D.	0° M.D.	0° D.	Virgo D.
57 30	29	5	29	4	36	6	41	7	21	8	17	9	13	10	8	10	0
36 29	28	5	28	5	28	6	0	7	0	8	55	9	51	9	46	9	1
16 28	27	4	27	5	46	5	38	6	34	7	34	8	30	9	25	8	2
54 27	26	3	26	4	24	5	15	6	11	7	11	8	7	8	3	8	3
32 26	25	3	25	4	2	5	53	5	9	5	49	7	45	7	41	7	4
10 25	24	2	24	3	49	4	35	5	31	6	27	5	31	6	27	5	6
49 24	23	2	23	3	27	4	9	5	9	5	5	5	9	6	5	5	7
26 23	22	1	22	2	3	4	47	4	45	5	43	4	45	5	41	4	8
4 22	21	1	21	2	32	3	24	4	20	5	20	4	16	5	12	4	9
41 21	20	1	20	2	10	3	2	3	58	5	58	4	54	5	50	3	10
19 20	59	0	59	1	49	2	46	2	42	3	42	3	38	4	27	3	11
59 19	36	0	27	1	23	2	23	2	18	3	18	3	16	3	5	2	12
36 18	13	0	3	1	59	1	2	2	55	2	55	2	52	3	41	2	13
13 17	9	0	40	0	36	1	36	1	31	2	31	2	28	2	23	2	14
9 16	32	0	18	0	14	1	13	1	9	1	8	2	5	1	0	0	15
55 14	45	0	56	0	51	0	46	1	42	3	37	3	31	4	32	5	16
19 13	23	0	33	0	28	0	23	0	18	3	13	3	9	4	8	4	17
41 12	0	0	14	0	5	0	0	0	55	2	50	2	45	3	45	3	18
10 11	45	0	41	1	41	0	36	0	31	1	26	1	22	2	21	2	19
52 10	23	0	18	0	18	0	13	0	9	1	8	1	5	1	58	0	20
52 10	2	1	0	1	6	1	49	1	44	2	42	1	39	2	34	3	21
15 9	25	2	34	2	29	1	26	2	21	3	18	3	16	2	11	3	22
38 8	48	3	47	3	53	1	2	2	57	3	55	3	52	1	47	2	23
2 7	12	3	21	3	17	2	22	3	41	2	33	2	28	1	23	2	24
26 6	36	4	35	3	36	2	46	3	8	2	10	1	5	1	0	0	25
50 5	0	0	34	3	3	3	10	2	44	3	15	0	41	0	36	1	26
14 4	14	0	34	4	34	3	21	3	11	3	39	0	17	0	12	1	27
37 3	37	0	47	4	47	3	57	2	57	2	3	0	7	0	48	0	28
2 2	2	0	21	5	21	4	41	3	41	2	27	1	31	0	24	0	29
25 0	25	0	35	5	35	4	45	3	45	2	50	1	55	0	0	0	30

c

DECLINATION.

Capricorn / Sagittary — Degrees of South Latitude

CAPRICORN D.D.	7° M.D.	6° M.D.	5° M.D.	4° M.D.	3° M.D.	2° M.D.	1° M.D.	0° M.D.	SAGITTARY D.D.
9 30	0 26	2 26	4 25	5 24	6 23	8 22	10 21	0 20	0 20
13 29	14 27	16 26	17 25	18 24	19 23	20 22	23 21	1 20	1 20
25 28	26 27	28 26	29 25	30 24	31 23	32 22	35 21	2 20	2 20
38 27	39 27	40 26	41 25	42 24	43 23	44 22	37 21	3 20	3 20
50 26	51 27	52 26	53 25	54 24	55 23	56 22	59 21	4 20	4 20
2 25	3 28	4 27	5 26	6 25	7 24	8 22	9 22	5 21	5 21
13 24	14 28	15 27	16 26	17 25	18 24	19 23	20 22	6 21	6 21
25 23	25 28	27 27	26 26	28 25	29 24	30 23	30 22	7 21	7 21
35 22	35 28	35 27	36 26	38 25	39 24	40 23	40 22	8 21	8 21
42 21	44 28	44 27	45 27	47 25	48 24	49 23	49 22	9 21	9 21
52 20	53 28	54 27	54 27	55 25	57 24	58 23	58 22	10 21	10 22
2 19	3 29	4 28	5 27	6 26	6 25	7 24	7 23	11 22	11 22
10 18	11 29	12 28	13 27	14 26	14 25	14 24	15 23	12 22	12 22
18 17	19 29	20 28	21 27	22 26	22 25	23 24	23 23	13 22	13 22
27 16	28 29	28 28	28 27	29 26	29 25	30 24	30 23	14 22	14 22
34 15	35 28	35 28	35 27	36 26	36 25	37 24	37 23	15 22	15 22
41 14	48 29	42 28	42 28	43 26	43 25	44 24	44 23	16 22	16 22
48 13	50 29	50 28	50 27	50 26	50 25	50 24	50 23	17 22	17 22
44 12	56 29	56 28	56 27	56 26	56 25	56 24	56 23	18 22	18 22
0 11	0 30	0 29	0 29	1 27	1 26	1 25	1 24	19 23	19 23
5 10	5 30	5 29	5 29	5 27	5 26	5 25	5 24	20 23	20 23
9 9	9 30	9 29	9 29	9 27	9 26	9 25	10 24	21 23	21 23
13 8	13 30	13 29	13 29	13 27	13 26	13 25	13 24	22 23	22 23
16 7	16 30	16 29	16 29	16 27	16 26	16 25	17 24	23 23	23 23
19 6	19 30	19 29	19 29	19 27	19 26	19 25	20 24	24 23	24 23
22 5	22 30	22 29	22 29	22 27	22 26	22 25	22 24	25 23	25 23
24 4	24 30	24 29	24 29	24 27	24 26	24 25	24 24	26 23	26 23
26 3	26 30	26 29	26 29	26 27	26 26	26 25	26 24	27 23	27 23
27 2	27 30	27 29	27 29	27 27	27 26	27 25	27 24	28 23	28 23
29 1	29 30	29 29	29 29	29 27	29 26	29 25	29 24	29 23	29 23
29 0	29 30	29 29	29 29	29 27	29 26	29 25	29 24	30 23	30 23

Aquarius / Scorpio — Degrees of South Latitude

SCORPIO D.D.	0° M.D.	1° M.D.	2° M.D.	3° M.D.	4° M.D.	5° M.D.	6° M.D.	7° M.D.	AQUARIUS D.D.
0 11	29 12	24 13	20 14	20 14	16 15	12 16	8 17	4 18	0 30
1 11	50 12	45 13	41 13	41 14	37 15	33 16	30 17	26 18	22 29
2 12	11 13	6 14	2 14	2 15	58 15	54 16	51 17	47 18	43 28
3 12	32 13	27 14	23 15	23 15	19 16	15 17	12 18	8 19	4 27
4 12	52 13	47 14	43 15	43 15	39 16	35 17	32 18	28 19	24 26
5 13	12 14	7 15	3 16	3 16	0 16	56 17	53 18	49 19	45 25
6 13	32 14	27 15	23 15	23 16	19 17	15 18	12 19	8 20	5 24
7 13	52 14	47 15	43 16	43 17	40 17	36 18	33 19	29 20	26 23
8 14	11 15	6 16	3 17	3 18	56 18	53 18	50 19	50 20	47 22
9 14	31 15	26 16	22 17	22 18	18 19	16 19	13 20	10 21	7 21
10 14	50 15	45 15	41 16	41 17	38 18	35 19	32 20	29 21	26 20
11 15	9 16	4 17	1 17	1 18	58 18	55 19	52 20	49 21	46 19
12 15	27 16	23 17	20 18	20 18	1 22	14 20	11 21	8 22	5 18
13 15	45 16	41 16	38 17	39 18	56 18	33 20	30 21	27 22	24 17
14 16	3 17	0 17	57 17	57 18	51 20	51 20	49 21	46 22	43 16
15 16	21 17	18 18	16 18	15 19	20 20	9 21	7 22	4 23	1 15
16 16	39 17	35 18	33 18	33 19	20 20	27 21	25 22	23 23	19 14
17 17	56 17	52 18	50 19	50 19	47 20	44 21	42 22	39 23	36 13
18 17	13 18	9 19	7 20	7 21	5 21	0 22	57 23	26 22	54 12
19 17	29 18	26 19	24 20	24 20	21 21	17 22	17 23	22 24	11 11
20 17	46 18	43 19	41 20	38 20	20 21	34 22	7 22	4 23	28 10
21 18	2 18	35 17	57 19	55 20	53 21	51 22	51 23	49 24	46 9
22 18	17 19	56 17	13 21	1 22	1 22	7 24	5 24	20 26	3 8
23 18	33 19	31 20	29 21	27 22	22 22	23 23	23 24	25 25	19 7
24 18	44 19	46 20	44 21	42 21	51 22	38 24	38 24	46 26	34 6
25 19	57 20	43 19	59 21	57 22	55 23	50 25	2 26	0 26	49 5
26 19	17 20	14 21	13 22	55 22	9 24	9 24	8 25	6 26	4 4
27 19	31 20	28 21	27 22	1 22	23 23	22 24	20 26	20 26	18 3
28 19	44 20	42 21	41 22	27 22	37 22	37 25	34 26	34 26	32 2
29 19	57 20	56 21	54 22	42 22	51 24	50 25	48 26	48 26	46 1
30 20	10 21	8 22	6 23	5 24	5 24	2 26	2 26	0 26	29 0

DECREASING IN LIGHT. The Moon passing from the full to the conjunction is decreasing in light. The same remark applies to the other planets. This is supposed to be a sign of weakness ; by this rule sinister aspects are not so powerful as the dexter.

DECUMBITURE. A scheme of the heavens erected for the time when persons take to their bed at the commencement of any sickness, by which the prognostics of their recovery or death are discovered.

DEGREE. The 360th part of the circle of the Zodiac, which contains 360 degrees ; its symbol is marked thus : °. Each degree contains sixty minutes, and each minute sixty seconds.

DEGREE RISING. The exact degree of the Zodiac rising at the time of birth is the most important point in the whole of the nativity. Its value should be discovered and fully ascertained, for it has a distinct colour and number, and corresponds to a peculiar vibration of its own, and to that particular sound those to whom it belongs will respond. See RISING SIGN.

DELINEATION. The reading of the map of the heavens at birth, in which the judgment is contained, or the reading of the nativity.

DESCENDANT. The seventh house, or western angle ; that part which is opposite to the ascendant.

DESCRIPTIONS. The sign rising generally describes the person to whom the figure relates. The following are the most reliable personal descriptions :—

♈ *Aries* produces a spare, strong body, rather above middle stature ; of strong limbs and large bones ; long face ; bushy eyebrows ; sharp sight ; long neck ; rough and wiry hair, usually brown or sandy, whiskers reddish ; swarthy complexion and thick shoulders ; disposition contentious and quick to anger and violence.

♉ *Taurus* generally gives middle stature with thick well-set body ; broad forehead, full face and prominent eyes—either dark or blue ; short neck and thick lips ; nose and mouth usually large or wide ; complexion swarthy, hair dark or black and often curly in front ; short, thick, broad hands ; strong appetites ; rather unfeeling, having *bull-like* stubbornness ; slow to anger but furious when roused.

♊ *Gemini* usually produces a tall erect figure with very long arms and fingers ; dark sanguine complexion, dark hair and eyebrows, hazel eyes with a sharp active look, a high and conspicuous nose and projecting chin ; understanding excellent though disposed to be fickle.

♋ *Cancer* gives moderate stature, generally larger from the middle upward than below : face full and round with a white or pale and delicate complexion, nose short and rounded, hair light brown, and small greyish or bluish eyes : rather effeminate and seldom of strong constitution : females prolific, timid, and dull.

♄ *Leo* usually produces a large noble person of tall stature and fine proportions ; shoulders broad and well set, head large and round, hair and beard often light and tawny, sometimes bushy and curly, eyes round and prominent, complexion ruddy or sanguine, and step firm and majestic : disposition free and courteous, resolute and courageous, and ambitious with an inclination to haughtiness.

♍ *Virgo* persons are usually of middle stature, well formed, neat and compact, full face, dark ruddy complexion, and dark or black hair ; a preponderance of the mental over physical qualities is usually exhibited : they are ingenious, industrious, and fond of learning, though rather changeable in opinion.

♎ *Libra* gives a person tall, graceful and slender, the last few degrees shorter and stouter ; hair brown and glossy, though sometimes black, face round and lovely, having generally great beauty, fine clear red and white complexion, eyes blue and handsome, the mind exquisite in taste, well principled and even-tempered, loving music and the fine arts and inclining to the nice avocations in life.

♏ *Scorpio* produces a thick well-set person of middle stature, strong and robust, face broad or square, dark complexion, dark hair curly and plentiful, neck thick, legs coarse and sometimes bowed, and feet ill-made or irregular : mind active and combative, reserved, secretive, and inclined to be deceitful.

♐ *Sagittarius* persons are tall and well formed, especially about the hips and thighs ; have a long oval face, high forehead, fine clear blue or grey eyes, ruddy complexion and open countenance, light brown or chestnut hair growing back from the temples, and inclining early to baldness in front ; they are strong and intrepid, fond of horses, athletic sports, and all the manly accomplishments.

♑ *Capricorn* usually produces slender and sometimes ill-formed persons, with long, thin visage, thin beard, neck long and small, hair dark and lanky, narrow chin and breast, weak knees, ill-formed legs and awkward gait.

♒ *Aquarius* usually gives a person above middle stature, comely,

robust, strong, and healthy in appearance ; having a long and rather
fleshy face ; complexion clear, sanguine, and delicate, hazel eyes, and
fair or flaxen hair ; disposition excellent, intelligent, and quick in the
acquisition of learning.

)(*Pisces* generally produces a medium or short stature ; body
fleshy, crooked or stooping and round shouldered, brown hair, large
bulging face, full, prominent and sleepy looking eyes, and rolling
lips ; arms and legs short and fin-like, and the feet ill-made ; disposition indolent, and unless the influences of the sign are much modified
by planetary position the native is given to drink.

*N.B.—These descriptions will be modified to a great extent, when many
planets are found in the ascendant, or rising sign.*

DESIRE. An emotion going out towards objects. Desire is,
therefore, often opposed to will, which demands. The whole of the
true desire nature is under the Sun, but Mars is king over the senses.

> His genius and his moral frame
> Were thus impaired, and he became
> The slave of low desires.—WORDSWORTH.

DESTINY. The end to which all forces are making. The part
we are to play in the scheme of evolution.

DESTRUCTIVE FORCE. Mars, if not transmuted into the elements
of Venus, would finally lead to destruction, the force being too great
for the vessel to contain it. The alchemists taught the transmutation of metals, the metal of Mars is iron, it is valuable when transmuted
into fine steel.

DETRIMENT. A planet is in its detriment when in a sign opposite to that which is its house or sign. The planets are then said to
be weak.

DETERMINATION. The fixed signs give fixity of purpose and
determination.

DEVIL, THE. Mars has been known as the devil, or rather the
influence corresponding to this supposed personage. Astrology
recognises the planet Saturn under the *nom de guerre* of Satan, and
Mars as that of the Devil. It is owing to the abuse of these great
principles of heat and cold that they have come to be considered as
evil forces. When the prince of darkness is imagined as heaping

flames of fire upon the wicked his appropriate title is the devil. If the knowledge of Astrology had not been lost we should have been saved the lamentable errors we have fallen into concerning Hell and the Devil.

DEXTER ASPECTS. Those taken in the opposite order of the signs.

DHANUS. The Hindu name for the sign Sagittarius, the ninth sign of the Zodiac, the name being equivalent to this number.

DIGNITIES. The dignities of the planets, which mean their strength, may be either essential or accidental, or they may be both. A planet is essentially dignified when in its own house, sign of exaltation, triplicity of joy. When a planet is in an angle, it is accidentally dignified. When angular, and in its own house, or exaltation, then essentially and accidentally dignified. The planets are in their debilities when the reverse of their dignities occur.

DIRECT. When a planet is not retrograde. Going in the order of the signs from Aries to Pisces.

DIRECTIONS. The calculations made after birth from the nativity for the purpose of ascertaining the time when events will happen ; properly speaking this is predictive Astrology, as it is concerned with the future of the person for whom the calculations are made. Directions are classed under two heads, primary and secondary, the former is similar to the small hand of a clock which marks off the hours, while the latter are like unto the long hand which marks off the exact time. There are various methods of making the calculations for directions, according to the choice of the student, several of which will be found under the various headings. There is one source of error common to the majority of students when taking out the directions, and that is the failure to judge the exact strength or weakness of the radix. All judgment with regard to directions must depend upon the quality of the nativity, a general interpretation is usually given to all directions indiscriminately, giving rise to much error and mistake in judgment.

In directions the Mid-heaven, Ascendant, Sun, and Moon, are the most important centres, and when working by what are called primary directions each of these points in the nativity may be turned into right ascension, this is found by measuring from the first point of Aries ($\Upsilon 0°$). It is usual to prepare a speculum as follows:

Planet	Latitude	Declin	Right Ascension	Meridian Distance	Semi-Arc	Position

the full explanation of which may be found under their various headings in this dictionary. The planetary positions at birth are always considered as stationary throughout the life, the influence as it were being impressed upon that spot which they held at the moment of birth. In finding out the arc of direction, as it is termed, the centres are moved until they meet certain aspects ; suppose the

M.C. to be 14°♉ 22′ ; Right Ascension is 41°53′

and ♅ ,, 11° ♊ 24′ ; ,, ,, 69°51′

To find out the arc of direction the smaller right ascension is deducted from the greater as follows :

A.R. ; ♅ 69°51′
A.R. ; M.C. 41°53′
_____
27°58′

By this we have the aspect of M.C. ☌ ♅ in zodiac direct. It is understood that each year of life is equal to 1°, and each month to 5′, therefore, had this aspect between M.C. and ♅ been exactly 28°, the arc of direction would have been complete at the twenty-eighth year of life.

The calculations may be made backwards, termed converse, or forward, known as direct motion.

The most popular, and certainly the most simple method of directing is that in which the Sun and Moon play the most prominent part, the plan adopted being to consider each day after birth as one year of life. The Sun, by progression each day after birth, forms aspects to the radical positions of the planets, mid-heaven, and ascendant ; these are termed primary aspects. The moon in her passage through the zodiac forms aspects to these primary aspects, setting them in motion as it were ; these are termed secondary aspects. In addition to these the planets are also moving from the radical to progressive positions, these are termed mutual aspects. These mutual aspects point out the nature of the events likely to happen, judgment being given from the signs and houses from which they occur, then, when the Moon forms any aspects to these primary or mutual aspects the time is known when the event will occur.

The simple rule to find out the directions in operation is as follows : Count the number of days after the birthday equal to the number of years that have elapsed since birth, and either fill into the radical map the planetary positions, also the Sun and Moon for the birth-time on that day, or tabulate the positions separately, but the object is to find the aspects between the radical positions and the progressive, as those for the birthday required are termed. The Moon moves about 1° 5' per month through the zodiac or 13° per year, the sun 1° per year, but by either using the nautical almanack or a good ephemeris the exact positions for each months may be found.

DISCORDANT ASPECTS. All aspects that occur from fiery and watery signs are discordant in nature, the same with regard to the earthy and airy signs. The square aspects are formed from these signs, and owing to their lack of sympathy they become discordant aspects. The following aspects are more or less discordant in nature : the semi-square, square, sesquiquadrate, and opposition. The position of the conjunction is also discordant when it is between two planets of opposing nature.

DISEASE. Certain planets when in affliction cause diseases as follows :—

Sun in Aries.—Internal headaches, generally right in the centre of the head. weakness in the eyes. and feverishness ; ill-health is usually produced by worry and over-excitement. or by outbursts of anger and impulsive expression.

Sun in Taurus.—The throat will be affected either by quinsy or some inflammation ; there may be diphtheria and throat complaints generally.

Sun in Gemini.—In this sign the blood is affected, and the chest and lungs become afflicted by inflammation ; two complaints may be going on at the same time, arising from congestion or an inflamed condition of the blood ; it gives a tendency to lingering complaints.

Sun in Cancer.—The disease of this position will be those arising out of indigestion, or a disordered condition of the stomach, tumours and cancerous complaints, and those affecting the fluidic system, such as dropsy, etc. The chest and breasts are affected.

Sun in Leo.—The heart and back suffer, and there is liability to all feverish complaints.

Sun in Virgo.—Diseases affecting the circulatory system, dysentery, and also obstructions in the bowels, with tendencies to consumption, etc.

Sun in Libra.—Kidney complaints and diseases affecting the reins and liver.

Sun in Scorpio.—Diseases connected with the private parts, affecting the urine and the generative organs ; it causes stone, gravel and all obstructions in that part of the body.

Sun in Sagittarius.—By reflection, this will affect the lungs, but generally it gives trouble with the anus, and sometimes affects the spine.

Sun in Capricorn.—By the same rule the stomach is affected, and generally the knees and joints also.

Sun in Aquarius.—The blood is affected, as also the eyes, and by reflection the heart and back.

Sun in Pisces.—Fluidic complaints, and sometimes trouble in the genitals. It should be noted that the signs that are in sympathy affect each other, the fixed signs governing all vital parts such as the throat, heart, generative system, and the blood : the cardinal signs govern the functional arrangement, and the common signs the limbs and extremities.

The Sun governs the structure, and from the afflictions to the Sun we may judge the nature of the hereditary complaints ; all so-called heredity comes under the solar influence, the real truth being that we are drawn toward those parents who can give us a vehicle suited to the working out of the results of those causes which we have set in motion in the past. The Sun governs all the vital parts and the structure generally, but the heart chiefly. The eyes will also be weak, and show signs of failure when the Sun is heavily afflicted ; in all vital diseases the Sun, and the direction from which the affliction to the Sun is coming, must be particularly studied, for the Sun alone has to do with diseases which cause fevers, or produce heat in those parts governed by the sign that he is in.

Taking the Sun alone, the diseases that may be expected to occur under his influence will be chiefly those connected with the heart, brain, and eyes. The most common complaints that may be attri-

buted to the Sun are palpitation, pimples on the face, heated flush-
ings, and a fullness of the system.   In the various signs, considering
the Sun generally as the centre to which the disease is making, and
also considering the sign as the vital spot (owing to the Sun's position
there), the following are the general indications :

At the head of the vital group stands the Sun, at the head of
the functional, the Moon, and governing the nervous system,
Mercury.

Saturn in Aries.—Colds in the head, catarrh, moist humours in
the head, trouble from mucus falling into the throat and deafness.
If the nativity indicates accidents, then blows and injuries to the
head.

Saturn in Taurus.—Colds in the throat, catarrh, or phlegm in
the throat affecting the breath.   Melancholy.

Saturn in Gemini.—Colds in the chest, bronchial affections,
pneumonia, coughs, colds, and rheumatic pains in the arms and
shoulders.   Consumption.

Saturn in Cancer.—Cold and flatulence, with obstructions of
mucus in the stomach, coughs, bad breath, and sometimes bruises
or cancer in the breast.   Weak digestion.

Saturn in Leo.—Heart disease, slow action of the heart, and
poor circulation of the blood ; rheumatism around the heart, falls,
bruises, and in many cases brittle bones.   Dangers from poison.

Saturn in Virgo.—Colds and cramps in the bowels, constipation,
cold, inactive liver, often a sallow complexion.   Melancholic.

Saturn in Libra.—Kidney diseases, pains in the back caused by
cold, mucus in the urine, and gravel, sciatica.

Saturn in Scorpio.—Urinary troubles, colds in the bladder,
gravel, retention of the urine, and in many cases piles.   In females
womb complaints.   Some tendency to gout.

Saturn in Sagittarius.—Bronchial affections, coughs, pneumonia,
rheumatic pains in the thighs, sciatica, falls, and bruises.

Saturn in Capricorn.—Rheumatic pains in the limbs, ague, colds
in the knees and ankles, poor circulation of the blood in the lower
parts of the body.

Saturn in Aquarius.—Rheumatism, also sores and bruises upon
the legs.   If the nativity shows it, broken limbs.   Blood affected.

Saturn in Pisces.—Cold, and liability to cramp in the feet and toes, poor circulation in the lower parts, coughs, colds, and lung troubles, infirmities in the feet and consumption tendencies.

Mars in Aries.—Fevers, heat, and violent pains in the head, sleeplessness, brain fever, cuts and scars in the head and face. Sometimes sunstroke, also small-pox.

Mars in Taurus.—Dry feverish throat, sore throat, quinsy, inflammation in the throat, swelling of the tonsils, and in many cases diphtheria.

Mars in Gemini.—Bronchitis, inflammation of the lungs, pains in the chest, pneumonia, and, when indicated, accidents to the hands and arms.

Mars in Cancer.—A weak, feverish stomach, gastric troubles, dyspepsia, in some cases consumption, biliousness, and the head affected by stomachic troubles.

Mars in Leo.—Heart disease, dilation and aneurism of the heart, fevers, malaria. In some cases burns and accidents.

Mars in Virgo.—Inflammation of the bowels, typhoid fever, liver disease, biliousness, and a sallow complexion.

Mars in Libra.—Kidney disease, inflammation of the kidneys, uric acid in the system, pains in the back, bronchial affections, and falls.

Mars in Scorpio.—Urinary troubles, inflammation in the bladder and of the womb, sediment in the urine, ulcers in the bladder, and venereal diseases in some cases.

Mars in Sagittarius.—Bronchial affections, inflammation of the lungs, fevers, accidents, pains in the thighs, weakness, and malaria.

Mars in Capricorn.—Pains, wounds, cuts, scars on the knees or leg, accidents to the lower parts, sometimes a broken leg, and in many cases malaria, flying gout.

Mars in Aquarius.—Pains in the legs, erysipelas in the lower parts, bruises, cuts, broken legs in some cases, lameness, and acute pains in the body.

Mars in Pisces.—Accidents to the feet and toes, swellings in the feet, impure blood, lung troubles, bronchitis, consumption, and sometimes dropsical affections.

Jupiter in Aries.—Headaches, dizziness, rush of blood to the head, congestion of the brain, and danger of apoplexy ; especially if the Sun afflict Jupiter.

Jupiter in Taurus.—Gout, and distempers in the throat, suffering through over-indulgence in eating and drinking, and luxuriant living.

Jupiter in Gemini.—Affections of the blood, sometimes pleurisies.

Jupiter in Cancer.—Dropsy, when much afflicted diabetes.

Jupiter in Leo.—Pleurisy, fevers, and danger of apoplexy when afflicted heavily.

Jupiter in Virgo.—Disordered liver, weakness and looseness of the bowels, impurities in the blood, sallow complexion. When afflicted in this sign disorders of the bowels are frequent.

Jupiter in Libra.—Inflammations, and obstructions in the reins through bad blood.

Jupiter in Scorpio.—Mucus in the urine, loss of seed ; especially if Mars affect Jupiter. Jupiter afflicted in Scorpio produces venereal diseases.

Jupiter in Sagittarius.—Over-heating of the blood through sports and violent exercise.

Jupiter in Capricorn.—Tired feelings, weakness in the legs, throbbing in the limbs, an excess of blood in the lower parts, caused by improper circulation of the blood.

Jupiter in Aquarius.—Lumbago, and flying pains from over-abundance of blood in the system.

Jupiter in Pisces.—Dropsy, poor blood.

Venus in Aries.—Headache. The health is affected by careless and impulsive habits.

Venus in Virgo.—Liver and bowel complaints, looseness of the bowels, and ruptures in some cases.

Venus in Scorpio.—Venereal diseases, loss of vitality, sickness through excess and improper habits, disease of the womb and ovaries, falling of the womb, profuse menses, and weakness of the bladder.

Mercury in Aries.—Worry, fear, anxiety of the mind, pains in the head, and nervous affections of the head.

Mercury in Sagittarius.—Weakness in the head, dizziness, nervousness, and weakness in the thighs.

Mercury in Pisces.—A poor memory, fear, worry, imaginary ailments, and nervous affections.

Moon in Aries.—Headaches, brain troubles, and restlessness.

Moon in Scorpio.—Loss of vitality, weakness of the bladder, falling of the womb, female complaints, irregular or profuse periodics, dropsical ailments, and diseases caused by outraging nature's laws.

Moon in Capricorn.—Weakness in the knees and legs, weak and tired feelings, sickness of stomach, sprains and bruises in lower parts.

Moon in Aquarius.—Dropsical complaints, and swellings in the lower parts.

Moon in Pisces.—Swellings and unpleasant odours from the feet, dropsical ailments, and a watery condition of the blood.

The diseases of the planets may be classified as follows :—

The Sun.—All hot and dry diseases, affections of the heart, back and arteries ; it has been said also that the Sun governs the right eye in man and the left in woman. His diseases are certainly palpitation of the heart, faintings, giddiness in the head, fevers, weak sight and brain troubles ; foul breath and affections of the mouth, catarrhs, and cramps. The Sun weak by house as well as sign should be noted. When the Sun is decadent in the nativity there will always be a tendency to the diseases of the Sun, more especially when the Sun is afflicted in the cadent house, or common sign ; but much less so when in Sagittarius, or the ninth house. The Sun angular gives power to resist disease, and less liability to sickness.

The Moon.—All feminine complaints come under the Moon, and also cases of insanity appropriately known as lunacy. The nature of the Moon is cold and moist ; therefore all cold and lymphatic diseases come under the Moon, such as cancer and stomachic complaints, and to her influence may be traced rheumatism and consumption. Her diseases are wind, vertigo, apoplexy, inflammation of the brain, convulsions, small-pox, measles, scrofulous diseases, and diseases of the skin. Women especially come under lunar diseases, and in their case the Moon affects the periodics and the liver. Children, during the first four years of life, come directly under the Moon.

The luminaries in affliction always weaken the eyesight.

Mercury.—This planet governs the brain as a whole, and also the nervous system. The parts of the body specially under his rule are the brain, tongue, hands, and feet. His diseases are madness, dumbness, stammering, apoplexy, stoppage in the head, headaches, lethargy, defective memory, gouty disorders in the hands and feet, flying humours, hoarseness, dry coughs, and nervous debility from worry or

over-work. When Mercury is much afflicted there is always danger
of consumption, fits, and madness, according to the affliction and the
signs from which it occurs.

Mars.—This planet has sympathy with the Sun, and accentuates
all the diseases mentioned under the Sun in the various signs ; all
fevers and inflammations come from Mars, but they are of the burning,
contagious, and destructive type ; they are quick, while those of the
Sun are slow, though severe. The diseases of Mars are yellow jaundice, and those which are the result of violent anger and passion ;
stone in the reins or kidneys, and those complaints which proceed
from the gall, from over-heated blood, and those caused by prodigal
life, and a wasting of the forces. Shingles, fistulas, diabetes, small-
pox, burns, scalds, wounds and bruises are all under Mars. This
fiery planet is dangerous in cases of child-birth, and he is responsible
for accidents, dog bites, and all sudden ruptures of the blood vessels.

The generative organs and the muscles and sinews, are chiefly
under Mars. He is said to govern the nose and forehand.

Saturn.—This planet is in sympathy with the Moon, and accentuates all the Moon's diseases. His diseases are those arising out of
melancholy, colds, and depression, and he produces consumption,
slow, lingering, and wasting diseases, such as atrophy, palsy, dropsy,
leprosy, severe catarrh, and acute nervous disorders. But his chief
diseases are rheumatism, and those which arise out of colds, such
as neuralgia, toothache, Under certain afflictions with the Moon
he causes epilepsy and fits of obsession. Saturn governs the bones,
joints, and spleen. The ears are also under Saturn, and when afflicted
in Aries deafness is generally the result.

Jupiter.—It can hardly be said that Jupiter causes any diseases,
but as he governs the blood and the seed, all afflictions to this planet
will act upon the blood, and thus affect the liver, lungs, and indirectly
the heart ; but the blood is the principal part of the system coming
under Jupiter's rule, so that pleurisy, apoplexy, boils, cramps, and
abscesses may be expected when he is much afflicted. Jupiter has
chief rule over the arterial system.

Venus.—When under affliction the diseases of Venus are those
affecting the generative system, causing disorders in the matrix,
genitals, bladder, the reins, spine, and breasts. Her diseases arise

from excess in pleasure, and all venereal disorders resulting from sensuality. Venus governs the throat, ovaries, and venous system.

Uranus.—The diseases of this planet are mostly nervous, and often incurable, being very difficult to understand. All sudden and unexpected complaints, such as accidents, suicides, and peculiar diseases, may be attributed to this planet. It governs what is known as the *etheric body*.

Persons with many planets in earthy signs are liable to have tumours in the fleshy parts of the body.

Mars in a fiery sign will give a liability to fevers and burns.

Venus has influence over the flesh, womb, complexion, and hair.

Mercury over the mind, intellect, nervous system, optic nerve, and the imagination.

The Moon, over the secretions of the body, the uterus, the ovaries and the eyes.

Saturn has influence over the bones, also the phlegm causing obstructions.

Jupiter over the blood, arteries, seed, teeth, and the circulation.

Mars has rule over the bile, liver, gall, inflammatory complaints, the temper, the heat of the body, and what is called animal magnetism, also the muscular system.

Herschel also has influence over animal magnetism and impulses, and sometimes causes numbness and electrical pains.

The Sun and Moon in affliction with each other will often give affections of the eyes, and if either be afflicted by planetary aspects, there will be ailments in connection with the eyes.

Venus afflicted by evil aspects will give womb complaints in females, and venereal diseases in males.

Mercury afflicted will produce brain troubles, mental derangement, nervous affections, and in some cases insanity.

Saturn afflicting Mercury indicates worry, fear, melancholy, catarrh, colds and dull pains in the head, and lack of confidence.

Saturn afflicting Venus, bad habits, and womb complaints.

Saturn in affliction with the Sun, palpitation of the heart, paralysis, wasting and lingering diseases, sore eyes, and sometimes cataract of the eyes.

Saturn afflicting Jupiter, sluggish action of the blood.

Mars affecting Mercury, fevers in the head, also nervous affection of the head.

Mars afflicting Venus denotes excesses, bad habits, venereal diseases, and womb complaints in females.

Mars and Herschel in affliction, strange accidents, cuts, shocks from electrical appliances, and dangers from explosions.

Mars afflicting Jupiter, impure blood, eruptions on the body, in some cases liver disease, also danger from explosions.

Herschel afflicting Mercury, nervous complaints, a muddled condition of the mind, and electrical pains in the head, also a numbness, and a peculiar pricking sensation in that portion of the body governed by the sign in which Herschel is posited at birth.

The part of the body governed by the sign in which the Moon is at birth is always a very sensitive spot. This also applies to the place of the Moon at any time, and operations should never be performed upon that part of the body which the Moon happens to occupy.

DISPOSE. A planet in the house of another disposes that planet. Venus in Aries disposes Mars, who is ruler of that sign. It is probably of more importance in horary Astrology, but it must also have some value in nativities.

DISPOSITION. The ascendant, with its ascending degree, together with the whole of the planetary positions and aspects, must be studied before any definite clue is obtained as to the disposition. According to the signs the disposition is as follows :

Aries.—Impulsive, courageous, ambitious, changeable and ingenious.

Taurus.—Patient, plodding, amorous, reserved, secretive, approbative.

Gemini.—Intellectual, artistic, dualistic, excitable, industrious.

Cancer.—Changeable, instinctive, magnetic, affectionate, timid, psychic.

Leo.—Ambitious, pompous, magnanimous, faithful, kind-hearted, liberal, determined.

Virgo.—Intuitive, generous, industrious, capable, receptive, kind, sensitive.

Libra.—Even-tempered, just, talkative, objective, fond of ease and comfort, and approbative.

Scorpio.—Reserved, sarcastic, proud, studious, psychic, contentious.

Sagittarius.—Generous, active, sporting, philosophic, hopeful, communicative.

Capricorn.—Ambitious, selfish, diplomatic, capricious, economical, envious.

Aquarius.—Patient, artistic, ingenious, intellectual, intuitive, refined.

Pisces.—Psychic, indolent, dualistic, thoughtful, mediumistic, sensitive.

DISPOSITOR. See DISPOSE.

DIURNAL. That which rules by day.

DIURNAL ARC. The measurement in degrees of a planet from its rising to its setting. See SEMI-ARC.

DRAGON'S HEAD.—The Moon's north node, when the Moon crosses the ecliptic into north latitude. Its symbol is thus ♌ ; it is supposed to be of good influence. Taurus is supposed to be its house or sign.

DRAGON'S TAIL. The reverse of the dragon's head ; it is supposed to be an evil influence, and is marked thus ♎. The dragon's tail is the Moon's south node, as the head is the north. Scorpio is supposed to be its house or sign.

DUMB SIGNS. The watery signs are said to be the dumb signs, and under certain conditions to cause impediment in the speech, but as Mercury has much to do with the speech, this planet would at the same time be afflicted.

DURATION OF LIFE. See HYLEG.

E. The fifth letter of the alphabet. The numerical value is five, and its symbol a window.

EAGLE. The king of birds, sacred to the sign Scorpio in a mythical sense. Held by the Greeks and Persians to be sacred to the Sun and Jupiter. The description of a pure Scorpio person would be that of an eagle, the eyes and nose being much like the eagle's.

EARTH. The name given to the globe which we inhabit. It appears to us to be the centre of the universe with the Sun and stars revolving round it, but this is an appearance only, due to the earth's

D

revolution upon its own axis, which is completed in about twenty-four hours, producing day and night. The earth is in reality a planet, like the other planets in the solar system which revolve round the Sun. The earth's passage round the Sun gives rise to the term, Sun in Aries or Taurus, etc. The Sun apparently passes through these signs owing to the position of the earth during the twelve months that form the year.

EARTHQUAKES. The shaking or quaking of the earth. The earthquake signs are Taurus and Scorpio. Severe afflictions from Herschel, Saturn, Jupiter and Mars in Taurus cause earthquakes. They are usually produced by eclipses, and can be traced by the various rules given for mundane Astrology; we have no record of earthquakes occurring when the planets were not in violent signs.

On the 26th of September, 1800, an earthquake destroyed the royal palace at Constantinople, ♄ was in ♌, and ♂ in ♉. At the new Moon of July 26th, 1805, 6,000 lives were lost at Frosolone, Naples; the ☉, ☽, ♀, and ☿ were in ♌, and ♃ in ♏. On the 11th of August, 1810, at the Azores, a village of St. Michael's sank, and a lake of boiling water appeared in its place, the ☉, ♂ and ☿ were in ♌, ♅ in ♏, and ♃ in ♉. On the 26th March, 1812, 12,000 persons perished by an earthquake in the City Leon de Carucus, ♅ was in ♏, and ♂ in ♉. On the 16th of June, 1819, the district of Kutch, in India, sank and buried 2,000 persons, ♂ was in ♉, and ♃ in ♒. On the 10th of August, 1822, Aleppo was destroyed and 20,000 persons perished, the ☉ was in ♌ and ☽ and ♄ in ♉. 6,000 perished in Spain on the 21st of March, 1829, ♅ was in ♒, ♂ in ♉. 6,000 perished at Canton on the 26th and 27th of May, 1830, ☽ and ♄ were in ♌, ♅ and ♂ in ♒. On the 29th of April, 1835, 1,000 persons were buried in Calabria. ☉ and ☽ in ♉, ♅ in ♒. On the 14th of August, 1851, 14,000 lives were lost in South Italy, the ☉ and ♀ in ♌, ♅ and ♄ in ♉. On the 16th December, 1859, 10,000 lives were lost in Calabria, ♅ and ♃ were in ♉. On the 23rd March, 1859, 5,000 persons were killed at Quito, the ☽ was in ♏, ♄ in ♌, ♂ in ♉, ♀ in ♒. There was an earthquake at 3hrs. 22mins. a.m., 6th of October, 1863, in the central, west, and north-west of England, ☽ was in ♌, and ♃ in ♏. 13th-15th of August, 1858, the cities of Arequipa and Iquique, and Tacna, and Chenencha and many towns in Peru, were destroyed, 25,000 lives lost and 30,000 rendered homeless, estimated loss of property sixty million pounds ; the ⊙ and ☿ were in ♌, and ♄ in ♏. A slight earthquake was felt in the West of England and South Wales on the 30th of October the same year, ⊙ and ☿ in ♏, ♂ in ♌. 16th-18th of May, 1875, 14,000 lives were lost at San José de Cuculá, ⊙ in ♅ in ♌, and ♄ in ♒. Zadkiel in 1834 published the following rules for predicting earthquakes :—

" 1.   Earthquakes generally follow close on the heels of eclipses.

" 2.   At the period of the earthquake, many aspects will be found between the planets in the heavens ; also, as regards the places of the planets at the preceding eclipse, but chiefly the place of the Sun and Moon.

" 3.   Earthquakes happen more frequently when there are planets—especially ♅, ♄ , ♃ and ♂ in the signs of ♉ and ♏.

" 4.   If there have been no recent eclipse of the ☽, within a month, look to the last eclipse of the ⊙.

" 5.   The planet ♃, in aspect with ♀ or ☿, more especially the conjunction, opposition, and parallel declination, has a powerful influence in causing earthquakes—especially when in ♉ or ♏.

" 6.   If no eclipse has taken place within three months, look to the planets' places at the last new or full Moon of the quarter, *i.e.*, the lunation nearest to the Sun's crossing the equator or tropic.

" 7.   Earthquakes generally happen when there are several planets in or near the tropics or equator.

" 8.   Earthquakes may always be expected near the perihelion of great comets, and when they approach within the orbits of the planets ♅ and ♄.

" 9.   Let all, or as many as possible, of these circumstances be combined before any very extensive earthquakes be predicted."

EARTHY SIGNS.   The signs forming the earthy triplicity.

EARTHY TRIPLICITY. ♉, ♍, ♑. These signs govern the physical and earthy condition of things, and are known as cold and dry signs.

EAST.   One of the four cardinal points ; a point toward the sunrise midway between the north and south poles of the heavens, and in which the Sun appears to rise at the vernal and autumnal equinoxes.

EASTER. A moveable festival. It is always the first Sunday after the full Moon which happens upon or next after the Sun's entry in Aries (21st March). If the full Moon happens on Sunday then Easter Day is the Sunday after.

EAST WINDS. These are caused by the planet Saturn.

ECCENTRICAL. A circle, the centre of which does not correspond with that of the earth.

ECCENTRICS. These are supposed by astrologers to be governed by ♅, this planet governing all uncommon and peculiar events.

ECLIPSE. The obscuration, total or partial, and not simply by clouds, of the light coming to us from a heavenly body.

ECLIPSE OF THE SUN. An obstruction of his light, occasioned by the interposition of the dark body of the Moon between him and our sight. An eclipse of the Sun can occur only at new Moon. Eclipses are partial or total.

ECLIPSES OF THE SUN AND MOON IN THE DECANATES OF THE TWELVE CELESTIAL SIGNS.

The Sun.

♈ 0° to 10°.—When the Sun is eclipsed in any of the first ten degrees of Aries, which is the first Decanate, it portends the sudden and frequent motion of armies, continual expeditions, assaults and batteries, with many tumults, seditions and controversies, and an inclination of the air to intemperate heat and drought.

♈ 10° to 20°.—In the following Decanate, from the 10th to the 20th degree of Aries, it denotes the imprisonment, trouble and sadness of some king, and danger of death to him ; a corruption of trees that are fruitful, or of such fruits as are produced of trees ; as also of the Earth.

♈ 20° to 30°.—In the last Decanate, from the 20th to the 30th degree of Aries, he bringeth grief and sadness to mortals, and the death of great women, and a scarcity or diminution of cattle (viz., those of the lesser sort, because it is signified by Aries).

♉ 0° to 10°.—An eclipse of the Sun, happening in the first Decanate of Taurus, afflicts negotiators, agents and solicitors, destroys businesses, and the corn upon the earth.

♉ 10° to 20°.—In the 2nd Decanate of Taurus, incommodities to such as bear children, and also to travellers.

♉ 20° to 30°.—In the 3rd, pestilence and famine, from whence we may imply the destruction of greater cattle, *viz.*, bulls, oxen and cows.

♊ 0° to 10°.—An eclipse of the *Sun* in the first Decanate of *Gemini* causes dissension amongst priests, whatsoever Order they are, inveterate hatred, seditions, and a contempt of both the Law of God and Man is to be feared.

♊ 10° to 20°.—In the 2nd, thefts and robberies, piracies and slaughters.

♊ 20° to 30°.—In the 3rd, the death of some king, and various mischiefs to such commonwealths as are under Gemini, and the frustration of such cities' affairs and negotiations.

♋ 0° to 10°.—Again, an eclipse of the *Sun* in the first Decanate of *Cancer* disturbs the air and causes various winds and alterations of weather.

♋ 10° to 20°.—In the 2nd, drieth up rivers and fountains, and causeth petulant and grievous mortalities.

♋ 20° to 30°.—In the 3rd, through Armenia and Africa and the rest of the regions and places subject to *Cancer*, hydropical diseases, seditions, etc.

♌ 0° to 10°.—Also an eclipse of the *Sun* in the 1st Decanate of *Leo* denotes the death of some eminent prince and the scarcity of bread and corn.

♌ 10° to 20°.—In the 2nd, troubles and anxieties to kings, princes, and great men or magistrates.

♌ 20° to 30°.—In the 3rd, captivities, slaughters, rapines and profanation of holy and sacred houses (churches, monasteries, etc.).

♍ 0° to 10°.—Moreover, an eclipse of the *Sun* in *Virgo* argues the grievous calamity and death of some certain king in the confines of *Virgo*.

♍ 10° to 20°.—In the 2nd, famine, pestilence and deadly seditions.

♍ 20° to 30°.—In the 3rd, to pictures, poets, and merchants, and such as live by their ingenuity and wit ; slaughters, destruction, banishment, and the like.

♎ 0° to 10°.—If an eclipse of the *Sun* be in the 1st Decanate of *Libra* it corrupts the air, causes pestilence and a scarcity and dearness of corn.

♎ 10° to 20°.—In the 2nd, portends the death of some great king under the dominion of Libra, seditions and famine.

♎ 20° to 30°.—In the 3rd, discords amongst great ones, and detriment in their estates.

♏ 0° to 10°.—Also, if an eclipse be in the 1st Decanate of *Scorpio*, it moves and stirs up wars and tumults, slaughter, hatred, captivities, plots and treacheries.

♏ 10° to 20°.—In the 2nd, mischief to some king, whose mind is averse to war.

♏ 20° to 30°.—In the 3rd, the rise of some tyrant ; the slothfulness and idleness of the former king being hateful to everyone.

♐ 0° to 10°.—In the 1st Decanate of *Sagittarius*, if an eclipse of the *Sun* be, it shows grievous dissensions and deadly feuds amongst men.

♐ 10° to 20°.—In the 2nd, the death of camels and cattle that chew the cud (especially the greater sort) and such like.

♐ 20° to 30°.—In the 3rd, prejudice to horses and armies.

♑ 0° to 10°.—Again, an eclipse of the *Sun* in the 1st Decanate of *Capricorn* denotes unhappiness, and chances to great men ; the transmigration of some king, and the rebellion of the nobles and rustics.

♑ 10° to 20°.—In the 2nd, soldiers are excited and animated against their commanders and superiors, and it frustrates all their devices.

♑ 20° to 30°.—In the 3rd it induceth the tumultuary motion of the king, and causeth famine.

♒ 0° to 10°.—An eclipse of the *Sun* in the 1st Decanate of *Aquarius*, causeth public sorrow and sadness.

♒ 10° to 20°.—In the 2nd, public thefts, rapines and robberies, earthquakes and famine.

♒ 20° to 30°.—In the 3rd, the death and slaughter of sheep and beasts of the field.

♓ 0° to 10°.—Lastly, an eclipse of the *Sun* in the 1st Decanate of *Pisces*, dries up rivers, and is unfortunate to the sea, and the affairs thereof.

♓ 10° to 20°.—In the 2nd, the death of famous and excellent men ; destruction of fish, earthquakes, etc.

♓ 20° to 30°.—In the 3rd sedition, cruelty, furiousness and inhumanity of soldiers.

OF THE MOON.

♈ 0° to 10°.—When the *Moon* is eclipsed in the 1st Decanate of *Aries*, she denotes fevers, destruction of woods by fire, and a dryness of the air.

♈ 10° to 20°.—In the 2nd, pestilence.

♈ 20° to 30°.—In the 3rd, abortive births, incommodities, and such like dangers to women.

♉ 0° to 10°.—An eclipse of the *Moon*, in the 1st Decanate of *Taurus*, denotes destruction and death to great cattle.

♉ 10° to 20°.—In the 2nd the death of the Queen of some region under *Taurus*, and a scarcity of seeds, and barrenness of the earth.

♉ 20° to 30°.—In the 3rd she shows cruelty on serpents, and such like.

♊ 0° to 10°.—An eclipse of the *Moon*, in the 1st Decanate of *Gemini*, threatens incursions, and rapines of enemies.

♊ 10° to 20°.—In the 2nd, the frequent motion of armies, and the solicitations of private and public things.

♊ 20° to 30°.—In the 3rd, the death of some illustrious and famous man.

♋ 0° to 10°.—An eclipse of the *Moon*, in the 1st Decanate of *Cancer*, excites and stirs up wars.

♋ 10° to 20°.—In the 2nd, grievous exactions, intolerable tributes, taxations, and such like burdens.

♋ 20° to 30°.—In the 3rd, death to the female sex, and sudden destruction and miseries.

♌ 0° to 10°.—An eclipse of the *Moon*, in the 1st Decanate of *Leo*, denotes the death of either some illustrious king, or famous man.

♌ 10° to 20°.—In the 2nd, the journey of the king, and imitation of things.

♌ 20° to 30°.—In the 3rd, she excites the people and armies to new actions and attempts.

♍ 0° to 10°.—An eclipse of the *Moon*, in the 1st Decanate of *Virgo*, causeth diseases and infirmities to the king, and various seditions and discords among men.

♍ 10° to 20°.—In the 2nd, mischief to counsellors, scribes, or such like men.

♍ 20° to 30°.—In the 3rd, brings deadly diseases.

♎ 0° to 10°.—A lunary eclipse, in the 1st Decanate of *Libra*, provoketh furious and tempestuous hailstorms.

♎ 10° to 20°.—In the 2nd, mischief and troubles to everyone.

♎ 20° to 30°.—In the 3rd, death to some famous and illustrious men.

♏ 0° to 10°.—An eclipse of the *Moon* in the 1st Decanate of *Scorpio* causeth much thunder and lightning, and sometimes earthquakes.

♏ 10° to 20°.—In the 2nd it causes a dry air and burning fevers.

♏ 20° to 30°.—In the 3rd the same is threatened, and death ; many seditions, quarrels and troubles, over and above.

♐ 0° to 10°.—An eclipse of the *Moon*, in the 1st Decanate of *Sagittarius*, sendeth thefts and rapines.

♐ 10° to 20°.—In the 2nd, destruction to horses and mules.

♐ 20° to 30°.—In the 3rd, the pestilence and many evils.

♑ 0° to 10°.—The *Moon* eclipsed in the 1st Decanate of *Capricorn*, shows untimely death ; or mischief to some illustrious and noble man.

♑ 10° to 20°.—In the 2nd, frequent incursions and assaults of soldiers, thefts, robberies and captivities.

♑ 20° to 30°.—In the 3rd, the death of some king in the dominion of *Capricorn*, also sedition.

♒ 0° to 10°.—The *Moon* eclipsed in the 1st Decanate of *Aquarius* denotes the misfortunes of some king under Aquarius.

♒ 10° to 20°.—In the 2nd, universally hurteth the seed of the earth.

♒ 20° to 30°.—In the 3rd, a change in all things.

♓ 0° to 10°.—The *Moon* eclipsed in the 1st Decanate of *Pisces*, brings sadness and anxiety to those we call priests, and religious houses.

♓ 10° to 20°.—In the 2nd, the death of some great and illustrious person.

♓ 20° to 30°.—In the 3rd, thefts, rapines, robberies by land, and piracies and troubles by sea.

ECLIPTIC. The circle in which the Sun appears to move. Its name is derived from the fact that eclipses occur therein. From patient observation the early astrologers discovered that the Sun appeared to make a circuit through the constellations, a complete revolution making one year. This belt around the heavens is known as the zodiac. See ZODIAC.

EGO. The " Self," or consciousness in man. That which is the " I am I." The consciousness is divided into two, apparently, as when identified with the personal, it is the Personality, but when identified with the higher consciousness, it is known as the Individuality.

ELECTIONS. The electing of a time to commence any new undertaking, setting out on journeys, for buying or selling, marrying, etc. " There is a time for everything." The nativity must be studied if the election is to be made reliable, and the directions that are in operation at the time of election must also be carefully considered, and in conjunction with this the Moon's daily position and aspects must be known. The following are some of the rules of the early astrologers :

First look to the Ascendant of the Nativity, or map for the question, and make your election accordingly, but note that if the ascendant and its lord be unfortunate in the radix, no election can be made that would produce results so advantageous as when the ascendant and ruler were well fortified. If the chief significator of any business be unfortunate in the radix, there can be no time elected to prevent the mischief threatened.

It may often be noticed that some men and occupations thrive and prosper some years more than others, at other times, on the contrary, do what they may, their business and endeavours, and all important undertakings, generally, prove unsuccessful. The reason is that their significator is more strong and fortified in the former case, but weak and debilitated in the latter.

When the true significator is known, with its essential and accidental fortitudes and debilities, the student cannot err, providing the rules are diligently observed, there being such an harmony and a concordancy between the celestial creatures and our terrestrial affairs, according to that excellent saying of " Hermes " :

> " There is nothing here beneath that is not
> Governed and ruled by what is above."

Know, then, that in the judging of elections special attention must be paid to the business in hand ; for according to the nature thereof must your business be ordered and the time chosen ; as for earthly business or affairs, as planting, sowing, and the like, an earthly sign must be chosen ; if appertaining to fire, a fiery sign ; if to the water, a watery one.   As, for example, if you would elect a time for the speedy despatch of any business, a movable sign must be chosen ; if for electing anything for a permanency, a fixed sign.

The student should mark well the planet signifying the affair in hand, and chiefly the Moon, because she has a general signification in all matters.   If the person would desire to consult superiors or ask favours ; the Sun should be well placed and aspected ; if concerning marriage or love affairs, Venus must be taken as chief consideration.   The sign and house signifying any such business in the nativity ought to be regarded and well dignified.   If you would elect a time for profit, let the Moon be in good aspect to the second house, any planet therein or its ruler, as well as the second in the figure for elections.

Note that Jupiter and Venus may sometimes be malevolent and unfortunate for the person signified by the nativity ; especially when ruling eight, twelfth and sixth houses ; they then, if badly aspected and unfortunately placed, occasion sickness, poverty, imprisonment, mischief and death as effectually as Saturn and Mars, and so by the same rule Saturn and Mars may be decidedly fortunate when strong and well fortified.

Avoid elections at such times as the ☽ separates from the ☌ or ☍ of the Sun, and immediately goes to the configuration of an infortune : for it shows that if the place of the ☌ or ☍ be unfortunate, the business then begun shall come to no good end ; but if the place of the ☌ or ☍ be fortunate, it shows that the beginning of the business then in agitation shall be good, but it shall not succeed in the end.

But if the Moon separate from ☌ or ☍, and apply to good aspect of Jupiter, Venus, or any planet that is fortunately placed and aspected in the nativity or question and the place of the ☌ or ☍ be unfortunate, it signifies that the beginning of the business shall be bad, and the end of it good, and if the place of the ☌ or ☍ be fortunate, and the Moon apply immediately to a fortune, it denotes that both the beginning and end of the works shall result in good.

The Influence of the Moon's Aspects.

☽ ☌ □ or ☍ ♄.—An unfortunate day. Avoid the company of aged persons ; commence nothing of importance ; defer desires.

☽ ✶ or ∠ ♄.—Good day for building and planting trees. Seek the company of aged persons ; fortunate for Saturnian things.

☽ ☌ ✶ or △ ♃.—A fortunate day. Begin any good work, take counsel, consult judges and ecclesiastical persons, lawyers and persons in public offices.

☽ ☌ □ or ☍ ♂.—An unfortunate day. Avoid contentions, take no journey, make no new friendships.

☽ ✶ or △ ♂.—A day for enterprise, activity, etc. Push all business matters.

☽ ✶ or △ ☉.—Seek employment, travel for health, ask favours of superiors and great men. This is also a good day for discovering anything lost.

☽ □ or ☍ ☉.—A day to be avoided in all things. Deal not with superiors and ask no favours ; not good for travel ; begin nothing of importance.

☽ ☌ ✶ or △ ♀.—A day for pleasure. Put on new garments, seek the love of women ; good for courtship and marriage, and all kinds of amusements that give pleasure to the many. Hire servants.

☽ □ and ☍ ♀.—Avoid the company of the opposite sex ; do not engage servants ; a bad day for courtship and marriage.

☽ ☌ ✶ or △ ☿.—Good for all kinds of clerical work, travelling. Apply yourself to study, make up accounts, write letters, commence things of an ingenious nature.

☽ □ and ☍ ☿.—Not good for study, or travel, or sending messages. Do not send out accounts or write anything important, such as editorial work, or anything that comes before the many.

Elections for :

Receiving and Borrowing Money.

In this matter the lord of the second house must be well fortified, also the cusp of the second house in the radix, and the lord of the house in which the ruler of the second occupies. If possible, Jupiter should be well aspected, as he is a general significator of wealth.

When the Moon is either in the first degree of Gemini, Leo, or Sagittarius, or on the cusp of the ascendant, it is not safe either to borrow or lend, for much trouble may ensue.

If you would borrow money privately so that none may know of it, let the Moon when you borrow or receive it be under the Sun's beams and going to conjunction of the fortunes when she is separate from the Sun, or some other good aspect of the fortunes in no way afflicted, and this will cause it to be kept private and close, but if the Moon be joined or apply by any aspect to Mars when she separates from the Sun, the business will be divulged and known by many ; see also that the Moon be not in conjunction with the dragon's head or tail.

Of Buying to Profit again by Sale

In buying anything to make advantage or gain from it, fortify the Moon especially. Let Mercury be well aspected, also the lord of the second and if possible the lord of the ascendant, let the Moon also be joined to Mercury by body or good aspect, and free from affliction and free from the bad aspect of Mars.

If you cannot fortify Mercury see that the Moon is well aspected, the eleventh house, and the lord thereof, but let Mercury be free from the evil aspects of Mars, and if you can by any means let him be in conjunction or good aspect of Venus.

On Selling to Advantage

To do this let the Moon be in Taurus, Cancer, Virgo or Pisces, free from affliction and separating from the conjunction or aspect of the fortunes and applying to the aspect (not conjunction) of the infortunes.

This is good for the seller, but the contrary for the buyer.

Removing from One Place to Another

For good success and end in this matter fortify the sign on cusp of fourth and its ruler, and if possible let Taurus or Leo be on the cusp of the fourth, for this denotes the goodness of the place. Also be careful that the above-mentioned places and significators be free from the aspects of the malevolents, and if possible not only so, but in con-figurations of the fortunes. If it is desirable to remain permanently, then let the Moon be in a fixed sign at the same time, if required temporarily the Moon in a cardinal or common sign ; for all new undertakings the Moon increasing in light in Taurus is good, signifying success and permanency in the affair.

Partnership and Agreement

The ascendant, its ruler the Moon and planet from whom the Moon last separated, are significators of the party who begins the business ; the seventh, its ruler, and the planet the Moon next applies to, of the other ; the tenth and its ruler shall signify what is, or shall happen between them ; and the fourth and its ruler, the end of the business. Look then whether the ascendant or seventh house be benevolently aspected by the lord of the tenth or in which he is most dignified, and judge that the party signified by the house he is most in favour with, to prosper or be most stable or firm in the matter.

Be sure that the Moon, the ascendant and its ruler, are placed at the time of making the agreement and partnership in common signs, and fortify them and let them be free from impediment, and the evil configurations of the infortunes, and if possible place them in the aspect with the fortunes. Moreover let the Moon be increasing in light and motion.

On the Making of Wills

When a will is made let not the Moon be in a movable sign nor the ascendant, nor its ruler, if it is intended to stand ; for this denotes its mutability, and that after a short time it shall be altered. Therefore let the ascendant be fixed and the Moon and the lord thereof placed in fixed signs ; for this denotes permanency.

Ninth House Journeys

In the beginning of any journey let the Moon be increasing in light and motion, free from impediment and affliction of the infortunes, for an infortune afflicting the Moon does more hurt than when it afflicts the ascendant, and let her not be in the second, eighth, fourth, sixth, nor twelfth, but in the fifth, and if possible beheld of the fortunes. Also let Mercury be free from combustion and evil aspects of the infortunes ; place also a fortune in the ascendant or an angle, for such an election denotes safety, joy and gladness in the journey ; and let not the Moon be in the ascendant, neither going nor returning, for it signifies sickness and grief in the journey.

Ninth House (on Learning of Science)

In commencing to learn any science see that the ascendant (for the time the study is begun) is a humane sign, and the lord of the ascendant in the tenth house or entering thereinto, the lord of the tenth in configuration of the ascendant, as also the lord of the ninth ; and let the Moon be joined to Mercury, or applying by good aspect, and Mercury strong and well dignified.   Make also Mercury lord of the ascendant in a good aspect and let not the Moon be decreasing in light nor descending in latitude ; and make the lord of the ninth to be in reception with the lord of the ascendant.

Of learning any Art or Occupation

In this matter you must judge the planet signifying the trade or profession you would learn.   Let the ascendant or tenth house be a sign wherein that planet beareth dominion by house ; for example, if you desire to be a merchant place Gemini or Virgo in the ascendant, or Libra, and the last fifteen degrees of Sagittarius or Aquarius. Fortify the lord of the ascendant, the cusp of the tenth and its lord Mercury and also the Moon.   Special care is needed with regard to Mercury because he is the planet signifying the trade or profession.

Marriage

Let the Moon be increasing in light and motion at the time of marriage, and see that she is not joined to any infortune in the ascendant, for that signifies that the parties then married shall be continually in strife and contention, brawling and discord, so likewise if in either of their nativities this position be found.

In this question Venus is the principal planet to be looked to. She should not be cadent, retrograde, combust, nor in her fall or detriment, nor in any evil configurations with the infortunes, for it is impossible the marriage should be good where Venus is impotent or afflicted ; neither can it be bad if she be strong and well aspected by the fortunes ; for in marriage she is the chief significatrix ; therefore, if possible, it would be best for Jupiter to be in sextile or trine with Venus, or if these two be in reception and the Moon in the house of either Jupiter or Venus, and if possible also in good aspect with them, or the ruler of the seventh in sextile or trine with Venus, the Moon, or lord of the ascendant, but make the lord of the seventh apply, or else be disposed of by them, either by house or exaltation.

ELEMENTALS.—Spirits of the Elements.   The creatures evolved in the four kingdoms or elements—fire, earth, air and water.   The fire elements are named Salamanders ; Earth, Gnomes ; Air, Sylphs ; and Water, Undines.

ELEVATED.—A term applied to a planet that is elevated over another. The planet nearest to the mid-heaven is the most elevated. If the ruler of the ascendant is in elevation over all the other planets, the position considerably strengthens it and gives it great power.

ELEVATION BY LATITUDE.—The planet having the most latitude is thus elevated.

ELEVATION BY SIGN.—Planets in ♈ are elevated over those in ♉ and so on through the signs of the zodiac.

ELEVATION OF THE POLE.—The latitude of the birthplace.

ELONGATION.—The angular distance of a heavenly body from the Sun, eastward or westward.

EMBOLISMIC LUNATIONS.—In every year there are twelve Moons of 29½ days each, this leaves an average of 11 days to complete the year of 365 days. When the odd days amount to 30, they complete another lunation, which Placidus termed embolismic. Each of these embolismic lunations are supposed to form a year of the native's life, commencing from the moment when the Moon is exactly at the same distance from the Sun as at birth. Judgment is then formed on these lunations in a method peculiar to those who use them as a means of directing.

EPHEMERIS.—A tabulation of the latitude and longitude, declination, etc., of the planets for certain days in the year. The astronomical ephemeris used by astrologers gives the geocentric positions of the planets each day and they may be obtained from the year 1800. That in most common use is *Raphael's Astronomical Ephemeris of the Planets' Places*. They are also issued each year by " Zadkiel " and others, and are mostly compiled from the *Nautical Almanack*.

EPOCH.—A birth moment, or the beginning of a period at a given point of time. This term is also used for a system of rectification, the rule being that the Moon's place about nine months previous to the nativity is the ascending or descending degree at the moment of physical birth. See RECTIFICATION.

EQUATION OF TIME.—The difference between mean and sidereal time at noon. It is now unnecessary to make any allowance for the equation of time, the ephemeris now published giving the sidereal time for each day ; the only equation therefore required is that for the time elapsed since noon on the previous day, which is explained under the heading of CORRECTIONS in this dictionary.

EQUATION OF ARCS OF DIRECTION.—One degree of arc equals one year of life, and every five minutes of arc one month in time, thus 30°45′ in arc would equal thirty years nine months in time.

EQUATOR.—A great circle of the celestial vault at right angles to its axis, and dividing it with a northern and southern hemisphere. It is constituted by the plane of the earth's equator, produced in every direction till it reaches the concave of the celestial sphere. In his progress north and south, and *vice versa*, the Sun is twice a year on the celestial equator, *viz.*, at the equinoxes (*q.v.*). The point in the equator which touches the meridian is raised above the true horizon by an arc which is the complement of the latitude.

EQUINOCTIAL SIGNS.—Aries and Libra.

EQUINOXES.—The two points of intersection of the ecliptic and equator. The days and nights are then equal. When the Sun crosses the equator at the north point, Aries, it is termed the vernal equinox ; the opposite point, Libra, is then the autumnal equinox.

EROS.—The Greek god of love. The name given to the new planet discovered by De Witt.

ESOTERIC ASTROLOGY.—The hidden or secret side of the divine science of Astrology. The branch of Astrology that is concerned with the inner growth of individuals, and that which deals with the science from an occult standpoint. It teaches us that the ego takes possession of many bodies, each of which comes under the planetary law operating at the physical birth. During each earth-life, the ego, through the personality, may sow fresh seeds for future reaping, and also reap the results of its thoughts, desires and actions in the previous birth or births. The fate of each individual is determined by what is known as its " karma," every action having its corresponding reaction, good thoughts producing good actions and selfish or evil thoughts the reverse. Esoteric Astrology may be illustrated as follows :—The luminaries represent the individuality and personality. The Sun the former, which is the light that rules by day, and the Moon the latter, which rules by night. The planet Mercury, the winged messenger of the gods, acts as intermediary between these two. The position and aspects of these three factors would therefore be very important in a study of esoteric Astrology. The signs and planets may then be considered as an expression of the man.

The twelve signs probably correspond to the aura (the cloud, or luminous mist which surrounds the man). The ascending sign might be taken to represent the physical body, and the Moon that which is now known as the "etheric," or the body drawn from the ether upon which the physical body is built ; the planets Mars and Venus as representatives of the "astral" or desire body ; Saturn and Mercury the mind body, and Jupiter what is known as the causal body or vehicle of the individuality. The various grades of matter, or the conditions through which the ego normally functions, are supposed to be indicated by the divisions of the signs into groups of fire, air, earth and water—the fiery signs giving the finest ethers, the air the mental, or "devachanic," the watery the "astral" matter, and the earthy the physical.

ESSENTIAL DIGNITIES. A planet is said to be essentially dignified, when placed in its own sign, or the sign of its exaltation.

ETHER. The highest substance at present known to physical science. "An almost infinitely attenuated and elastic medium, which fills all space, and which we name the *æther*."—TYNDALL. The truth as taught by occult science, is that it is not a special substance, but rather a state of ordinary matter, far more refined than the gaseous condition.

EVOLUTION. The development and growth of all things from the lowest to the highest order. All is progress, from the first ensoulment of pure spirit, through the various kingdoms to man, and from thence to God, the central power of the solar system.

EXALTATION. The planets are exalted in certain signs. The Sun in Aries ; Moon in Taurus ; Mars in Capricorn ; Saturn in Libra ; Jupiter in Cancer ; the Venus in Pisces. There are many explanations to account for the reason of these exaltations. The best explanation is based upon the esoteric idea that the planets correspond to the principles. The Sun, ruler of the heart, life and vitality, is exalted in Aries from the standpoint of illumination, Aries, ruling the head, would be illuminated by the presence of the Sun in that sign. The Moon, ruling the etheric double, also a wandering and changeable influence, would be exalted in Taurus, owing to the fixed and earthy nature of this sign. Mars, king of the passional, emotional and sense nature, would be exalted in the house of the lower mind, Capricorn, having more power in this sign by its saturnine nature. Saturn, the

E

planet of the lower mind, is exalted in Libra, by reason of this sign being the house of balance and Justice. Venus in Pisces, this being the end of the zodiac, the sign of understanding and universal love. Jupiter in Cancer; owing to the purity and philanthropy of Jupiter, is the sign governing the feelings and emotions, the idea being that emotion may be turned into devotion.

EXOTERIC. The outer or exposed. The opposite to esoteric.

F. The sixth letter of the alphabet.

FACE. The sixth part of a sign of the zodiac, containing 5°, as a decanate, being the third part, contains 10°. Each face when rising impresses its influence upon the disposition of those born under that part of the sign ascending. Many descriptions of these faces have been given, but the following are those used in practice by the author. *N.B.*—The planet rising in the ascendant at birth will always modify the influence of the face ascending.

Aries

1° ♈ 5°.—A martial face. A fearless person, ambitious, and one able to lead others. Quick and ingenious and generally a good speaker.

5° ♈ 10°.—A mixture of Venus and Mercury, with an undercurrent of Mars. This face generally gives pride and conceit, and some tendency towards resentment or indignation. The Taurus influence in this face causes jealousy. The fortunes are mixed.

10° ♈ 15°.—A face of change and lively fancy. There is a love of fame and activity, or unrest.

15° ♈ 20°.—A face of ingenuity, tact and keen intellect, giving good commercial instincts.

20° ♈ 25°.—Deception and an amorous tendency indicated; the life may be affected through the death of others with whom the native may be concerned.

25° ♈ 30°.—Fortune through impulsive action; a very ambitious nature, often reckless in the early part of life, but attains position at the close.

Taurus

1° ♉ 5°.—A steady nature with artistic tastes. Very determined and industrious. Gaining success through concentration and resolution.

5° ♉ 10°.—A peevish nature, having many sorrows in the life through lack of energy and enterprise.

10° ♉ 15°.—Careless, indifferent and subject to many temptations are those coming under this face. This face gives a good form.

15° ♉ 20°.—Lack of energy and want of courage is denoted ; the nature is too soft and negative with psychic tendencies.

20° ♉ 25°.—A tendency towards deception or dogmatism with fully acquisitiveness is indicated. This face generally denotes persons alive to their own ends.

26° ♉ 30°.—This is not a good face ; those born under these degrees should be temperate and avoid excesses in all so-called pleasures.

Gemini

1° ♊ 5°.—There are two natures born in this face. Those in the first portion will be mentally active but fond of double-dealing. In the latter portion approbativeness and self-esteem may be very marked. It is not a good face.

5° ♊ 10°.—A dignified person is indicated, and one who overrates his abilities.

10° ♊ 15°.—A clever person is denoted. Those born in this face may accomplish much by their intelligence and ingenuity.

15° ♊ 20°.—A subtle nature, full of deep motives, but one who may outwit himself, is described by this face.

20° ♊ 15°.—Those born under this face are liable to deceive themselves and may become hypocritical. They will find it difficult to understand their own nature.

25° ♊ 30°.—Artistic, ingenious, active and witty are the characteristics of this face. Good ability for scientific research is indicated.

Cancer

1° ♋ 5°.—A somewhat suspicious nature is denoted ; resentment and anger may often be easily provoked.

5° ♋ 10°.—Oratory, and a desire to come before the public, are indicated, but unless morally developed the native may be tricky and unreliable.

10° ♋ 15.°—A face of power, tenacity and quiet endurance. This face is very considerably affected by the Moon's position in the nativity.

15° ♋ 20°.—More show than reality is denoted, and the native is much affected by surroundings ; the nature may be peevish and re-pining.

20° ♋ 25°.—A psychic nature, easily moved by sensation, very impressionable, and often reflecting others.

25° ♋ 30°.—Very aspiring and somewhat ambitious ; but inclined to religious feelings.

Leo

1° ♌ 5°.—This face denotes a person full of pride and self-esteem, somewhat boastful and daring. This nature is considerably im-proved through experience.

5° ♌ 10°.—A very harmonious and peaceful nature, kind and sympathetic ; very courteous and amiable.

10° ♌ 15°.—This face denotes an unforgiving spirit, and one who retains evil. The secret for this face is chastity, by that means love and wisdom may be obtained.

15° ♌ 20°.—An inharmonious face ; there is much danger of sel-fishness and an undesirable ambition into which hypocrisy may enter.

20° ♌ 25°.—This face gives a good understanding, and denotes one who is loyal, sincere and sympathetic.

25° ♌ 30°.—Those who are born under this face should avoid all tendencies to gambling. The head and heart may be too easily drawn into pleasure.

Virgo.

1° ♍ 5°.—This face indicates a dual nature, and the motives are inclined to be selfish, and the native may think too highly of himself ; but real ability is denoted.

5° ♍ 10°.—This is a good face, indicating a wise and discreet per-son, loving truth and honour.

10° ♍ 15°.—A successful face. It denotes a lover of justice, and one inclined to be very discriminative.

15° ♍ 20°.—The face of mysticism, denoting one who may be-come wise and skilful. If chaste, a seer and a prophet.

20° ♍ 25°.—An ambitious nature, thoughtful, diplomatic and contemplative ; rising in life through sincerity and attention to details.

25° ♍ 30°.—A very talkative person indicated, but one who will display much ingenuity. Very impressionable and psychic.

Libra

1° ♎︎ 5°.—The face of ability. Those born under this face are sincere, just, honest and prudent.

5° ♎︎ 10°.—This denotes one who may become devotional. There will be much discretion and the desire to do right.

10° ♎︎ 15°.—Ambitious, mentally energetic, thoughtful, chaste and intuitive, are the chief characteristics of this face.

15° ♎︎ 20°.—This face gives perception, discretion, prudence and a quiet, inoffensive nature.

20° ♎︎ 25°.—The form and objective side of life will be much appreciated by those born in this face; they will be lovers of beauty.

25° ♎︎ 30°.—Much will depend upon the position of Venus, as to the influence this face will have upon the native. The nature is versatile and well disposed.

Scorpio

1° ♏︎ 5°.—This face gives dignity, confidence and a strong will. The character is faithful, sincere and intuitive.

5° ♏︎ 10°.—A lover of justice is denoted; those born under this face possess some real talent which may be latent.

10° ♏︎ 15°.—This face gives keen criticism; and denotes one who may excel in judgment and the power to dive into nature's secrets.

15° ♏︎ 20°.—Tact and diplomacy are promised to those born under this face. There will be a serious and thoughtful tendency. This face indicates a strong character.

20° ♏︎ 25°.—Those born under this face may become good judges of human nature, and obtain magical ability.

25° ♏︎ 30°.—The first portion of this face may be quite different from the last—the former being positive and intellectually bright, while the latter inclines to feeling and the senses.

Sagittarius

1° ♐︎ 5°.—This face gives a good mind and disposition, and denotes one who is honest and trustworthy. The first half gives benevolence, the last half acquisitiveness.

5° ♐︎ 10°.—Those born under this face have pure desires, and love all things that make for the good of others. They have a religious spirit and study subjects connected with higher thought.

10°♐ 15°.—This face gives a fullness of vitality, and a full share of animal spirit ; the nature is generous and free, and often too expressive.

15°♐ 20°.—Those born under this face are often a misfit, generally too effeminate, and they find it difficult to express their true nature. They are not always real and sincere.

20°♐ 25°.—This face gives deception, and an over-anxiety for fame and public approval. The native may pretend to more than he can fulfil. It is an unfortunate face.

25° ♐ 30°.—A sincere nature, and one who loves to be active and busy is denoted. The passions are active and they are often too hasty.

Capricorn

1° ♑ 5°.—An ambitious but just and well-balanced person is denoted. The natives of this face may rise in life and hold prominent positions ; they have high ideals.

5° ♑ 10°.—The motive temperament abounds in this face ; but there may some be signs of weakness in the nature, and the native may seek to perform more than he is really capable of.

10° ♑ 15°.—This face gives a strong character of a pronounced type. There will be plenty of tact and diplomacy and a very ambitious nature.

15° ♑ 20°.—An easy-going disposition with more behind than appears on the surface. The native is affected by others.

20° ♑ 25°.—A successful face with regard to mundane affairs ; acquisitiveness well developed.

25° ♑ 30°.—A weak nature is denoted ; too much vacillation and a tendency to become too effeminate.

Aquarius

1° ♒ 5°.—A clever person is denoted, or one who is fully alive to his own desires ; at times too positive, at others too weak and negative ; rather unreliable.

5° ♒ 10°.—An undesirable nature, inclined to be dogmatic, suspicious and mistrustful. At times too aggressive.

10° ♒ 15°.—This face gives caution and some lack of hope ; yet there is ingenuity and foresight.

15° ♒ 20°.—The character of this face will be influenced by the position of the Moon. The native will desire recognition of what he does, but will not always obtain it.

20° ♒ 25°.—There is much selfishness in this face unless the native is well-developed morally. If the mind is under control much may be accomplished by those born in this face.

25° ♒ 30°.—The first portion of this face gives a good disposition, a just and faithful nature. The last portion indicates cunning and deceit.

Pisces

1° ♓ 5°.—A double life may be lived by those born under this face. It gives a lack of decision and a wavering disposition.

5° ♓ 10°.—This face gives understanding, prudence and a peaceful disposition.

10° ♓ 15°.—A mutable disposition ; somewhat lacking in firmness.

15° ♓ 20 ♅.—External firmness, but internal indecision. Affable, kind and well disposed.

20° ♓ 25°.—A psychic nature, very impressionable, fond of company, and able to cater for many.

25° ♓ 30°.—This face indicates one who may talk too much, and be too easily affected by surroundings ; the mind is generally very active.

FALL. A term applied to a planet when in the sign opposite to that in which it has exaltation. The Moon " falls " in Scorpio ; Venus in Virgo ; Mars in Cancer ; Saturn in Aries ; Jupiter in Capricorn ; and the Sun in Libra. The term applies more to horary than natal Astrology.

FAMILIARITY. When planets are in mutual aspect they are said to be in familiar aspect.

FATE. That which is irrevocable, predestined and fixed. The modern teaching of Astrology supposes a certain amount of fate in all lives until freedom from planetary influence is attained. When the will is active and is used, all may rise above the limitations of fate. Fate is made by desire, which attracts men to the objective side of existence ; to be free from desire the will must be strong enough to overcome all attractions towards physical bondage. The Moon and Mars are the principal factors in making fate, and also the planet

Saturn, but there is also free-will as well as desire in the latter, therefore everything must depend upon the position and aspects of Saturn in the judgment of fate and free-will. Mercury, owing to its dual nature, may be either on the side of one or the other. See also FREE-WILL.

FEMININE SIGNS. The even or negative signs are said to be feminine in nautre, but it is probable that the term negative or receptive signs would be more appropriate. They are ♉, ♋, ♍, ♏, ♑, ♓.

FERAL. An old term used to denote the bestial nature of certain signs. Its meaning is vague, and could only apply to undeveloped civilisations.

FIERY SIGNS. Aries, Leo, and Sagittarius. These signs belong to the fiery triplicity. They are the life-giving and vital signs of the zodiac

FIGURE. The scheme or map of the heavens, at any particular time. The term is a common phrase used by astrologers.

FIXED SIGNS. Taurus, Leo, Scorpio, and Aquarius. These signs always come between the cardinal and common ; they represent the vital centres of the physical body, ♉ the throat, ♌ the heart, ♏ the generative organs, and ♒ the blood.

The fixed signs give an important clue to the interpretation of a nativity, and usually indicate that which is fixed, and difficult to remove. When the majority of the planets are found in fixed signs at birth the character is very determined, steadfast and reliable. They give reserve power, self-reliance, patience, endurance, and authority. The fixed signs also give originality, power of thought, concentration and industry.

The most rigid of the fixed signs is Taurus, which is unbending, stubborn and obstinate ; it represents the neck fixed to support the head. Taurus signifies external will-power. Leo signifies the internal will prompted by the heart and its motives. Scorpio, the externalising will of action, and reproduction. Aquarius, the will of expressed thought and motive combined. The fixed signs taken as a whole represent a serpent, each sign symbolising a stage of uncoiling.

FIXED STARS. The fixed stars are supposed, by a few astrologers, to have effect according to the aspects of the luminaries to them ; it is very doubtful if these influences are felt to any appreciable extent in any nativity. The following is the table of some of the fixed stars, their magnitude, longitude and supposed nature :

Name.	Magnitude.	Longitude.	Nature.
β Arietis - - - -	3½	2 ♉ 29	♄♂
α Arietis, Ram's following Horn	2	6 ,, 10	♄♂
η Tauri - - - -	3	28 ,, 30	♂☽
γ Tauri, Hyades - - -	4	4 ♊ 19	♂☽
ε Tauri, Oculus - - -	3½	6 ,, 59	♀
α Tauri, Alderbaran - -	1	8 ,, 18	♂
β Tauri, Bull's North Horn -	2	21 ,, 5	♂
γ Geminorum - - -	2½	7♋37	☿♀
α ,, Castor - -	1½	18 ,, 46	♂♀♄
β ,, Pollux - -	1½	21 ,, 45	♂
Praesepe - - - -	Nebula	5♌47	♂☽
γ Cancri - - - -	4½	6 ,, 4	♂☉
δ ,, - - - -	4½	7 ,, 14	♂☉
α Leonis, Regulus - - -	1½	28 ,, 21	♂
α Virginis Spica - - -	1	22♎21	♀♂
α Librae, South scale - -	2½	13♏35	♄♀
β ,, North ,, - -	2	17 ,, 53	♃♂
β Scorpii - - - -	2	1 ♐ 42	♄♀
α ,, Antares - - -	1	8 ,, 16	☿♂
η ,, - - - -	2½	16 ,, 29	♄♀
δ Capricorni - - -	3	22 ♒ 3	♄

FORM. The form is governed by the degree of the rising sign, and the position of the Moon at birth. The features are sometimes expressed through the position and aspects of Mercury. The planets in a general way have some influence in affecting the form of the body, but particularly when rising or near the ascendant.

FORTITUDES. A planet is said to be well fortified when exalted angular and well posited in the map.

FORTUNES. The planets Jupiter and Venus are known as the fortunes or fortunate planets. The Sun also, when free from afflictions, and well placed.

FORTUNATE SIGNS. The positive signs ♈, ♊, ♌, ♎, ♐, ♒, are considered fortunate when rising.

FREE-WILL. The exercise of will to overcome obstacles or influences, and so change the direction of the operating force that it works in harmony with the will as opposed to the yielding to the influence which is called fate.

FRUITFUL SIGNS. The watery signs, Cancer, Scorpio, and Pisces.

FRUSTRATION. The application of one planet to another intercepted before becoming complete by a third planet receiving the application. This term is used in Horary Astrology, and whatever is promised is said to be frustrated.

G. The seventh letter of the alphabet.

GABRIEL. The angel of the Moon.

GEMINI. The third sign of the zodiac. A common sign, and the first of the airy triplicity. Its position on the cliptic is from 60° to 90°. This is known as a double-bodied and positive sign. The Sun appears to enter this sign about the 20th of May each year.

GENETHLIACAL. A name given to that branch of Astrology which deals solely with nativities, from the word geniture. See NATAL ASTROLOGY.

GENETHLIALOGY. A system of Astrology directly concerned with the birth of individuals, by which the character, mind and senses of those born at any given moment are judged, also the fate and fortunes as described by the map of the heavens then cast. From this figure, horoscope or nativity, a delineation is obtained from its twelve divisions or mansions as follows :

The first house governs the form or personality, the health, constitution and general characteristics. Its rules the head.

The second house, the property, wealth and poverty, or general financial condition. It rules the neck and throat.

The third house governs the educational mind and mental capacity. It is also connected with the relatives. It tules the chest, lungs and shoulders.

The fourth house governs the end of life, the residence or dwelling place, also the father's affairs, inheritance, and the household generally. It rules the breasts and stomach.

The fifth house governs the offspring, nature of pleasures enjoyed, courtships and speculation. It rules the heart and back.

The sixth house indicates the nature of the sickness to which the native is liable during life. It rules the bowels and intestines.

The seventh house governs marriage, law, partnerships and public affairs generally. It rules the veins and kidneys.

The eighth house governs the nature of the *terminus vitæ*, the occult ability, and the prospects of gain by will or legacy. It rules the secret parts and generative system.

The ninth house governs the religious and scientific tendencies, travels, etc. It rules over the thighs.

The tenth house or mid-heaven governs the employment, business or profession, honour and fame, also the mother's affairs. It rules over the knees.

The eleventh governs the hopes, wishes and desires, also the friends and acquaintances. It rules the blood and ankles.

The twelfth house governs the self-undoing, and the occult or hidden side of the life. It rules the feet.

GENITURE. The birth or beginning.

GEOCENTRIC. As viewed from or having relation to the earth as centre, as, the geocentric latitude or longitude ; or what is distinguished from the Heliocentric—that is, as seen from the centre of the Sun. (1) Of a planet ; its latitude as seen from the earth. (2) Of a place on the earth's surface : the angle included between the radius of the earth through the place and the plane of the equator. It is contra-distinguished from geographical latitude, which always exceeds it slightly in amount.

GEOCENTRIC LONGITUDE (of a planet). The distance measured on the ecliptic between the geocentric place and the first point of ♈.

GEOMANCY, ASTROLOGICAL. A system of divination, by which a map containing twelve divisions is used, and the ordinary symbols of geomancy placed therein in conjunction with the ruling planets and signs.

GEORGIUM SIDUS. Another name for the planet Uranus.

GIVER OF LIFE. The Sun. See HYLEG.

GNOMES. A name given to the invisible Nature-spirits belonging to the earthy triplicity.

GNOSTICS.   Philosophers of the early Christian centuries.

GEOMANCY.   A system of divination by lines, or dots, originally made on the earth, but more generally marked on paper.   To practise geomancy the mind must be calm, tranquil and concentrated, or the results will be unsatisfactory.   The symbols used in geomancy appear to have been adopted from a former use of the planetary signs, and may have arisen out of practice of horary Astrology.   The sixteen geomantic symbols are as follows :

Fortuna Major.

Via.

Acquistio.

Puella.

Conjunctio.

Puer.

Carcer.

Caput Draconis.

Fortuna Minor.

Populus.

Lætitia.

Amissio.

Albus.

Rubens.

Tristitia.

Cauda Draconis.

H.   The eighth letter of the alphabet.

HADES.   The land of shadows.

HEABANI.   A famous Chaldæan astrologer.

HEALTH. The life and health are governed by the rising sign. The part of the system, or physical body, which is the most vital or sensitive, will be that ruled by the ascending, or rising sign ; long illnesses often result in this part of the body being weakened. The nature of the complaints a person is liable to may be seen by the sign upon the ascendant at birth.

Aries governs the head and face.

Taurus, the neck and throat.

Gemini, the chest, lungs and extremities.

Cancer, breasts and stomach.

Leo, heart and back.

Virgo, the bowels and intestines.

Libra, the reins and kidneys.

Scorpio, the secret parts.

Sagittarius, the thighs.

Capricorn, the knees.

Aquarius, ankles and blood.

Pisces, feet.

The luminaries have much to do with the state of the health. When in affliction the health is poor and sickness more frequent. When the lights are well placed and free from affliction the constitution is strong and able to resist disease. The Sun governs the structure and the organic conditions ; the Moon the functional arrangements. The health is generally better when the Sun is rising than when it is setting.

The fiery signs rising give vitality, and the watery signs less vitality and a liability to absorb disease. The planets afflicting the Sun, Moon or Ascendant, indicate the nature of the ill-health.

Saturn afflicting the luminaries denotes ill-health from colds, constipation, depression, obstruction, aches and pains, such as rheumatism and osseous complaints.

Mars, from fevers, inflammations, ruptures, and sharp pains from swellings, etc.

Jupiter, bad blood, apoplexy and pleurisy.

Venus, complaints of the generative system, kidneys, etc.

Mercury, nervous and mental troubles.

Uranus, peculiar and uncommon complaints.

It is generally found that signs opposite to the Ascendant, and those holding the malefics, are affected by sympathy and should always be studied, also those of the same nature, such as the cardinal, fixed and common. See DISEASE.

HEART OF THE SUN. See CAZIMI.

HELL. Probably a corruption of the word bel, meaning the Sun, which is supposed to be as hot as the term hell is supposed to imply. It is also said to have been derived from Helios, the Sun.

HELIOCENTRIC. Taking the Sun as the centre.

HELIOCENTRIC ASTROLOGY. A system of so-called Astrology that has sprung up in America in modern times. By this system an attempt is made to read the character of all persons born on the same day, who by this system would have identically the same characters, there being no allowance made for rising signs and houses, this method having no ascendant sign to work from. A map of the heavens is arranged with the signs of the zodiac starting from the cusp of the ordinary fourth house in regular order from Aries to Pisces going westward, and into this map the heliocentric positions of the planets are placed. The planets Uranus, Neptune, Saturn and Jupiter are always 180 degrees distant, or in the opposite houses from their positions as tabulated in the ephemeris. [This is entirely incorrect.—ED.] As a system of Astrology it has no value ; although it may be used as a character delineator, as set forth in *Solar Biology*.

HELIOS. The Greek Sun God, who went home every evening (sunset) in a golden boat which had wings.

HEMISPHERE. Half of the circle in the heavens surrounding the earth. The oriental or eastern is that part of the hemisphere ascending. The *Imum Cœli*, that part from the M.C. to the west. [No. The Imum Cœli is the cusp of the 4th house.—ED.] The occidental that which is setting.

HERCULES. A Northern constellation.

HERBS OF THE PLANETS :

Sun.—Almond, angelica, ash tree, bay tree, celandine, centaury, chamomile, corn hornwort, eyebright, heart trefoil, juniper, male peony, marigolds, mistletoe, olive, pimpernel, rosemary, rue, saffron, St. John's wort, sun dew, tormentil, turnsole, vine, viper's bugloss, walnut.

Moon.—Adder's tongue, cabbage, chickweed, clary, coral-wort, cuckoo flowers, daisy, dog-tooth, duck's meat, iris, lettuce, mercury, moonwort, mouse-ear, pearlwort, privet, pumpkin, purslain, rattle grass, spunk, wallflowers, water arrowhead, watercress, water lily, water violet, white lily, white poppy, white rose, white saxifrage, whitlow grass, wild wallflower, willow, winter green.

Mercury.—Azaleas, bitter sweet, calamint, caraway, coralline, dill, elecampane, endive, fennel, hare's foot, hazel, horehound, hound's tongue, lavender, lily of the valley, liquorice, male fern, mandrake, marjoram, mulberry, myrtle, olive spurge, parsley, pellitory, southernwood, star-wort, trefoil, valerian, wild carrots, winter savory.

Venus.—Apples, archangel, artichoke, beans, bear-berry, bishop's weed, black alder, bugle holly, burdock, cloves, cock's head, couch grass, cowslip, cranesbill, cudweed, elder, featherfew, foxgloves, ground ivy, groundsel, kidney-wort, little daisy, marsh mallows, mint, pennyroyal, pennywort, peppermint, red cherries, sanicle, sea holly, sorrel, spear-mint, tansy, throat-wort, vervain.

Mars.—All-heal, aloes, anemone, arsmart, barberry, basil, box tree broom, butcher's broom, capers, catmint, coriander, crowfoot, flax-weed, furze-bush, garden cress, garlic, hawthorn, honeysuckle, hops, horse-tongue, hyssop, lead-wort, leeks, madder, masterwort, mousetail, nettles, onions, plantain, savin, tobacco, wake-robin, wormwood.

Jupiter.—Agrimony, aniseed, apricots, asparagus, balm, balsam, betony, blood-wort, borage, chestnut, cinquefoil, dandelion, fig tree hart's tongue, house leek, jessamine, lime tree, liver wort, maple, myrrh, nailwort, oak, polypody, sage, scurvy grass, small samphire swallow wort, thistle, thorn apple, wild pinks, wild succory.

Saturn.—Aconite, barley, barren wort, beech, black hellebore, blue bottle, comfrey, crosswort, flax-weed, flea-wort, fumitory, gladwin, ground moss, hemlock, hemp, henbane, holly, horse-tail, ivy, jew's ear, knap-weed, knot-grass, mangel, medlar, navelwort, pansies, quince, rupture wort, rushes, tye, sciatica wort, shepherd's purse, sloes, Solomon's seal.

HERMAPHRODITE. Dual-sexed ; male and female ; a term attributed to the planet Mercury owing to his dual nature.

HERMES. A mystical name of the planet Mercury, meaning wisdom.

HERMETIC. Esoteric teaching connected with Hermes. Treatises on Astrology are found in the Hermetic writings. The teaching is " as above so below."

HERSCHEL. The planet Uranus, also known as *Georgium sidus.*

This planet was so named after the astronomer who re-discovered it—Sir Wm. Herschel.

HEXAGON.   Sextile.

HIEROGLYPHICS.   See SYMBOLS.

HINDU ASTROLOGY :

[NOTE.—It is only fair to mention that practically the whole of this section is by SEPHARIAL.   It first appeared in *Modern Astrology*, from which Mr. Leo reprinted it for the dictionary without acknow- ledgment.—ED.]

THE AYANÂMSHA

Having the horoscope of birth in hand, made in the usual European manner, the first thing is to convert it into terms of the Hindu zodiac. This is done as follows :

1.   From the year of birth subtract 498.   This will give the *Ayanâmsha* period.

2.   Multiply the *Ayanâmsha* period by 50⅓" and reduce to degrees, minutes and seconds of space.

3.   Uniformly subtract the number of degrees, minutes and seconds from

(*a*)   The cusps of the houses in the European figure of birth.

(*b*)   The planet's places.

The figure thus obtained is the figure of birth according to the Hindu system.

N.B.—A serious error, which may not be at first apparent, will occur in the event of the student subtracting the *Ayanâmsha* from the mid-heaven only, and then erecting the figure, with this new M.C., from the Tables of Houses, for the oblique ascension of the signs and planets will be falsified.

To avert this possibility, observe that if, in the original European figure, a planet holds a certain place, distant say 5° from the cusp of the Second House, it ought to be in the same relative position in the Hindu figure derived by the above rules.   The only difference will be that the planet may have changed its sign, which is the case when the degrees held by it in any sign are less than the *Ayanâmsha*.

THE ASTERISMS

The Asterisms, or *Nakshatrams*—as they are called in Sanskrit— are twenty-seven in number.   A twenty-eighth Asterism, falling in

Capricorn, is sometimes used in Hindu Astrology for the purpose of some branches of *Prashna*, or Horary Astrology. Its name is *Abhijit.* The twenty-eight Asterisms correspond to the " Mansions of the Moon," used sometimes by Hermetists and Kabalists, but very seldom in ordinary European Astrology.

Every Asterism has its own specific nature just like the signs of the zodiac ; a change corresponding thereto usually takes place in the life of a native at the Moon's transit from one to another of them. The Asterisms count from the beginning of the Hindu zodiac for purposes of the present systems, and are each exactly 13°20' in extent. Each Asterism is divided into four parts, called Pâdams, or quarters, but for simplicity we may call them merely parts.

As there are 30° in each sign, and 13°20' in each Asterism, it follows that a sign contains just 2¼ Asterisms, *i.e.*, two whole Asterisms and one " part." The following table shows the Asterisms contained in each of the signs ; a separate column indicates the planet ruling each Asterism, and another, the period through which it is said to rule :

Table of Asterisms.

♈	♌	♐		
4. Ashvini	Magha	Mula	☊	7
4. Bharani	Purva Phalguni	Purvashadha	♀	20
1. Krittika	Uttara Phalguni	Uttara Shadha	☉	6
♉	♍	♑		
3. Krittika	Uttara Phalguni	Uttara Shadha	☉	6
4. Rohini	Hasta	Shravana	☽	10
2. Mrigashirsha	Chitra	Dhanistha	♂	7
♊	♎	♒		
2. Mrigashirsha	Chitra	Dhanistha	♂	7
4. Ardra	Svati	Satabhisha	♌	18
3. Punarvasu	Vishaka	Purvabhadra	♃	16
♋	♏	♓		
1. Punarvasu	Vishaka	Purvabhadra	♃	16
4. Pushya	Anuradha	Uttarabhadra	♄	19
4. Aslesha	Tyeshta	Revati	☿	17

F

If attention be paid to the following explanation the table will be soon understood. In the first column we find ♈, and beneath it four Ashvini, four Bharani, one Krittika, which means that in the sign Aries there are four parts of Ashvini, four of Bharani and one of Krittika. Under ♉ we find the remaining three parts of Krittika, the whole of Rohini and half of Mrigashirsha. Under ♈ again and opposite to Ashvini we find in the second column the Asterism Magha under Leo, and Mula under Sagittarius ; while still further in the same line we find ☋ (Dragon's Tail, called *Ketu* by the Hindus), and the figure of which means that Ashvini, Magha, and Mula are all ruled by Ketu, and that Ketu's period is seven years.

The Hindu equivalents for the planets are as follows : The Sun is *Surya* ; the Moon, *Chandra* ; Mars, *Kuja* ; Mercury, *Budham* ; Jupiter *Curu* ; Venus, *Shukra* ; Saturn, *Shani* ; the Dragon's Head or Moon's Ascending Node, *Rahu* ; the Dragon's Tail or Moon's Descending Node, *Ketu*.

THE PLANET'S PERIODS

The total of the different periods is 120 years, which the Hindus regard as the natural life-period. This period, therefore, in some way corresponds to the complete circle of 360, which is three times 120. The zodiacal circle is divided into twenty-seven Asterisms, each of 13°20', and the life-period of 120 years, when divided by nine, the number of the signification employed, gives thirteen years, four months, so that there is a proportion of one degree for each year of life, as in the Western systems.

It will be readily seen, moreover, that the basis of the system lies in the triad :

$$360 = 3 \text{ times } 120$$
$$120 = 3 \quad ,, \quad 40$$
$$40 = 3 \quad ,, \quad 13\tfrac{1}{3}$$
$$9 = 3 \quad ,, \quad 3$$

THE SIGNS OF THE ZODIAC

The Hindu zodiac is similar to the Western, having twelve equal divisions. The order of the signs is the same, and the natures of both the signs and their rulers are, in all essentials, the same as those obtaining among Western astrologers.

The signs have no symbols among the Hindus, who always suppose Aries to be in the first house, and merely mark the Ascendant

(*Lagnam*) either by a line or by the letter L. In the north of India, another system is in vogue ; but all tend to the same end, *viz.*, to determine the rising sign. From this, as a starting-point, the rest of the signs are equally and uniformly distributed through the twelve houses, though there are no symbols to indicate the fact. At the present day there are many astrologers in the north of India who use Tables of Houses and indicate oblique ascension of the signs, but these are mere copyists of the more mathematical systems of the West. In the famous and most ancient of all Nâdis, the *Brighu Samhita*, numerous figures are given, but in none of them is any attention paid to oblique ascension.

The names of the zodiacal signs corresponding to ours are :

Aries,	*Mesham*	Libra,	*Tulam*
Taurus,	*Vrishabham*	Scorpio,	*Vrishchika*
Gemini,	*Mithuna*	Sagittary,	*Dhanus*
Cancer,	*Kâtakam*	Capricorn,	*Makaram*
Leo,	*Simha*	Aquarius,	*Kumbha*
Virgo,	*Kanya*	Pisces,	*Mînam*

The meanings of the Sanskrit words are the same as those of the Latin names in general use.

THE HOUSES

It is at this point that the Hindu system of Astrology really becomes perplexing to the European student. The great variety of seemingly unconnected things attributed to the several houses by the Jyoshis, renders anything like a systematic statement of the rulership of the houses a matter of great difficulty.

The five physical senses (*Gnanendriyas*) are attributed to this, the first house, also. But the *eyes* are ruled in the same system by the second house, the *ears* by the third house. In the same way the religion is said to be ruled by the first house, while all that constitutes it, and from which it is built up, comes under the ninth house, *e.g.*, education, temples, religious instruction, the " thread ceremony " (*upadesha*), the occult or spiritual powers (*siddhis*), etc. Hindu astrologers uniformly attribute the fourth house to the *mother*.

The tenth house, while indicating honour, fame, the family titles and the profession, also denotes in the Hindu system the *father*.

The sixth house, enemies.

The twelfth house the Hindus regard as an *evil* house, but they likewise give *monetary losses* as ruled by this house.

The aspects in Hindu Astrology are counted from sign to sign. There are no half-signs employed, as in the ∠ and ⊡. The *trikonam,* or trine aspect, is the chief aspect, and the half-trikonam, or sextile, belongs to the same order. Both these are good. The *Kendra,* or square aspect, gives good results when good planets are so placed, and evil when the planets are evil. The method of signifying aspects is to refer to the number of signs from the significator which the aspecting body may hold. Thus : if the Sun be in the second house, and Venus in the third house of the figure, Venus is spoken of as in the second from the Sun, and third from *Lagnam* or Ascendant.

In the judgment of a figure the conditions of the planets are taken by sign and house, *i.e.*, by essential and accidental dignities or debilities. The signs and their rulers are the same as with Europeans. The houses are also the same : *Kendra* (angular) first, fourth, seventh, and tenth ; *Panapara* (succedent) second, fifth, eighth, and eleventh ; *Apokalima* (cadent) third, sixth, ninth, twelfth.

Of these houses, the third, fifth, ninth, and eleventh are uniformly good ; and the sixth, eighth, twelfth, evil. The first, second, fourth, seventh and tenth depend upon the planets occupying them. These aspects may be counted from any significator, and must not be restricted to the houses bearing those numerals in the figure itself. *Example* : Ascendant, Aquarius ; Saturn, in the eighth house of figure in the sign ♍, the Sun in Taurus in the fourth of the figure. Here Saturn is evil in regard to the first house ; but accidentally in good aspect to Sun, being in the fifth from that luminary. So that in judging of the things ruled by the fourth house, Saturn would be taken as favourable ; but in relation to the things of the first house, unfavourable.

The planets Jupiter and Venus, Sun and Moon in the fourth from a significator are friendly, unless in their *nicham* or "fall" ; while Saturn and Mars Rahu and Ketu, are evil, unless in their dignities.

It may be mentioned here that the sign ♏ is identified with Rahu and ♉ with Ketu, in which signs they are respectively strong.

The above remarks have reference to judgment from the Radix only.

In judging the general effects of the combination of the planets by period and sub-period, the general rule in regard to the planetary relations is that of *temporal* position. Thus : all planets in the tenth, eleventh, twelfth, second, third, and fourth houses from the significator, and those also which (being themselves *good*) are in the same sign as the significator, are *benefic* ; all other are *evil*. This is the simplest and surest rule that is known in all the books, and, if due allowance be made for the accidental and essential *strength* of the planets, a sure judgment can be given. Yet the essential or natural sympathies and antipathies of the planets among themselves must not be lost sight of, for a temporal relationship cannot entirely prevail against a natural and inherent one that is contrary to it.

ILLUSTRATION

Example : Horoscope of Her Majesty Queen Victoria. The Ayanâmsha, or difference between the Vernal Equinox and the star Revati, is thus determined : 1819 - 498 A.D. = 1321 years, ♅ 50¼″ = 66,490″ = 81°28′10″.

This amount must be subtracted from the Ascendant and the planets' places, and the signs must be set in the figure without regard to oblique ascension, as in the example given below. The subtraction of the Ayanâmsha is not for the purpose of marking the exact degrees held by the planets in the Hindu zodiac, but to determine merely what change of sign, if any, is due to them by the conversion from one zodiac to another. And in the example given, we find that the Ascendant falls in Taurus (*Vrishabham*), the Sun and Moon are in the same sign of the Hindu zodiac, Mercury passes into Aries, Jupiter into Capricorn, and Mars into Pisces. Uranus, not being included in the system of Parashara and of the Hindu writers generally, is left out of the figure, while the Moon's Nodes, ☊ and ☋, are included therein. The signs, too, are differently placed in regard to the houses, being equally distributed throughout. Shorn of all the elements which properly belong to the European figure, and which are not required by the Hindu Jyoshi, the result would be as follows :—

Saturn. Mars.		Jupiter.	
Mercury. Venus. D. Head.	EMPRESS		
Taurus. Sun. Moon.	OF INDIA		Dragon's Tail.

There are different methods of drawing the figures among the Dravidians in the South of India and the Aryans in the North ; and the first house is placed indifferently in various parts of the figure by the several schools of astrologers ; but all would agree in placing the planets and signs in the same relative positions as above. It will be remarked that the ascending sign only is given ; the rest are understood as being identified with the several successive houses of the figure. Reading this figure we say : Taurus rising, with Sun and Moon ; Dragon's Tail in Libra in the sixth ; Jupiter in Capricornus in the ninth ; Saturn and Mars in Pisces in the eleventh ; Venus, Mercury, and Dragon's Head in Aries in the twelfth. A southern Hindu would say : Vrishabha Lagnam, Durya and Chandra ; Ketu in sixth ; Guru in ninth ; Shani, Kuja in eleventh ; Shukra, Budhan and Rahu in twelfth ; and with these elements he would go to work, remarking that Chandra (Moon) is in " Svocham " (its exaltation), and Shukra in " svanîcham " (its debility).

The accidental relations of the planets are as follows : Dragon's Tail is an " enemy " to all the planets except Jupiter ; Jupiter is friendly to Dragon's Tail, Saturn, Mars, Venus, Mercury, and Dragon's Head, and also to the Sun and Moon ; Saturn, Mars, Venus, Mercury, and Dragon's Head are friendly to all except the Dragon's

Tail ; and the Sun and Moon are friendly to all except the Dragon's Tail. Now, to determine the asterism of birth, observe the *exact* longitude of the Moon in the Hindu zodiac. The longitude given in the European figure of birth is ♊ 3'39°, and that, being reduced by the Ayanâmsha 18°28', gives ♉ 15'11°. Reference to the Table will show that in the sign ♉ there are three parts of Krittika, four of Rohini, and two of Mrigashirsha. Each of these parts we know to be 3°20' in extent ; therefore, three of Krittika = 10° ; and 15°11' – 10° leaves 5°11' to be accounted for. These 5°11' form part of the next asterism—Rohini. Therefore we say that at the Queen's birth the Moon was in Rohini, having passed through 5°11' of that asterism, and being in the second " part " thereof. Looking at the Table again, we see that Rohini is ruled by the Moon, whose period is ten years. We have therefore to find how much of the ten years is due to the 5°11' of Rohini, through which the Moon has passed up to the birth-time. Each asterism being 13°20' in extent, we say in this case : If 13°20' gives ten years, what will 5°11' give ?

13°20' (800') : 5°11' (311') : : 10 : 3 yrs. 10 mths., 19 days. Then, with this expired portion of the Moon's period of ten years, we are able to determine under what sub-period in the Moon's period the Queen was born.

THE SUB-PERIODS

The Sub-periods are obtained by multiplying together the years due to the planet ruling the Period and Sub-period ; then, cutting off the last figures in the product, multiply it by 3, and call the result *days*, the first figure in the product being so many *months*. Thus, to find the Sub-period due to the Moon in its own Period :—The period of the Moon is ten years—10 × 10 = 100 = 10 months. There is a cypher for the last figure of the product, and therefore the Sub-period has no odd days. Take another example :—

Find the Sub-period due to Mars in the Period of the Sun, the Sun's period being six years, and that of Mars seven years.

7 × 6 = 42 = 4 months 6 days. These Sub-periods are called in Sanskrit *Bukthi*.

They are further divided into *antaram* periods. The rule for determining their duration is as follows :—

1. Divide the *months* of the Bukthi period by 4 ; this will give so many *days, hours, etc.*

2. Divide the *days* of the Bukthi period by 5 ; this will give so many *hours, minutes, etc.*

3. The days, hours, and minutes thus produced must be multiplied by the total period (Dashâ) of the planet whose *antaram* period is required.

Example.—Required the *antaram* period of Jupiter in the Sub-period (*Bukthi*) of Saturn, and the period (*Dashâ*) of Dragon's Tail (*Ketu*).

           ☡ Period   =   7 years.
           ♄ Sub-period =   13 months 9 days.
           ♃ Inter-period, or *Antaram* = ?

By Rule 1, $13 \div 4 = 3$ days 6 hours.
By Rule 2, $9 \div 5 = 1$ hour 48 minutes.
          Total.—3 days 7 hours 49 minutes.

This period, multiplied by 16, the total period of Jupiter, whose *antaram*, or inter-period, is required = 1 month 25 days 9 hours 48 min., which is Jupiter's inter-period in the sub-period of Saturn and the period of Dragon's Tail, or, as the Hindus would say, *Ketu, Dashâ Shani Bukthi, Guru Antaram.*

It is stated that the ancient Hindu astrologers subdivided these periods into most minute fractions, and stayed only at the *Swara*, or breath, a period of a few seconds. Whether or not they were able to determine the *phalam*, or effects, due to these minute periods is a matter of question. For all practical purposes, the inter-periods of the planets will be found sufficient.

The order of the planets in the successive subdivisions of the periods is as follows :

In all cases the planet whose period is subdivided takes the first place, and the rest follow on in the order observed in the Table of Asterisms, *viz.*, ☡ ♀ ☉ ☽ ♂ ☊ ♃ ♄ ☿.

So, if the period belongs to ☽, then ☽ will rule the first sub-period, and the first inter-period of that sub-period. Then follows the sub-period of Mars in the period of the Moon, and the first inter-period of the sub-period will likewise be ruled by Mars ; ☊, ♃, ♄, etc., following in their order.

EXAMPLE OF PLANETARY SUB-DIVISIONS

Moon's Period

	Sub-Periods.					Inter-Periods.				
1.	Moon	☽	♂	☊	♃	♄	☿	☋	♀	☉
2.	Mars	♂	☊	♃	♄	☿	☋	♀	☉	☽
3.	Dragon's Head-	☊	♃	♄	☿	☋	♀	☉	☽	♂
4.	Jupiter -	♃	♄	☿	☋	♀	☉	☽	♂	☊
5.	Saturn -	♄	☿	☋	♀	☉	☽	♂	☊	♃
6.	Mercury -	☿	☋	♀	☉	☽	♂	☊	♃	♄
7.	Dragon's Tail -	☋	♀	☉	☽	♂	☊	♃	♄	☿
8.	Venus -	♀	☉	☽	♂	☊	♃	♄	☿	☋
9.	Sun -	☉	☽	♂	☊	♃	♄	☿	☋	♀

The above example will, no doubt, make the preceding intelligible to all. The letters P., S.P., and I.P., will stand for Period, Sub-Period, and Inter-Period.

The Birth-Period

We have seen that, in the case of the Queen, the period in force at the time of birth was that of the Moon ; but it was also seen that of the ten years due to the Moon as its full period, three years ten months nineteen days had expired at the moment of birth. We need therefore to determine the sub-period which is operating at the time of birth, and to set out the scale of periods and sub-periods for the whole term of life.

Moon's Period—10 years

	Yrs.	Mths.	Dys.
Moon's Sub-Period - - - - -	0	10	0
Mars' ,, - - - - -	0	7	0
Dragon's Head's Sub-period - - -	1	6	0
Jupiter's ,, - - -	1	4	0
Saturn's ,, - - -	1	7	0
Mercury's ,, - - -	1	5	0
Dragon's Tail's ,, - - -	0	7	0
Venus' ,, - - -	1	8	0
Sun's ,, - - -	0	6	0
Total	10	0	0

Of these sub-periods, the whole of the Moon's, the whole of Mars',. the whole of the Dragon's Head's, and eleven months and nineteen days of that of Jupiter, in all amounting to three years ten months nineteen days, had expired at the time of birth, thus leaving for months eleven days of Jupiter's sub-period to be worked out.

The ages at which the various sub-periods of the Moon's period will expire can thus be set out in order :

Moon's Period

				Yrs.	Mths.	Dys.	
Moon's	Sub-period	-	-	0	10	0	expired.
Mars'	,,	-	-	0	7	0	,,
Dragon's Hd.'s	,.	-	-	1	6	0	,
Jupiter's	,,	-	-	0	11	19	,,
	Total			3	10	19	,,

					Yrs.	Mths.	Dys.
Jupiter's Sub-period expires at the age of	-				0	4	11
Saturn's	,,	,,	,,	-	1	11	11
Mercury's	,,	,,	,,	-	3	4	11
Dragon's Tail's	,,	,,	,,	-	3	11	11
Venus'	,,	,,	,,	-	5	7	11
Sun's	,,	,,	,,	-	6	1	11

It will thus be seen that the Queen's age at the expiry of the Moon's period was six years one month eleven days.

The next period is that of Mars, which rules for seven years. Add this to the above age and we get thirteen years one month eleven days, the age of expiry of Mars' period. After Mars comes the Dragon's Head, which rules for eighteen years, bringing us to the age of thirty-one years one month eleven days. Then Jupiter, with a period of sixteen years, reaching to the age of forty-seven years one month eleven days. Next Saturn, with nineteen years for its period, rules to the age of sixty-six years one month eleven days. Next Mercury,. whose period is seventeen years, brings us up to the age of eighty-three years one month eleven days.

These periods can be set out according to the example given in the Moon's period, and the age progressively shown at the expiry of each sub-period.

It will now be more or less clear to the student of Hindu Astrology upon what basis the zodiac rests ; how the Nakshatrams (or Asterisms) are counted, and what planets rule over each of them, together with the period of their rule. It will further be clear after what manner the Periods, Sub-periods, and Inter-periods (the Hindu method of computing the time of events) are to be calculated.

LOCALITY

In judging of the direction in which a person will travel when such is shown in the horoscope, or again in the P., S.P., and I.P. effects, the following rule is usually taken :—The first house, with its complements twelfth and second, governs the *South*. The tenth, with ninth and eleventh, governs the *East*. The seventh, with fifth and eighth, governs the *West* ; and the fourth, with third and fifth, governs the *North*.

So in the signs : ♓ ♈ ♉ = South ; ♊ ♋ ♌ = North ; ♍ ♎ ♏ = West ; and ♐ ♑ ♒ = East.

Therefore, Mars rules the East ; the Moon rules the North ; Venus governs the *West* ; and Saturn the South.

Judgment is chiefly to be made from the *houses*, and next, but subserviently, from the signs occupied by the planets.

Judgment by Planetary Position

In judging the effects due to the planets in the horoscope and their successive combinations in the P., S.P., and I.P., after birth, the following general dominion of the planets must be taken into account :—

The Sun governs honour, fame, nobles, advancement, profession, father, health.

The Moon governs females, marriage, travelling, change of residence, wealth, health, the mother, the house of residence, and native place.

Mars governs fire, fever, madness, quarrels, ambitions, energy, prowess, courage, adventures, poison, hurts, passions, and death.

Jupiter governs the religion (*dharma*), religious duties, the law, the father's brothers and sisters, teachers and preceptors, journeys to foreign lands, devotion, religious ceremonies, good fortune, increase.

Saturn governs the father, disease, wasting, chronic affections, ill-health, poverty, condition of the family.

Mercury governs the mind, the memory, hearing, brothers and sisters, mother's relatives, sickness, servants, food, journeys in one's own country, pilgrimages, and messages of all kinds.

Venus governs money, apparel, wealth in kind or specie ; trinkets, jewellery, articles of *vertu* ; the speech, learning, the wife, marriage, alliances, pleasures, arts and sciences.

Rahu and Ketu (Dragon's Head and Tail) governs such things as are denoted by the houses occupied by them at the time of birth.

In general, it is necessary to take into consideration, when judging of the effects of a planet : (1) Its natural rulership in the order of the signs ; (2) the house (*bhâva*) occupied by it ; (3) the house, or houses, over which it rules in the horoscope.

Râhu has affinity with the sign Scorpio where it is strong, and *Ketu* with Taurus. These signs are called their *uchha*, or exaltations.

From these descriptions it will be seen that judgment concerning any planet is derived from a consideration of its rulership in the signs, and the houses occupied by those signs, in addition to the place of the planet itself, its general nature and its sympathies and antipathies in the natural world and in man.

For this reason the Moon is strong in the second and fourth houses ; the Sun in the fifth and first ; Mars in the first and eighth ; Saturn in the tenth and seventh, etc., irrespective of the signs in which they are found ; for they have affinity with these several houses by their affinities in the world-soul, the horoscope of which is *Meshalagnam* (Aries for rising sign), during the whole of *Kali Yuga* (the present age), *i.e.*, the Dark or Iron Age.

PERIODS.

As the general *phalam* (effects) of the horoscope is derived from the configurations and conditions of all the planets, taken as significators for the whole life, so, in judging of the effects of any *period* of the life, attention must be paid to the condition (by position and configuration) of the planet ruling that period as determined by the calculation called *Kâlachakradashâphalakathna*, *i.e.*, the dividing of time (the life-period) into its periodical effects, as set forth in the periods, sub-periods and inter-periods. Its basis is the Moon's place at birth. According to the condition of the planets ruling the required period, so the life and fortunes of the native will be affected.

SUB-PERIODS

These are considered in relation to the general effects due to the planet governing the Period in which they fall, and they are subsidiary to the fortunes promised by the Period planet. In this respect they may be considered in the same manner as Lunar and Solar Directions, which will, perhaps, simplify matters. Then, if the Period planet shows *good* effects, it does so from its position and aspects at birth, and an *evil* Sub-period planet cannot counteract its effects wholly, but some good will remain behind. The result is similar when, *mutatis mutandis*, the P. planet is evil and the S.P. planet good. But when both agree in nature and point to the same end, then the effects are forcible, and decided either for good or evil as the case may be.

INTER-PERIODS

These are taken as subsidiary to the Sub-periods in the same manner that transits or lunations are considered in relation to Lunar or Secondary Directions in our European methods. The longest of these reaches over a period of six months twenty days, *viz.*, the ♀ I.P. of the ♀ S.P. in the ♀ P. ; the shortest period is that of the Sun in its own Sub-period and Period ; it lasts only five days nine hours thirty-six minutes. The condition of the I.P. planet must be taken into account, and its relation to the Sub-period planet properly estimated. Its effects may then be accurately known.

RULES TO JUDGE OF PLANETARY PERIODS

1. Consider well the positions and affections of the period planet, for even a good planet will not bear good fruit during its period if it be ill affected by sign or position, or afflicted by the majority of planets.

2. The sub-period planet must be considered in the same way as the period planet, but in addition thereto its *relations* with the period planet must be taken carefully into account ; for though the planets have a natural enmity and friendship existing between them, and due to their respective natures, yet when the sub-period planet is in good aspect to the period it will produce good, even though these planets be natural enemies. Similarly, friendly and benefic planets will not produce good fruits if weak or afflicted, or themselves afflicting (by position) the period planet to which they are related.

3. The effects of the ruling planets are intensified at such time as the Sun may be passing through the sign occupied by them or the signs over which they rule.

N.B.—The Sun does not enter the Hindu signs until twenty days after its entry into the European signs bearing the same name.

4. The inter-period planets are considered in the same manner, in regard to the sub-period planets to which they are related, as these latter are to the period planets. It thus happens that even when the period is a good one, as shown by the position and affections of the period planet, yet there are sub-periods, and again inter-periods, when evils may naturally arise.

5. The general effects of the planets thus related must be taken into account, and their natural relations, as well as the temporary relations in the horoscope, must be well considered. Thus, Saturn and Sun, although natural enemies by sign and exaltation, may be respectively in Libra and Leo, in which case they are in temporary good relations, occupying the third and eleventh signs respectively from one another. Judgment is made accordingly, but it is to be understood that a temporary friendship will not entirely overcome a radical and constitutional enmity.

6. The effects will further have relation to the nature of the house corresponding to the sign occupied by the sub-planet, in the period under consideration. Thus, if the period be that of Sun, and the sub-period be that of Venus, and Venus be in the sign Aquarius, the effects will fall out in relation to the eleventh house affairs ; if Venus be in Libra the seventh house affairs will be affected.

7. The sign, counted from the rising sign, will give a further element of interpretation. Thus, if in the sub-period of any planet, that planet occupies Leo, and Scorpio be rising, the effects will fall on the tenth house affairs.

8. The number of the signs counted from the period to the sub-period planet will give the house corresponding thereto, over which the effects will hold sway. Thus, Sun in Virgo and Venus as sub-period planet in Scorpio will show the third house affairs to be affected.

9. The houses in the horoscope ruled by the planet whose period, sub-period, or inter-period is considered, must also be regarded as affecting.

N.B.—Rahu and Ketu (Dragon's Head and Tail) have no houses, but transmit the influence of the signs they are in, and of the planets to which they are conjoined. The Dragon's Head has affinity with the sign Scorpio, and the Dragon's Tail with the sign Taurus.

THE KÂLÂMRITAM

The effects of periods and sub-periods, measured from the Asterism held by the Moon at birth, and known as the *Dasâ Bukthi Phala*, are given variously in different Sanskrit and vernacular works current in India. But that which seems to be held most in esteem among the astrologers in Southern India is the *Kâlâmritam*, a small but explicit treatise upon the system of *Parâshara*. The following statement of the effects of the periods and sub-periods of life (measured according to the rules already given in this exposition) are taken from its pages. Like most treatises of its kind, the original takes the form of a Kaviata or poem.

In making this translation, respect has been had to the customs of European life, and this fact alone draws it away from the domain of scholastic criticism, which would only be concerned with a work of scholarly pretensions. The sense and import of the text have been chiefly considered, and the ideas embodied have been put into simple English.

Thus, instead of enumerating the "gold, pearls, granaries, carriages, soft cushions, sunshades, rich clothes and turbans" that certain periods and sub-periods will confer upon the native, it is quite English enough to state that his "wealth and property will increase." With these reservations, and bearing in mind what has been said in regard to the radical relations of the different planets, the following may be accepted as the general effects of periods and sub-periods.

PERIOD OF SUN

Sun's Sub-period.—There will be trouble among relatives, quarrelling and difficulties with superiors and those in office above the native. Anxieties, headaches, pains in the ears, some tendency to urinary or kidney affections. Sickness is to be expected between April 12th and May 12th (if included in this period) or again between 12th August and 12th September, *i.e.*, when the Sun is in *Mesham* (Aries) or *Simha* (Leo).

Moon's Sub-period.—Benefits from superiors or patrons, gain and success in business, new enterprises, troubles through women, pains in the eyes. (This will be augmented in the month of *Katakam*, 12th July to 12th August, and on those days when the Moon passes through Cancer.)

Mars' Sub-period.—Rheumatic or some sharp pains, feverishness, quarrelling, some danger of enteric fever, dysentery, or other wasting diseases ; troubles fall on the relatives ; the native wastes his money or may lose it by theft or carelessness. His efforts will not be very successful.

Dragon's Head Sub-period.—A great many troubles and fears, crosses and changes, according to the condition and place of the Dragon's Head. Entire break-up of the family. The native will be away from his home at the time.

Jupiter's Sub-period.—Friends will benefit him. He will increase in knowledge and give evidence of his powers in some form or other. Employment among people of good position ; association with people of high rank. Will overcome all obstacles, and, if married, may have the birth of a child.

Saturn's Sub-period.—Sickness of children, much anxiety, trouble on account of the wife or children. Enemies will be made. Loss of property. Bodily sickness ; much unhappiness. He may leave his home or country. Accidental or enforced estrangement.

Mercury's Sub-period.—Even his own friends will be against him ; many will become his enemies ; and there will be cause for grave anxiety and fear. The health will be afflicted ; children will cause trouble. He will be involved in disputes and trouble by a superior, a ruler or a judge. He will suffer some disgrace. Irregular meals and sleep. Many short journeys, wanderings, etc. ; a predominance of mental and physical pain in this sub-period.

Dragon's Tail Sub-period.—Memory will decrease ; the mind will be afflicted with troubles ; there will be fainting or nervous exhaustion ; and the mind will be filled with doubts and misgivings. He will go to a distant country or place. Owing to disputes he will live in a different house. Troubles among relatives and associates. There will be no benefits in this sub-period unless Dragon's Tail is well placed and in good aspect to the sun.

Venus. Sub-period.—A possibility of marriage. Increase of prosperity. Some bodily sickness. The eyes may be affected. This will be cured. He will do good actions in this period, and will reap their reward.

MOON'S PERIOD, *Sub-periods*

Moon.—Marriage frequently occurs during the rule of this sub-period, and is fortunate. The native does heroic actions and noble deeds. He inclines to public life. He will have changes of residence. All he wishes will be fulfilled. A child may be born to him.

Mars.—Useless quarrels and litigation ; disputes of all kinds ; rashness ; impetuosity ; loss of property ; cutaneous affections ; danger of fire in the month from April 12th to May 12th. Danger of disputes between husband and wife, or between lovers, or in regard to marital affairs.

Dragon's Head.—Loss of money ; danger of stirring up enemies, sickness according to the sign the Dragon's Head occupies. Anxiety on account of friends ; enmity of superiors and those in power. Anxiety or trouble through the wife or lover.

Jupiter.—Property will increase ; food and comforts will be plentiful ; there will be prosperity. Benefits from persons in good position, masters, governors, the father, or the ruling powers. The native may beget a child at this time.

Saturn.—The partner (wife or lover) may die or be separated from the native. Much mental trouble. Loss of wealth, or a state of impecuniosity. Dishonour or slander will be experienced. Loss of friends ; some ill-health.

Mercury.—Disputes will cease. The native will have pleasure through children or love affairs. Wealth will increase. All intentions will be accomplished. In the month of Virgo, 12th September to 12th October, he will give evidence of some intellectual achievements.

Dragon's Tail.—There will be sickness of a feverish nature, or hurt by fire. The body will be subject to some eruptions or swellings. The eyes may suffer. The mind will be filled with cares, and the native will experience much trouble. He may incur some public criticism or displeasure ; may meet with dishonour or be the means of his own undoing.

G

Venus.—According to the position of Venus in regard to the Moon and rising sign, there will be sickness, pain, loss of property, enmity and loss through enemies—or, the reverse of this.

Sun.—Biliousness and feverish complaints. Some change in the bodily appearance. Severe pain in the eyes. Success, or the reverse, according to the relative position of the Sun and Moon.

MARS' PERIOD, *Sub-Periods*

Mars.—Danger of hurts according to the sign held by Mars. In the month of Aries or Scorpio (if included) he will have trouble with superiors, and some anxiety through strangers, foreigners, or people abroad, and through Mars men generally. In the month of Cancer, *i.e.*, July 12th to August 12th, there will be danger of open violence.

Dragon's Head—He will suffer from poisonous complaints, according to the sign held by Dragon's Head. Loss of relatives. Danger of scrofulous or skin affections. Change of residence. Some severe form of cutaneous disease.

Jupiter.—Loss of property. Enmity of superiors. Enemies will be created in the place of residence and beyond it. But the end of this sub-period will be more fortunate ; and favours from superiors and persons in position may be looked for.

Saturn.—Quarrels, disputes, litigation, loss of property, cutaneous affections, loss of office or position, much anxiety.

Mercury.—He will be inclined to marry at this time, and if so will be fortunately wedded. Knowledge, and the fruits of knowledge, will increase. Wealth will increase. Existing evils in body and mind will disappear. But in the month of Gemini or Virgo (if included) he will be subject to slander, or may be poisoned in his body by hurts from animals or insects, or by abrasions.

Dragon's Tails.—Family disputes ; troubles with his own kindred. Disease. Poisonous complaints threaten him ; trouble through women. Many enemies.

Venus.—He will acquire property or gain money. Will have domestic happiness and successful love affairs. He may feel more inclination to religious observances and festivities. His associations are beneficial. He is influenced by churchmen or sectaries. Skin eruptions, boils, or sloughings may be expected. Travelling will give him pleasure at this time.

Sun.—Anxieties. Fever or other inflammatory affection. Danger of fire. Troubles through persons in position. The wife is likely to be afflicted with disease. He will have many enemies.

Moon.—Profit ; gain of property and the acquisition of valuables, There is likely to be renovation of the house or improvements made therein. But in the end of this sub-period there will be a decrease of all these good effects.

DRAGON'S HEAD PERIOD, *Sub-Periods*

Dragon's Head.—Death of the King, superiors, senior partner, master or the head of the family. Mental anxiety. Danger of blood-poisoning. The wife is afflicted. The native will have some removals. All sorts of quarrels and scandals will take place in regard to him.

Jupiter.—Pleasure will increase. Gain through nobles or persons of position. Benefits and comforts through his superiors. All his efforts will succeed. He will be married, engaged, or if married will be re-united to his wife.

Saturn.—Enemies will arise. There will be cause for mental anxiety. Disease will appear. Incessant disputes and contests. Rheumatism, biliousness, etc., will attack his health. Trouble will prevail.

Mercury.—Of the thirty months ruled by this sub-period planet, the first eighteen will be very busy. The native will thrive well. He will be seriously-inclined and will gain money. In the last twelve he will experience enmity through his own actions.

Dragon's Tail.—Danger of physical hurts and poison. Ill-health to his children. Some swellings in the body. Troubles on account of the wife. Danger from superiors.

Venus.—Acquisition of money and other advantages. Friendly alliances will be formed. The wife will be fortunate and a source of happiness. Benefits from superiors or those in office above the native. Some trouble will happen through deceit being practised upon the native. False friends will come to light in their true colours. But all evils will pass away.

Sun.—Quarrels on account of the family. Benefits from persons in good position. Fear and suspicion will arise in connection with the wife, children and relatives. Changes of position or residence will occur.

Moon.—Loss of relatives. Loss of money through the wife. Pains in the limbs. He will leave his native place or his present residence. There will be danger of personal hurts. The health will be unstable.

Mars.—Danger of fire, burns and other physical hurts. Dangers to the person through the malice of enemies. A tendency to lax or dissolute habits will show itself. Danger of loss by theft. Disputes and mental anxiety.

JUPITER'S PERIOD, *Sub-Periods*

Jupiter.—Much prosperity. Fame, good position. Property will increase. There will be domestic plenty and happiness. Benefits from the employment or occupation. Lawyers, priests (clergy), and superiors favour the native.

Saturn.—There will be an increase of wealth or property. After this, pains in the body will be experienced, rheumatic pains in the limbs. Troubles through the wife or partner. A falling off of profit and credit in the place of abode. But these troubles will pass away.

Mercury.—Gain by knowledge in the fine arts. Birth of a well-favoured child, in the case of married people. Wealth increases and advantages from superiors fall to the native.

Dragon's Tail.—The partner, although strong, will die. The native will change his place of abode. He will be separated from his relatives and friends, and he may leave his business or forsake his occupation because of all this.

Venus.—There will be a reunion in the family. Good success in the profession or business. He will gain land in the month of Taurus or Libra (*i.e.*, when the Sun is in these signs). Much enjoyment. Relatives are friendly, and he will live in peace.

Sun. Gain. Good actions are performed or the fruits of past good action come to the native at this time. Loss of bodily strength may be experienced. Some disease will appear according to the sign held by the Sun. But these evils will not endure.

Moon.—Property increases. He gains honour and fame. Acquires property. Benefits through children and happiness to them. All good efforts in the past will collectively render their fruits to the native.

Mars.—Annoyances and troubles of various kinds. Danger of loss by theft. Loss of a friend, elder brother, or parent. Some inflammatory disease arises in the system. He will move from his present place, and will fail to accomplish his engagements.

Dragon's Head.—Relatives give trouble. Small quarrels are numerous. There is some loss of property. Troubles to the wife or through her. The native becomes the object of deception, which occasions some loss or trouble.

SATURN'S PERIOD, *Sub-Periods*

Saturn.—Disease appears, and the body languishes. Loss of children and money is to be feared. Serious enmities arise ; relatives cause disputes. Troubles come upon the native through his relatives.

Mercury.—Knowledge in some particular direction will increase. The native will be wise and discreet. Children will prosper. Relatives will meet with success. The native will prosper and receive favours and approbation from superiors.

Dragon's Tail.—Rheumatism in the right leg. Some biliousness, or sickness. Danger of poisonous elements in the system. Danger from the native's own son. Loss of money. Contentions and quarrels. A bad time generally.

Venus.—Attentions and favours from others. Gifts. Profit in business. Increase in the family circle by a birth or marriage. Victory over enemies and the overcoming of obstacles.

Sun.—Danger of blood-poisoning. Hemorrhage of the generative system. Chronic poisoning. Intestinal swellings. Affections of the eyes. Even healthy children and wives come to the sick-bed under this influence. The body is full of pains and disorders. Danger of death.

Moon.—Trouble and sickness fall upon the native. There are family disputes. Losses both of money and property. The native will be reduced to great need and will sell or mortgage his property, and will recover it only after a lapse of time.

Mars.—Some disgrace will fall upon the family. Very serious enmity and strife will ensue. Much blame will attach to the native. He will go from one place to another, and will lead an unsettled life at this period. He will have many enemies ; will be deprived of money by fraud or theft. He will leave his home or kindred.

Dragon's Head.—Loss of money. Will be in danger of physical hurts. Various physical troubles will ensue. Even foreigners will become his enemies. Troubles increase under this influence.

Jupiter.—He will find favour and refuge with good men or clergy. Will have some increase in his bodily comforts. Through the aid of superiors he will accomplish his intentions. He will abide happily in one place, and have an increase of family.

MERCURY PERIOD, *Sub-Periods*

Mercury.—The native gains a brother or sister, either by marriage or birth. An increase of the family is shown. He gains in business, and receives advancement. Learning will attract his attention and engage his efforts.

Dragon's Tail.—The native leaves his place of abode. He experiences some sickness, loss of property, misfortune to his relatives, etc. He has some trouble through doctors, and danger in regard to his medicine. Mental anxiety.

Venus —The native has good children born to him. Happiness in the married state. Relatives prosper. Trade increases. Knowledge is gained. He returns from a long journey. If not already married, he will form an alliance at this time.

Sun —Danger of fire. Anxieties. Sickness of the wife. Enemies give trouble. Many obstacles in all his affairs. Troubles through superiors.

Moon.—Loss of health. Some swellings or hurts in the limbs. Quarrels and trouble through females. Many difficulties will arise. Will have troubles through women, and will consequently try to avoid them.

Mars.—Some danger of jaundice or bilious fever. Affections of the blood. Neuralgic pains and severe headaches. Neighbours cause troubles. Sickness due to trouble ; wounds or hurts. This period will end in quarrels.

Dragon's Head.—The native is removed from his present position. Fear and danger through foreigners. Disputes concerning property, in which the native loses. Evil dreams, headaches, sickness, and loss of appetite.

Jupiter.—Will have a fair degree of happiness ; some renown or esteem ; good credit ; advancement through superiors. Birth of a child, or marriage (if not already married). Good fortune generally.

Saturn.—Bad fortune. He becomes a stranger to success and happiness. Severe reversal. Enmity is incurred. Some disease or pain in the part governed by Saturn. Relatives suffer a downfall or some disgrace. The native suffers in consequence. The mind is filled with gloomy forebodings and grief.

DRAGON'S TAIL PERIOD, *Sub-Periods*

Dragon's Tail.—The native has some mental troubles. Will be separated from his relatives. Will be subject to some estrangement, restraint or detention.

Venus.—A child may be born to the native. Wealth increases. All his efforts are crowned with success. In the end of this period, however, he will have sickness. His wife also will be ill. But these troubles will soon pass away.

Sun.—He will have a long journey, and will return. Some disease or sickness will disfigure the body. Anxiety on account of the partner in marriage.

Moon.—Disputes on account of the actions of the other sex. Trouble through the children or on account of them. Gain and financial success. All troubles will vanish.

Mars.—Obstacles bar the path of progress. There is cause for fear and anxiety. Disputes and contests of different kinds. Enemies arise. Danger of destruction through one of the opposite sex. Danger fire, fever, or an operation.

Dragon's Head.—Danger of blood-poisoning will come and go. Females will suffer. The native is in danger of ruin. Loss of property, fame, and honour is to be feared.

Jupiter.—Profitable transactions. Association with people of good position. Danger of poison. The wife becomes the cause of pleasure. If unmarried, his love affairs progress well. Wealth will increase considerably.

Saturn.—All properties will be in danger of ruin. The native will suffer heavy losses in different ways. He will change his place of abode. Some cutaneous disease is to be feared. Anxiety owing to the sickness of the wife or partner.

Mercury.—Changes will occur. Danger from relatives. Anxiety on account of children. His plans will not succeed.

VENUS' PERIOD, *Sub-Periods*

Venus.—Financial success. Good servants, and the accessories of good fortune. Many pleasures. Money will be plentiful, but in the month of Libra (12th Oct. to 12th Nov.) there will be sorrow.

Sun.—He will have cause for anxiety and fear. Prosperity will decline. This will be caused by superiors. There will be disputes with the wife or partner, with children and others. Family and domestic troubles. Even in sacred places or in regard to spiritual matters he will be involved in disputes and quarrels.

Moon.—He will accomplish all his intentions. There will be troubles through the wife, but they will pass away, and domestic happiness will ensue in full measure.

Mars.—Property will increase. Through the influence of women he will not perform his duties, and will become lax in his efforts, neglecting his duties. His mind will be upon earthly things, bent upon pleasure and neglecting religion. Some affection of the eyes and skin will appear and pass away.

Dragon's Head.—"Like a perfect *muni* (one under a vow of silence), he will perform Tapas (religious austerity). Foreseeing quarrels among his people or relations, and between them and himself, by a very rare medicine, he will withdraw himself from them, and become as distant as possible." In some cases an entire change of surroundings may be expected to happen.

Jupiter.—Means of livelihood will increase. Profit through the occupation. Many benefits through superiors or employers, or persons ruled by Jupiter. He will gain fame, but will experience some anxiety in the end.

Saturn.—Affections of the excretory system, piles, etc. Sciatica or rheumatic pains in the legs and hands. Disease in the system. Danger of the eyesight being affected at this time. Distaste for food, loss of appetite. The physical condition in a very poor way.

Mercury.—Pleasure through the wife and children. Increase of wealth. Gain of knowledge in the arts and sciences. Successful period.

Dragon's Tail.—Troubles in love affairs or through the wife.

Danger from quadrupeds. Someone in the house will come by an accident, and may have blood-poisoning, but it will be cured.

HORARY ASTROLOGY. This is an entirely separate and distinct branch of Astrology, with rules peculiar to its system which is used for the solving of important questions. The value of Horary Astrology rests upon the correct interpretation of the figure of the heavens taken for the moment when the mind is deeply anxious, or when an important question has been asked. This branch of Astrology, which is in reality a form of astro-divination, is concerned with the birth of objective thoughts into the physical world, and has some connection with a definite object, or question connected with the past, present, or future. A map of the heavens may be erected for the moment of reading a letter, or first hearing of an event, or at the moment that a question is asked, but in all cases the mind must be clear, definite, anxious, and in earnest. It is usual to see if the figure is radical before giving a judgment upon it, which means that the sign rising must have advanced three degrees, or that the sign is not within three degrees of passing from the ascendant. It is never safe to judge the map unless the sign has advanced into the house, the very beginning or the end being indefinite, and often indicating that the mind of the querent (or questioner) is vague and not clear upon the point at issue. It is essential that all doubts be placed on one side, also all prejudice in the matter, otherwise the judgment will not be sound ; but to have the best success the querent will always do well to consult an astrologer, or one who is disinterested in the matter, unless an unbiased mind is preserved at the time of consulting the figure erected. Horary Astrology should never be used to solve frivolous or foolish questions.

The map of the heavens is erected in the manner adopted in the case of nativities, but without the seculum, and with the addition of the Dragon's Head and Tail, also the Part of Fortune. Special attention is paid to the significator and the lords of houses. Each house is made to represent the general affairs of the personality, as follows :

The first house represents the querent, or the person asking the question ; the rising sign, the significator, which is the ruler of the ascendant, and any planets placed in the first house describe the enquirer in a general way. The various descriptions of signs and planets in signs will be found under their separate headings ; the more decided and earnest the querent the more precise will be the description. A clever artist can give accurate descriptions.

The second house describes the financial condition, and answers all questions in connection with the worldly welfare, monetary matters and finance generally.

The third house describes the brethren, and kindred, all matters relating to short journeys, travelling, and movement ; also neighbours, and affairs connected with learning and education. It is also the house that indicates answers to questions concerning letters, papers, and documents of all kinds.

The fourth is the house concerned with the residence, and the end of the matter enquired about ; it describes the father and his affairs, also interprets all matters connected with removals, changes, inheritance, house property, land and estates.

The fifth house deals with questions concerning children, and child-birth, pleasure, speculation, and general happiness.

The sixth house concerns servants, sickness, food stuffs, hygiene, small animals, and phenomenal magic.

The seventh house relates to all matters of partnership, marriage, legal affairs, love matters. It describes the physician attending the sick, the defendants in law suits, and all matters of a joint issue.

The eighth house is concerned with deaths, wills, legacies, and goods of the dead.

The ninth house relates to science, philosophy, and religion ; long journeys, shipping affairs, books and publications, clergymen, etc.

The tenth house describes the nature of the employment or the employer, the mother and her affairs, the honour and general success.

The eleventh house is concerned with hopes, wishes, and desires ; also with friends, acquaintances, and fortunate issues.

The twelfth house is the unfortunate house of the figure, indicating imprisonment, persecution, enemies, sorrow, tragedy and romance.

In addition to these interpretations, there is also the consideration of the houses in relation to the other houses. The figure may be reversed for interpretation as follows : The second is the eighth from the seventh, therefore would indicate all that the eighth house of the map would govern, as the death of the partner, business or marriage, also lovers and adversaries. Its relation may be taken with regard to any of the other houses, and this may be done with them all ; the third, friends of children ; fourth, employment of marriage partner ; eighth, finance of partners, etc., etc.

In all horary questions the Moon plays the most important part. Her application or separation to and from the planets must always be carefully noted.

The planets generally represent the matters and personalities enquired about, and from the position of the planets, etc., the descriptions are obtained ; in a general way the planets describe persons as follows :—

Saturn indicates persons of middle stature, small eyes—usually green or greenish grey ; dark hair, melancholic in appearance, body spare, bones large, and the motive temperament predominating. The sign that Saturn occupies will modify the description. The disposition is cold, austere, and selfish ; it describes persons who are aged, acquisitive, reflective, laborious, patient, slow, and persevering.

Mars indicates those who are muscular, strong and well built ; roundish face ; sharp, piercing hazel eyes ; florid complexion with reddish or sandy hair, although Mars gives dark hair also. The Mars man is generally quick and active, moving about freely. The disposition is aggressive, combative, militant, courageous, fearless, but hasty.

Jupiter indicates one who is tall and of commanding appearance, pleasant and genial in manner, usually with high forehead, soft blue eyes, hair chestnut or dark brown, and a robust body with long legs and feet. The disposition is hopeful, benevolent, sincere, peaceful, and religious, representing ministers, clergymen, etc.

The Sun indicates one of large frame ; broad, high forehead ; light, or golden hair ; large eyes, often grey. The solar man is commanding in appearance. The disposition is firm, conscientious, self-reliant, and approbative. It represents persons holding authority, and those having command or power.

Venus generally indicates women in Horary Astrology, or those who are fair and have good complexions, beautiful features, and graceful forms. The eyes are blue, and the hair light brown, and the vital temperament abounds. The disposition is agreeable, social, pleasant, and loving. It represents musicians, singers, artists and actors.

Mercury indicates persons who are rather tall and thin, or of medium height, sharp features, brown and sometimes grey eyes, thin lips, narrow chin, a pyriform face, a sallowish complexion, long hands and arms, hair auburn or light brown; the disposition active, nervous, restless and anxious, fond of learning, quick-witted and given to study. It represents writers, orators, clerks, printers, schoolmasters, etc.

The Moon indicates persons full in stature, pale complexion, round face, greenish-grey eyes, fair hair, of phlegmatic temperament ; disposition romantic, imaginative, fond of travel and change. It represents sailors, nurses, and those engaged in liquid pursuits, and females generally.

Uranus indicates uncommon persons, eccentrics, bohemians, and those who are original, abrupt, and not of the ordinary type.

DESCRIPTIONS ACCORDING TO SIGNS

Aries.—A dry, spare body and strong limbs. The early part of the sign gives more flesh. The face and neck are generally long, the complexion rather sallow and swarthy, hair dark and wiry, full eyebrows, which are usually very dark, the eyes piercing, round, and prominent. The face usually resembles the ram.

Disposition : Impulsive, rash, and intemperate, but dauntless, fearless, and bold. When undeveloped, liable to be violent, rough and rude.

Diseases : Small-pox, fevers, epilepsy, apoplexy, and all complaints that affect the head. Planets in this sign generally give some mark on the head.

Taurus.—A short, rather corpulent and well-set stature ; the face is generally full and the complexion swarthy ; a wide nose and mouth with thick lips. The forehead is broad and the neck resembles the bull's. The hair is usually rough and curly, and the hands plump, short, and broad.

Disposition : Rather melancholy, slow to anger, but when provoked very violent and furious, like the bull.

Diseases : Those that effect the throat, such as quinsy, swellings, etc., gout, and diseases arising from errors in diet.

Gemini.—Rather tall, but well-formed body, sanguine complexion, long arms and hands, dark eyes, often hazel, with a very quick and penetrative sight ; dark brown hair.

Disposition : Very intelligent and humane, well-disposed and very judicious.

Diseases : Those affecting the blood and nervous system.

Cancer.—Short stature, the upper part of the body usually much larger than the lower ; pale complexion, small round face. The eyes are generally grey, and the hair dark brown, sometimes black.

Disposition : Very sensitive, phlegmatic, lethargic, and very impressionable.

Diseases : Those affecting the stomach and digestion ; sometimes dropsy and cancer.

Leo.—A well-built person, broad shoulders and large head, oval face, full round eyes, light hair, sometimes rather curly, a ruddy or sanguine complexion.

Disposition : Courageous, firm, high-spirited, and austere, very generous and courteous.

Diseases : Those affecting the heart and back, also the eyes.

Virgo.—A slender body, of middle stature, but well made ; a roundish face, well favoured, yet not handsome ; a dark, ruddy complexion ; dark brown hair ; a small shrill voice.

Disposition : Ingenious, studious, witty, fond of history and literature ; judicious and well-spoken, but unstable, fickle-minded, and frequently melancholy.

Diseases : All those of the bowels, spleen, and diaphragm ; such as worms, wind, obstructions, colic, dysentry, also hernia.

Libra.—A tall, well-framed body, elegantly made, with a round beautiful face and lovely expression ; all the features regular ; in youth a fine, sanguine complexion ; but in age pimples, or a very high colour ; the eyes generally blue ; hair, light auburn or flaxen, shining, smooth, and long, yet sometimes a jet black and glossy. This sign gives more beauty than any other.

Disposition : Even-tempered, well-principled, and affectionate.

Diseases : All those of the veins, kidneys, and bladder ; such as stone, gravel, corrupt blood, and weakness.

Scorpio.—A middle size ; a corpulent, short, strong, able body ; broad visage ; dark, muddy complexion ; sad brown, curling, plentiful hair ; thick neck and legs ; hairy and coarse body ; often bow-legged, always ill-formed feet.

Disposition : Active, but very reserved and thoughtful in conversation.

Diseases : All those of the groin, bladder, urethra, fundament, etc., such as gravel, stone, hernia, fistulas, piles, strangury, strictures, etc.

Sagittarius.—Well formed, rather tall, strong person, with a very handsome, open countenance ; rather a full face, but long and oval, with the head formed like that of a horse ; high forehead ; the hair growing off the temples, rather bald ; hair chestnut-coloured ; fine clear eyes, complexion honey-coloured, or sunburnt.

Disposition : Active, bold, and intrepid ; very partial to active sports, as hunting, riding, etc., and fond of *horses.*

Diseases : Gout and rheumatism ; falls, broken bones, fevers, hurts to the thighs, etc., and gunshot wounds.

Capricorn.—A dry constitution and short stature ; long, lean, and slender visage ; sallow complexion ; thin beard ; black hair ; narrow breast ; small, long neck ; narrow chin ; weak knees and inclined to be crooked ; thin person.

Disposition : Subtle, collected, witty, changeable and melancholy ; active in manner, sometimes skipping about like a young *goat.*

Diseases : All those of the knees and hams ; gout, sprains, fractures, hysterics, scirrhous tumours, and all cutaneous diseases.

Aquarius.—A middle stature, not tall ; robust, well set, strong, plump, healthy make ; long face, delicate complexion, fair and clear, rather pale ; sandy-coloured hair, or dark flaxen, and hazel eyes ; a very pure skin.

Disposition : Very good, kind, and humane.

Diseases : All those of the legs and ankles ; such as broken legs, gout, sprains, cramp, rheumatism, foul blood, etc.

Pisces.—A short stature, crooked or stooping ; thick, round shoulders ; an ill figure, and the head bent forward ; pale and fleshy large face ; dark, soft, brown hair ; dark eyes and plump body.

Disposition : Timid, dull, and phlegmatic.

Diseases : All those of the feet and toes ; as gout, lameness, corns, bunions ; ulcerous sores, and cold, moist diseases, and colds by damp feet ; putrid blood, blotches, boils.

IMPORTANT CONSIDERATIONS

In Horary Astrology the planets must be taken as symbols or significators, each representing its own special property. The planets may be considered as the life, and the signs as the form or expression. The Sun will always represent power and authority, magnanimity, grandeur, and is always very high, noble, and lofty, its influence being modified according to the sign and aspect. It represents persons having authority and those holding the greatest power.

Mercury represents all literary affairs and matters connected with books, papers, and correspondence, also with travel and children. It also represents food-stuffs in a general way, but much depends upon the aspect to this planet and the sign that it is in. It represents secretaries, clerks, messengers, and all those who are connected with the transference of thought.

Venus represents the female sex generally, and all matters that are effeminate, or of a pleasure-giving and sensuous nature. It is concerned with finance, love, courtship, and marriage. It is the planet of mirth and pleasure.

Mars represents the male sex generally, military men, doctors, surgeons, and all persons who use force and energy, and those who are assertive, positive, and at times aggressive. It is the planet of activity, that stirs into action all life of every description. It is always hot in its nature and its tendency is to set everything boiling.

Jupiter is temperate ; the great social planet, bringing success, and governing all matters of a benefic nature. It represents the truly religious, and everything that is jovial, happy, and free. It is the planet of benevolence, mercy, and compassion, and governs all those who are well-disposed, generous, loyal, and noble-spirited. It always represents superiors, moral and mental.

Saturn is the planet of cold and limitation. Its general tendency is to restrict, hinder, and delay. It brings things to perfection by slow degrees, patience, industry, and thoroughness. It is considered a malefic, owing to the long period of time which it governs. It represents inferiors generally ; also persons who are cold-natured but just and exacting.

Uranus governs everything that is eccentric and wonderful ; all things that are uncertain and inevitable. It is the great metaphysical planet and governs all things that are original, such as inventions, etc.

The Moon represents the public generally, all persons who follow common employments and everything of a fluidic nature. It represents change, and those things used for the public benefit.

The influence of Neptune is not generally known ; but, when afflicted, it is said to govern frauds, shams, and deceptions, and when well placed and aspected, all things that are uncommon and advanced. It is probably a higher Venus.

OBJECTS GOVERNED BY THE PLANETS

The Sun governs gold and diamonds, and everything that is valuable and scarce.

Mercury governs papers connected with money, and legal documents, also books and pictures, all writing materials, and everything connected with education and learning, also quicksilver.

Venus governs jewellery and ornaments, copper, women's wearing apparel, also all linen connected with the bed-chamber.

Mars governs war-like instruments, everything that is sharp, such as cutlery, and all iron materials, also steel, etc.

Jupiter governs tin, men's wearing apparel, all sweet things in merchandise, also horses and domestic pets.

Saturn governs lead, all heavy materials, such as those connected with agriculture and garden implements, also land and minerals.

The Moon governs all common objects such as utensils in common use, all things connected with washing and laundry, work in metals, silver and silver-plated articles.

Uranus governs machinery, baths, public institutions, old coins, and antiques, also everything that is uncommon and out of the ordinary.

PROFESSIONS

The Sun governs positions of power and authority, and would thus represent magistrates, high sheriffs, superintendents, directors, goldsmiths, and all business where huge sums of money are handled.

Jupiter governs judges, lawyers, clergymen, and all professions connected with religion and the law, and businesses connected with woollen clothing.

Venus represents all professions connected with music and the fine arts, also jewellers, embroiderers, perfumers, and all businesses connected with women and their adornment.

Mars governs all military professions, also surgeons and chemists, and when this planet is weak, butchers, barbers, smiths, etc. It generally represents tailors, bakers, and dyers, and all common employments.

Saturn governs all employments of the laborious type, and all employments where much labour is necessary to acquire gain.

The Moon governs all common employments ; and persons dealing with public commodities, holding inferior positions, etc., chiefly in connection with transit.

Uranus governs uncommon employments such as astrology, lecturing, mesmerism, metaphysic, etc.

Colours of the Planets and *Signs.*—In Horary Astrology the Sun governs yellow ; the Moon, white or silver ; Mercury, light blue or striped ; Venus, white ; Mars, fiery red ; Jupiter, red mixed with green ; Saturn, black. The signs of the zodiac have colours assigned to them, respectively—♈, white and red ; ♉, red mixed with citron ; ♊, red and white mixed ; ♋, green or russet ; ♌, red or green ; ♍, black spotted with blue ; ♎, black or dark brown ; ♏, dark brown ; ♒, sky blue ; ♓, pure white or glistening.

COUNTRIES, CITIES, AND TOWNS RULED BY THE SIGNS

Aries

Countries : Britain, Denmark, Galatia, Germany, Lithuania, Lower Poland, Palestine, Syria or Judea (especially Lebanon and near Damascus).

Cities and Towns : Brunswick, Capua, Cracow, Florence, Leicester, Marseilles, Naples, Padua, Saragossa, Utrecht.

Taurus

Countries : Aderbijan, Archipelago, Asia Minor, Caucasus, Cyprus, Georgia, Holland, Ireland, Media, Mozendaran, Persia, Poland, White Russia.

H

Cities and Towns : Dublin, Franconia, Leipsic, Mantua, Palermo, Parma.

Gemini

Countries : Armenia, Belgium, Brabant, Egypt (Lower), England (West), Flanders, Lombardy, Sardinia, Tripoli, United States.

Cities and Towns : Cordova, London, Louvain, Mentz, Nuremburg, Versailles.

Cancer

Countries : Africa (North and West), Anatolia (nr. Constantinople), Holland, Scotland, Zealand.

Cities and Towns : Amsterdam, Berne, Cadiz, Constantinople, Genoa, Lubeck, Manchester (29th and 30th degrees), Milan, New York, St. Andrews, Tunis, Venice, York.

Leo

Countries : Alps, Bohemia, Cappadocia, Chaldea, France, Italy, Puglia, Sicily, Coast of Sidon, and Tyre.

Cities and Towns : Bath, Bolton-le-Moors, Bristol, Damascus, Philadelphia, Portsmouth, Prague, Ravenna, Rome, Taunton.

Virgo

Countries : Assyria, Babylon, Candia, Corinth, Croatia, Country between Euphrates and Tiber, Greece, Lavadia, Mesopotamia, Morea, Silesia (Lower), Switzerland, Thessaly, Turkey.

Cities and Towns : Basle, Bagdad, Cheltenham, Heidelburg, Jerusalem, Lyons, Navarre, Padua, Paris, Reading.

Libra

Countries : Austria, China, Egypt, Japan, Livonia, Savoy, Thibet (part), Upper Egypt.

Cities and Towns : Antwerp, Charlestown, Frankfort, Fribourg, Lisbon, Speyer, Plasencia, Vienna.

Scorpio

Countries : Algeria, Barbary, Bavaria, Catalona, Fez, Judea, Jutland, Morocco, Norway.

Cities and Towns : Frankfort on the Oder, Ghent, Liverpool, and Messina.

Sagittarius

Countries : Arabia, Cape Finisterre, Dalmatia, France (between

Masien and La Garon), Hungary, Italy (especially Tarante), Moravia, Provence, Spain, Slavonia, Tuscany.

Cities and Towns : Avignon, Buda, Cologne, Narbonne, Naples, Sheffield (in Toledo).

Capricorn

Countries : Bosnia, Bulgaria, Circars, Hesse, India, Illyria, Khorassan, Lithuania, Macedonia, Mexico, Morea, Mecklenburg, Punjab, Thrace, Styria, Saxony.

Aquarius

Countries : Arabia, Abyssinia, Circassia, Lithuania, Lower Sweden, Prussia, Poland, Piedmont, Russia, Tartary, Westphalia.

Cities and Towns : Bremen, Hamburg, Ingoldstadt, Salsburg, Trent.

Pisces

Countries : Asia (Southern), Africa (North), Desert of Sahara, Calabria, Egypt, Galicia (Spain), Nubia, Normandy, Portugal.

Cities and Towns : Alexandria, Cilicia, Compostela, Ratisbon, Seville, Tiverton, Worms.

Having erected the horoscope, it becomes essential to know which is the strongest planet in the figure. Each planet has a sign over which it is lord or ruler ; in certain signs some of the planets are exalted, in others in their fall, etc. All this can be seen at a glance from the following table :

Sign.	Ruler Planet.	Planet Exalted.	Planet's Fall.	Weak or Detrimen.
♈	♂	☉	♄	♀
♉	♀	☽	—	♂
♊	☿	—	—	♃
♋	☽	♄	♂	♄
♌	☉	—	—	—
♍	☿	—	♀	♃
♎	♀	♄	☉	♂
♏	♂	—	☽	♀
♐	♃	—	—	☿
♑	♄	♂	♃	☽
♒	♄	—	—	☉
♓	♃	♀	—	☿

A planet is always strongest when placed in its own sign, that is, the sign over which it is lord or ruler ; next when in the sign of its exaltation, but weak when in either fall or detriment.   There are certain dignities allowed to the planets when in certain positions.   A planet is essentially dignified when in its own sign and angular, especially if elevated in the M.C. ; accidentally dignified when in an angular position, but not in its own sign, etc.

Attention should be paid to the application or separation of planets.   The Moon, being the fastest traveller, applies to all the planets, and the planets apply to the others in the following order : Mercury, Venus, Sun, Mars, Jupiter, Saturn, Uranus, and Neptune. The application of one planet to another, or the Moon to planets, shows that the event is about to happen but is not complete ; but when separating, that it is passed or just completed.   The aspects and orbs of the planets must be studied in this particular.

Table of Aspects

No. of Degrees.	Aspect.	Symbol.	Nature.
30°	Semi-sextile	⚺	Harmonious.
45°	Semi-square	∠	Inharmonious.
60°	Sextile	⚹	Harmonious.
72°	Quintile	Q	Harmonious.
90°	Square	□	Inharmonious.
120°	Trine	△	Harmonious.
135°	Sesquiquadrate	□	Inharmonious.
144°	Bi-quintile	Bq.	Harmonious.
150°	Inconjunct	150	Harmonious.*
180°	Opposition	☍	Inharmonious.

A conjunction ☌ is the position of two planets that are within five degrees of each other.

There is a very simple method of quickly arriving at the aspects, viz :—The fiery signs are always in trine aspect to each other, i.e., if Mars were in fifth degree of Aries, then a planet in either the fifth degree of Leo or Sagittarius will be in trine ; and this holds good with the earth, water, and air signs.   The fixed signs are always in square aspect to each other.   These signs are Taurus, Leo, Scorpio, and Aquarius ; so that a planet in the tenth degree of Taurus

* Depending upon the nature of the planets that are Inconjunct.

would be square to another in the tenth degree of Leo or Aquarius, but in opposition to one in tenth degree of Scorpio. This will also hold good with the common and cardinal signs.

There are also the dexter and sinister aspects as follows :

Aspect ⚹ □ △ ☍	Aspect ⚹ □ △ ☍	Aspect ⚹ □ △ ☍
Dexter ♒ ♑ ♐	Dexter ♊ ♉ ♈	Dexter ♎ ♍ ♌
Sign ♈ ♎	Sign ♌ ♒	Sign ♐ ♊
Sinister ♊ ♋ ♌	Sinister ♎ ♏ ♐	Sinister ♒ ♓ ♈
Dexter ♓ ♒ ♑	Dexter ♋ ♊ ♉	Dexter ♏ ♎ ♍
Sign ♉ ♏	Sign ♍ ♓	Sign ♑ ♋
Sinister ♋ ♌ ♍	Sinister ♏ ♐ ♑	Sinister ♓ ♈ ♉
Dexter ♈ ♓ ♒	Dexter ♌ ♋ ♊	Dexter ♐ ♏ ♎
Sign ♊ ♐	Sign ♎ ♈	Sign ♒ ♌
Sinister ♌ ♍ ♎	Sinister ♐ ♑ ♒	Sinister ♈ ♉ ♊
Dexter ♉ ♈ ♓	Dexter ♍ ♌ ♋	Dexter ♑ ♐ ♏
Sign ♋ ♑	Sign ♏ ♉	Sign ♓ ♍
Sinister ♍ ♎ ♏	Sinister ♑ ♒ ♓	Sinister ♉ ♊ ♋

Table of Dexter and Sinister Aspects

The semi-sextile aspect ⚺ occurs on either side of the sign, and the inconjunct 150° on either side of the sign that is in opposition : thus to ♈, ♓ is dexter ⚺ and ♉ sinister ; ⚺ the 150° dexter ♏ sinister ♍, and so on with the other signs.

The nature of the dexter and sinister aspects in the houses are as follows :

Dexter Aspect	⚺	⚹	□	△	150°
House	12th	11th	10th	9th	8th
Sinister Aspect	⚺	⚹	□	△	150°
House	2nd	3rd	4th	5th	6th

When dealing with the aspects of the planets, it is necessary to know how many degrees to allow for the sphere of influence, and this sphere is known as the orb of the planet, each planet having its own orb, to the extent of which it acts upon other planets within aspect of that orb. It is safer, having learned the value of the application and separation, to allow an orb of seven degrees in which the planets affect each other when in aspect ; but this will not apply to the minor aspects of semi-square, semi-sextile, quintile, sesquiquadrate, bi-quintile, and 150°, which should be within one degree of a complete aspect.

It is important, before judgment, to decide which is the signifi-cator of the matter or person enquired about, also to link with this the Moon as co-significator. The one who asks a question is always the querent, and that which is enquired about is the quested. If Aries ascend at the time of erecting the figure, then Mars, which is the ruler of the sign Aries, is the significator of the querent. The strength and position of this significator should be well understood and its power fully known, so that the fortune or success of the querent may be known. If finance is the matter enquired about, then the ruler of the Second House will be the significator of the mone-tary affairs at the time ; or if the enquiry is about relatives, the lord of the Third House is taken as the significator ; if concerning children, then the Fifth House and its ruler must be studied for the signifi-cator, etc.

There are certain considerations which make the judgment sure and easy and the task a pleasure, the result being attained without much labour. When the joint significators are hastening to a conjunc-tion, the question will be clearly answered. If free from all complica-tions, angular, swift in motion, accidentally or essentially dignified, then the matter may be brought to a speedy termination ; if in suc-cedent houses, after some little delay ; but when in cadent houses, after much difficulty, delay, and hindrance. If the aspect is trine or sextile, then all will go well, but no evil aspect must come between— that is, the trine or sextile must be the first aspect met ; if in well-dig-nified positions, then all will go well, but if out of dignities, delay, etc. Events are brought to pass by square aspect, and opposing position ; but the matter is not usually of a satisfactory nature. Attention should be paid to the mutual receptions. The applications of planets are promising of good and evil ; but the separating aspects show that the matter is passing off, and that there is not much hope attached to the question. It often happens that when the significator meets a planet in no way affecting the question, before the significator of the matter is aspected, that some other influence intervenes, which may be brought about by some other person. The nature of the sign and house from which the intervention comes, will show the nature of the person, help or hindrance that is interposing. There is also another method of obtaining judgment ; when the significators are not in aspect but aspect a more ponderous planet, then the matter signified by this planet will assist, or be the means of bringing the matter to a satisfactory or adverse termination. A good general knowledge of Astrology is necessary before correct judgment can be given, and it will be better to study some of the examples before attempting to form any definite judgment, also to know the nature of each of the houses and all the questions that may be solved by a reference to them.

THE FIRST HOUSE

Life, Health, Description, and Condition of the Querent

The First House, commonly called the ascendant, is the house of the person making the enquiry, or of the thing enquired about in a general way, if the querent is erecting the figure for his own private study. In conjunction with a consideration of the ascendant, the Moon must also be taken into account, the Moon being the principal factor in all astrological questions.

The sign upon the ascendant must be carefully noted, also its lord or ruler, which is known as the significator. If the ruler be weak, then judge of the querent's condition accordingly, noting well the position of the ruler.

The significator is weak if retrograde, in a cadent house, or heavily afflicted ; but strong and favourable if well aspected, direct in motion, or angular. The significator should never be too close to the Sun ; it is then unable to express its own character, and cannot be judged apart from the solar influence.

Planets in the ascendant are co-significators with the ruling planet, the influence of the ascending planet often coming to aid or retard the querent.

If the querent enquires concerning health, life, character, or general welfare, the ascendant must be studied.

Uranus rising, promises sudden and unexpected events. It may indicate either sudden journeys or romantic adventures. It will describe one who is original, fond of metaphysics, Astrology, and those things pertaining to the higher mind. If much afflicted, the person is abrupt, irritable, and sometimes dangerous.

Saturn in the First House describes one advanced in years, a sober, tactful, just, and prudent person ; very reserved, cautious, and earnest. If afflicted, it indicates a discontented and melancholy person, heavy with grief or sorrow, unfortunate and laborious. It denotes long life and great age. Saturn in the ascendant at the time of asking a question is often a sign of hindrance, sickness from cold complaints, and shows the matter under consideration to be enduring, or connected with a long period of time.

Jupiter in the First House denotes that the querent is sociable, cheerful, happy, and hopeful for the future ; desirous of gaining justice with mercy, and inclined to be liberal, generous, and free. Afflicted, it denotes some hypocrisy and pretence to false claims, severe affliction from inferiors, or those who are unjust. It is an indication of good health, full life, and good fortune ; but afflicted, the blood is affected and the health suffers, according to the sign ascending.

Mars in the ascendant describes a consequential person, who will know more, in his own estimation, than he has realized. It denotes one who is courageous, more inclined to use force than tact, and to argue, contend, combat, and show an aggressive attitude. Afflicted, it shows the person to be quarrelsome, untruthful, and unreliable. It indicates cuts, blows, wounds, strife, danger of accidents and sudden death, probably arising from impulsive and foolish acts.

Venus in the First House denotes one fond of life and pleasure, loving ease and comfort ; one who is affable, agreeable, peaceful, loving fortune and freedom from care ; afflicted, one who is untidy, careless and indolent, too fond of pleasure and company, a gossip and time-waster ; if afflicted by Mars, unchaste or sensuous.   This position shows good health, a vital temperament, and success ; afflicted, kidney troubles, and a life that may be foolishly and quickly expended.

Mercury in the First House generally describes persons who are young ; those who are shrewd, quick-witted, clever, competent, fond of learning and activity ; afflicted, much depends upon the nature of the affliction, this planet absorbing the whole of the influence of the planet that it aspects. It indicates, when afflicted, one who is a rambler, too talkative, and unfortunate. The health is afflicted through the nerves, worry, or dissolute habits. Much depends upon the aspects, as to the length of life.

The Moon in the First House denotes one who is fond of change, and movement ; romantic and fanciful or imaginative. Afflicted, the character is weak, and liable to fall into temptation. The health is not good and the life precarious.

The Sun in the First House describes one who is noble and majestic, holding authority, power and influence ; it indicates success and prosperity. Afflicted, it shows the querent to be a boaster, and one who is ambitious beyond his capacity for attainment ; appro- bation, and self-esteem predominating. This indicates an average life and a very strong constitution.

The Part of Fortune in the First House is good for wealth and success in life.

The ruler of the First House must be well studied ; according to the sign and house that it is in will its strength be, but never fail to give the querent the credit of the rising planet first, as this shows his condition at the time of asking the question. The ruling planet shows his general condition of spirit, mind or body.

When studying the ascendant for length of life, note the Fourth, Sixth, and Eighth Houses, the strength of the ruling planet, and the rising sign.

The Times of Events occurring

It is necessary to know how the length of time may be judged. First count the number of degrees between the application of the sig- nificators—which must always be calculated with extreme care— choosing the rule of the figure as chief significator. Note the Moon's application and the number of degrees the aspect requires before completion, and judge time by the following table :

Angles.	*Succedents.*	*Cadent Houses.*
Cardinal Signs	Cardinal Signs	Cardinal Signs
♈ ♋ ♎ ♑	♈ ♋ ♎ ♑	♈ ♋ ♎ ♑
Indicate Days.	Indicate Weeks.	Indicate Months.
Mutable Signs	Mutable Signs	Mutable Signs
♊ ♍ ♐ ♓	♊ ♍ ♐ ♓	♊ ♍ ♐ ♓
Indicate Weeks.	Indicate Months.	Indicate Years.
Fixed Signs	Fixed Signs	Fixed Signs
♉ ♌ ♏ ♒	♉ ♌ ♏ ♒	♉ ♌ ♏ ♒
Indicate Months.	Indicate Years.	Time Indefinite.

THE SECOND HOUSE

Finance and all matters connected with money, wealth, or property. The sign upon the cusp of this house and its lord must be noted, also where the ruler is placed and how it is aspected. Then note the planets in this house. Neptune is supposed to indicate frauds and deceptions. This remark will apply to all the other houses in regard to Neptune. Uranus in the Second House indicates some sudden and unexpected loss or gain, according to how it is aspected. Taken generally, it indicates sudden events in connection with finance. Saturn in the Second House causes hindrances and delays in money matters, or gain by labour and industry ; also success with building, or land transactions when not afflicted. Jupiter therein indicates wealth, success, and prosperity, also Venus and the Part of Fortune, according to how they are aspected. The Sun or Mars in the Second House indicates much finance, which melts away with excess of expenditure ; Moon or Mercury, much fluctuation, according to the aspect.

The Second House is also the eighth house of the partner. It is the fifth from the mother's house—the tenth ; the eleventh from the father's—the fourth ; and the tenth from the children's house— the fifth.

THE THIRD HOUSE

The Third House answers all questions concerned with brethren, neighbours, letters, writings, and short journeys. Uranus in this house indicates originality of mind. It is good for all mystical studies, but infavourable for all affairs connected with relatives, unless well aspected. It indicates sudden and unexpected events connected with papers and relatives, and the probability of some sudden travel. Saturn located in this house denotes delay, hindrance and loss in travel, also long and protracted disputes with relatives. Jupiter herein promises success in travel, letters and writings, and concord with relatives. Mars in the Third House indicates quarrels and disputes with relatives, accidents in travel, or unpleasant companions, and angry disputes in correspondence. Venus indicates pleasure in connection with relatives, travel, and correspondence. Mercury in this house deals more with correspondence and literary affairs. Note, the planet ruling this house placed therein, is good for matters described by the planet. The Sun in the Third House is a good testimony for harmony and success in all questions relating to this house. The Moon therein indicates much travel and change, also uncertainty ; but with fruitful results if well aspected.

THE FOURTH HOUSE

This is the house of the parents ; it governs all home affairs and the environment generally, also the residence of the native. Uranus herein shows sudden mishaps, unexpected changes and removals, and it is generally very evil for the parents and the home life in all horary questions. Saturn in the Fourth House, a bad termination to all matters connected with this house, with the probability of sorrow, worry, and anxiety. It indicates delay in regard to the matter under consideration. Jupiter in the Fourth House, gain by inheritance ; it is a sign of prosperity, with a successful termination to affairs. Mars herein indicates death and destruction, home quarrels and sad endings. Venus in the Fourth House promises pleasure and a successful issue to all questions connected with this house. Mercury in this House indicates an intelligent environment. When the Sun is placed in the Fourth House it is good for the father and the character of the home life. The Moon herein indicates changes, etc., the nature depending upon the aspects.

FIFTH HOUSE

This governs all matters connected with children, pleasure, and speculation. Uranus in this house denotes dangers in connection with child-birth, strange and romantic love experiences, sudden gains and losses in speculation, according to aspect. Saturn in the Fifth House indicates troubles from children, delays in matters connected with pleasure, and when well aspected, profit from lands and mines. Jupiter in the Fifth House, gain through speculation or through children. Mars in this house indicates trouble through children ; it shows gambling tendencies and riotous pleasure. Venus in the Fifth shows success and gain in speculation and all matters connected with pleasure and children. This is good for all love affairs. Mercury in the Fifth House indicates correspondence through children and speculation. The Sun in this house is a good influence, but the Moon will act according to the aspects.

THE SIXTH HOUSE

This governs all matters connected with sickness and servants ; it is also connected with food stuffs and animals. Uranus in this house indicates incurable diseases, strange servants, and trouble through uncles and aunts. Saturn in the Sixth House shows slow diseases, and it is connected with elderly servants. Jupiter in this house is good for the health, but if afflicted the blood may be affected. It denotes good servants. Mars in the Sixth House indicates sickness and feverish complaints, and inflammatory diseases. When afflicted it indicates disorderly servants. Sun, Moon, Venus, and Mercury will act in accordance with the aspects.

THE SEVENTH HOUSE

This house is concerned with love, courtship, and marriage, partnerships, legal affairs, strangers, and opponents. Uranus in the Seventh House denotes peculiar and romatic love affairs, strange marriages, and if much afflicted divorce, separation, and peculiar proceedings. Well aspected it may indicate platonic unions. Saturn in this house shows faithfulness in marriage, elderly partners, but when afflicted, much sorrow and grief. Jupiter in the Seventh House denotes success at law, also in marriage and partnership. Mars in the Seventh House shows disputes and disturbances. This planet is very evil in the Seventh House, as it is out of harmony there. Venus in the Seventh House is good for all love affairs, and promises a successful marriage and a happy partnership. Mercury in the Seventh House denotes much correspondence through love affairs. and great activity in legal matters. The Sun in the Seventh House promises a noble union, or to one holding a high position in life. The Moon in this house will act according to aspects. Part of Fortune in this house denotes gain by marriage.

THE EIGHTH HOUSE

This house indicates the nature of death, it is concerned with wills and legacies, the goods of the dead and the partner's financial affairs. It is also the house of co-workers. Uranus in the Eighth House denotes peculiar deaths of a sudden and unexpected nature.

Well aspected, it may bring unexpected legacies, but often attended with much trouble. Saturn in the Eighth House spoils the hope of legacies and affects partners, and co-workers' financial affairs. Jupiter in the Eighth House denotes gain by legacy or marriage. Mars in this house indicates sudden deaths and disputes over legacies. Venus in the Eighth House promises legacy. Mercury in the Eighth House denotes much correspondence concerning the dead. The Part of Fortune in this house indicates gain through Eighth House matters.

THE NINTH HOUSE

This is concerned with higher thought, science, philosophy and religion, long journeys, and shipping affairs. Uranus in this house indicates unexpected travel and peculiar experiences in foreign lands. It is good for all metaphysical affairs. Saturn in this house is good in all philosophical questions. When afflicted, much deception may be expected, also sorrow in matters connected with foreign affairs. Jupiter in this house is very good for religion, and denotes gain from partners' relatives. Mars in the Ninth House denotes atheistical tendencies or bigoted opinions concerning religion. It is evil for all matters connected with travel, shipping, etc. Venus in the Ninth House shows agreement with marriage relatives. Mercury in this house is good for scientific research. The Sun herein denotes success and religion. The Moon in the Ninth House shows changes in regard to religious affairs and much travelling.

THE TENTH HOUSE

This house is concerned with honour, credit, profession, and success in life. It is the most important angle. Uranus in this house will affect trade and honour according to aspect. Saturn in the Tenth House shows discredit and danger of a fall from position. Jupiter indicates wealth and honour. Mars denotes some violence. It indicates much assertiveness and ambition ; also scandal. Venus in the Tenth House indicates gain through feminine affairs. Mercury in the Tenth House shows gain by learning. The Sun in the Tenth House shows honour and good fortune. The Moon in the Tenth House denotes gain by changes in public affairs.

THE ELEVENTH HOUSE

This is concerned with friends, acquaintances, public institutions, hopes and wishes. Uranus in the Eleventh House denotes occult friends and persons who are interested in metaphysics, etc., but is very evil when badly aspected. Saturn in the Eleventh House well aspected indicates faithful friends, but when afflicted, false friends. Jupiter in the Eleventh House is good for sociability and friendship. Mars in the Eleventh House indicates acquaintances according to the aspects. Venus in the Eleventh House, good female friends. Mercury in the Eleventh House, literary acquaintances. The Sun in the Eleventh House shows friends holding good positions. The Moon in the Eleventh House indicates friends among the common people.

THE TWELFTH HOUSE

This house is both fortunate and unfortunate, and everything depends upon how the planets are aspected that occupy it. It requires to be judged with very great care. Planets afflicted in this house may indicate treachery, imprisonment, and confinement. Generally speaking, it governs hospitals, prisons and places of confinement.

ILLUSTRATIONS IN HORARY ASTROLOGY

The following examples will show how the judgment of horary questions by this branch of Astrology is obtained. They are authentic cases.

EXAMPLE I

A Horary Figure for Lost Money

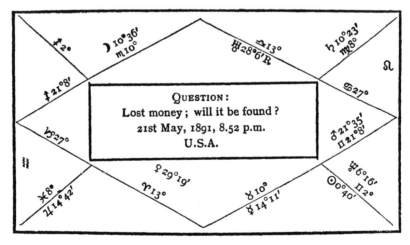

QUESTION:
Lost money ; will it be found ?
21st May, 1891, 8.52 p.m.
U.S.A.

On May 21st, 1891, at 8.45 p.m., a female consulted an astrologer in regard to money and a pocket-book which had been stolen from
her mother, who was ill and could not call to see him.

The Sun ruled at the hour, and described the female, who was
stout, with full eyes, round full face, ruddy complexion, and had
rather a strong voice, and as the Sun ruled the Eighth House, which
denotes the money of others, it was said she wished to know whether
the money would be recovered or not, and that she also wished to
know if deaths would occur in the family. She stated that such were
her thoughts.

Finding Mars in the Seventh House, in a double sign, and in
sextile to Venus, which was badly placed in Aries, in opposition to
Herschel, the Astrologer said there were two persons connected with
the theft of the money, and that neither bore a good reputation ; that
the man was tall, dark, with sun-burnt complexion of a quarrelsome
disposition, quick and impulsive, which Mars in aspect with Herschel
would denote ; and that he was connected with a female who was
rather lean, of doubtful character, and one who was given to bad
habits. Finding both planets in an angle, he said they were both at
her home at the hour of consultation, and were connected with her
house, as lodgers or residents, and the sooner she got rid of them the
better it would be for her. Mars the lord of the Fourth House being
in Gemini, an airy sign, and in an angle, he said the money was upon
the premises, and in the west part, upon a high airy place, where
there were tall posts or partitions, and where the air could blow
around it ; that the man was to blame, and that it was his intention
to remove the money at some convenient time ; and finding the Moon
in close trine to Jupiter, the querent was told she would probably find
the money, late that night or early next morning, when the Moon
would be in perfect aspect with the planet.

The querent then stated that there were two lodgers of the description which he had given, a male and a female, who rumour
said, were unmarried. The man had said he was about to leave the
female and go easterly, but as the astrologer found Mars leaving a
westerly sign and about to enter Cancer, he told her he would go east,
probably to New York, as Cancer ruled that place ; this he told before
she knew the facts. On the following Saturday, at 5 p.m., a brother
of the female came and told him that the money was found on the

morning of the 22nd.   It was found under a grape arbour, which was
upon tall posts and in an airy position, and from other facts it transpired that the thief had taken the money and hidden it upon the
arbour, and in the morning, when they had accidentally agitated the
arbour, the money fell to the ground and was found.

EXAMPLE II.

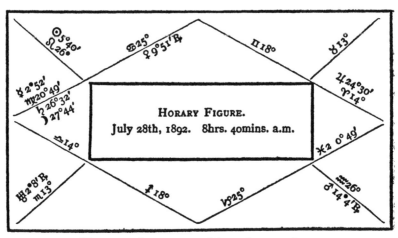

HORARY FIGURE.
July 28th, 1892. 8hrs. 40mins. a.m.

Three questions answered from the same figure.

1.   Will the querent do right by remaining in his present
     situation ?
2.   If he leave, is he likely to improve his position ?
3.   Is the person by whom he is employed reliable, and what he
     professes to be ?

The lord of ascendant cadent in Twelfth House shows the enquirer to be in a most desponding state of mind, and were it not for
the approaching semi-sextile of the Moon, he would throw up the
situation.

As the Moon is only five degrees from the semi-sextile of Mercury,
in five weeks' time some great concession will be made to him.
Venus being posited in the Tenth House and the Sun favourably inclined from the eleventh, signifying hopes and wishes, is a strong
argument that he should continue in his situation.   The fact that the
Moon is leaving a malefic and hasting to sextile of the Sun in the
Eleventh House is another favourable argument.   As Uranus in

Second House has the square of Sun, there will be delay in payment of salary or commission. As Jupiter, lord of the Fourth House, has no aspect to Mercury or Moon, yet comes within four degrees of a trine to Mercury, lord of ascendant, on September 4th, it is a convincing argument that in about five weeks the cloud will disappear. As Mercury comes to the opposition of Jupiter, October 10th, he should be cautious so as not to cause a rupture on that day.

To sum up :

1. He should stay, but be circumspect.
2. Not for some months.
3. His employer is too exacting, yet an honourable man. If not careful, he will have notice to leave on October 10th.

EXAMPLE III.

Three questions answered from the same map.

1. Are my ideas sound and practical ?
2. Will it pay to patent ?
3. Should I retain or sell my invention ?

1. The ☽, chief significator of the ninth, the house of inventions, having the △ ♄ from eleventh, the house of hopes and wishes, also the ✳ ♄ from the fifth, house of speculation, being angular in the seventy and fixed, and ♀, the lady off ascendant in tenth, with ♅

angular in first ⚹ to ☿, part ruler of ninth, are all arguments that the theory is genuine.

2. ♂, lord of second, conjoined with ♀, lady of ascendant in tenth, the co-significator being strong and in △ aspect to the lord of the fourth, it will pay to bring out.

3. The enquirer should sell the idea to some ship-builder, as ♒ signifies the captain or owner of a vessel, and that sign being on the cusp of the fourth, an engineer evidently known to him, and as ♂ is conjoined with his significator, he can help him materially in bringing the matter to a successful issue ; he will be a man of good height, chestnut hair, sun-burnt complexion and full eyes.

EXAMPLE IV.

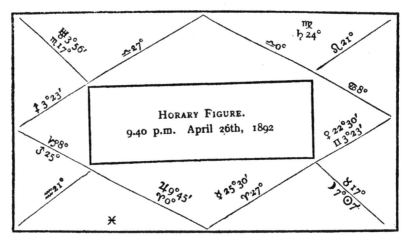

HORARY FIGURE.
9.40 p.m.   April 26th,   1892

Question : Is a vessel overdue lost ? Will she return to port in safety ?

As no planets are posited in the Eighth House, and the lady of the Eighth House conjoined with Sun, and lately suffered from the opposition of Herschel, it is patent she has been in extreme danger, yet certainly not lost.

The Moon combust looks exceedingly black, and would show entire loss if the Moon signified the ship.

As Jupiter signifies the ship and he has the semi-sextile of Sun and Moon, she is safe.

The presence of Mars in second in trine to Saturn in the house of voyages, is a further argument of safety.

As Aries represents the bows, and Taurus the cut-water, and as Mercury has the square of Mars, whilst the Sun and Moon have the opposition of Herschel, and Venus has the semi-square of the Sun and Moon, it is conclusive the bows, cut-water, and rudder are injured.

As Taurus is an earthy sign, she has run aground and sprung a leak.

As Herschel is in Scorpio in opposition to Sun and Moon, it is conclusive of injury to the ship's bottom also.

As Scorpio represents the seamen, it would appear that some fresh track was chosen by a new hand.

As there is no evil aspect to the ascendant or lord of ascendant, we conclude the ship and cargo are quite safe.

The lord of ascendant in the Fourth House is an argument that she will return to port, and as Jupiter is a heavy planet, she will proceed but slowly back to dock.

EXAMPLE V.

HORARY FIGURE.
March 29th, 1892, 8.45 a.m.

Question: Will the querent benefit from his uncle's will? If the contrary, who will?

As Mercury, his significator, is in the Eleventh House, signifying hopes and wishes, it is an argument that he expects something substantial and has built his hopes thereon, which, however, will be frustrated, as Mercury is disposed of by Mars, the significator of his uncle. As the Moon is lady of his second, and approaching the conjunction of his significator, Mercury, and she being lord of the uncle's ninth, the house of law, etc., his name will appear in the will. As the uncle's significator, Mars, is not in any aspect to the querent's significator, Mercury, neither is the lord of his second, Jupiter, in any aspect to the significator, he certainly will be left out in the cold. Following Lilly's rules : as the lord of the fourth is close square to Mars, *no legacy even* may be expected. As the lord of the fourth is conjoined with Jupiter, *i.e.,* within orbs, he will be one of the executors, and have a nominal sum for his trouble—nothing more.

As Jupiter signifies persons in power, a solicitor will be his co-executor. Saturn is always a potent significator of deceased persons, and as the second fortune, Venus, is hastening to a trine, it is most palpable that his uncle's late wife's relations are coming into favour, and the bulk of the property will most certainly be left to them.

As Venus is in the twelfth, evidently some persons he has considered as enemies, though mistakenly, will benefit by the will, as the co-significator is in semi-sextile to her. The Moon having the semi-sextile of Venus, and she being chief ruler of the fifth of the figure, it is a convincing argument that the querent's children will benefit to a small extent.

EXAMPLE VI.

HORARY FIGURE.
July 18th, 1892, 1.45 p.m.

One Map for two Enquirers

Questions :

1.   Shall I dispose of my stock well ?

Shall I get out of business and go south of birthplace ?

2.   *Another Letter.*—Is it advisable for me to go on with the medical profession ?

Should I do any good on the stage ?

Would it be wise to go abroad ?

1.   Finding the lord of first retrograde cadent, and afflicting the Moon by a close square, he is in a most desponding state respecting it.

The significator has no good aspect from either planet, and Jupiter, lord of the second, having recently fallen from an angle, the stock, although in good condition, will remain a drug in the market some months to come.   As Mars becomes direct in the beginning of September, prices will improve a little, but the middle of December, when Jupiter becomes direct, and sextile Mars' place in figure, will be the best time to dispose of the stock.   At the same time, Mercury, lord of the eighth, will be in Sagittarius, in sextile to Mars, and trine to Jupiter ; also favourable.   Venus, lady of the seventh, passing cusp of second, is another argument.

As the Sun is lord of the tenth, and sextile to Saturn, part ruler of the second, it will be well to dispose of it to a company, in preference to a private individual.   And early in January go South, with perfect success.

2.   Mars, lord of first retrograde in cadent house, signifies the querent to be most despondent and irresolute ; he has an idea that he will never do any good in the world.

As Mars has the square of the Moon from the seventh, it is concluded that a certain lady has absorbed much of his time that should have been given to study.

As the Moon is approaching square of Mercury, the latter being on the M.C., he will have a severe letter from his mother, upbraiding him for waste of time, and not without good reason, for he has been most dilatory.

As Mercury, lord of the eleventh, has no aspect to Mars, another examination cannot be recommended, for he will fail.

As the Moon is lady of the ninth, in close square to Mars, and he retrograde and cadent, he cannot be recommended to go abroad, nor on the stage, as Sun, lord of the tenth, is square to Jupiter, lord of the fifth (Theatres).

HORIZON. The circle round the earth that separates the visible hemisphere from the invisible. The terms Sensible, Visible or Physical Horizon are often used. The Astronomical Horizon is termed the Rational Horizon and this is obtained by supposing a line drawn from the earth's centre to be parallel with the horizon. Astrologically, the Eastern Horizon is that point on the earth's surface that is rising in the East, the sign of the Zodiac then seen is called the rising sign, this impressing its influence upon the Ascendant. See RISING SIGN.

HOROSCOPE. This is a term generally used for what is properly known as the Nativity. The horoscope is taken to represent the aspect of the heavens at the time of physical birth, but the word more properly applies to Horary Astrology. This is a convenient term, however, for a plan of the heavens at the time of casting a Figure, as it is called. To cast the Horoscope the following is the method adopted :

Obtain an Ephemeris of the planets' places in the year for which the horoscope is wanted. Open the Ephemeris at the month required, and note the sidereal time on the day of the month for which the horoscope is to be cast. On January 15th, 1900, the sidereal time *at noon* was 19hrs. 37mins. 55secs. If the time of birth for which the Horoscope is to be cast, occurred *after* noon, then the time elapsed since noon is to be *added* to the sidereal time at noon ; for example, to erect a map of the heavens for 4.35 p.m., January 15th, 1900, the method is as follows :

	h.	m.	s.
S.T. at noon - - - - -	19	37	55
Add time elapsed - - - -	4	35	0
Correction (See CORRECTIONS) -	0	0	45
	24	13	40
Deduct time of natural day 24 hrs. -	24	0	0
	0	13	40

To erect the map it is now necessary to refer to a table of houses for the latitude of the birth-place. If the birth occurred at London, then refer to the London table of houses, to be found at the end of Raphael's Ephemeris, or by using Dalton's tables. Open the table of houses at the page showing the sidereal time at ohr. 14m. 41s., this being the nearest sidereal time to ohr. 13m. 40s. At the head of the column marked 10 will be found the sign ♈, and in line with this for sidereal time ohr. 14m. 41s. is the figure 4 ; this indicates that 4° of the sign Aries is upon the cusp of the Mid-heaven or Tenth House. In the next column under 11 is placed the symbol of ♉ and in line with the S. T. the figures 13 indicating that 13° of Taurus is upon the cusp of the Eleventh House. In the next column under 12 is the symbol ♊, and in line with S. T. the figures 25, showing that Gemini 25° is upon the Twelfth House. In the next broader column at the head is marked " Ascen." and under it ♋ ; and in line with S. T. the figures 29 17, showing that Cancer 29° 17′ was upon the cusp of the ascendant. In the next column at the top is found the figure 2, and in line with S. T. 15, showing that ♌ 15° is on the Second House ; and, finally, in the last column is 3, and in the required line 6, denoting that ♍ 6° is upon the cusp of the Third House. These signs and degrees marked into their proper houses on the map will be represented as follows :

10th.	11th.	12th	Asc.	2nd.	3rd.
♈ 4°	♉ 13°	♊ 25°	♋ 29°17′	♌ 15°	♍ 6°

To complete the map, the six opposite signs of the zodiac with the same number of degrees are to be marked into the opposite vacant spaces.

Having placed the signs in their correct positions, it is then necessary to find the planets' places from the Ephemeris. Under the column ☉ Longitude on the 15th day of the month are found the figures : 24, 55, 52, and at the head of the figures the symbol ♑. This denotes that 24°55′52″ of the sign Capricorn was the place of the Sun at noon on that day. If the Sun's place be noted for the following day at noon, it will be found that he has moved 1°1′5″ in 24 hours ; this is very little over 2¼′ per hour ; in half an hour he will move 1′15″ ; and in 4 hours the ☉ will have moved 10′ ; therefore, roughly, 11′15″ will have to be added to the place at noon of the Sun, making his place 25°7′7″ at 3.30 p.m., or, to be exact, 25°7′20″ ♑. This place of the Sun is now filled into the map. Passing now to the column marked ☿ Longitude, we note

that Mercury at noon on the 15th is in 9°11′ of ♑, and the movement in 24 hrs. is 1°30′, a uniform rate of 3′45″ per hour, and
showing that ☿ has moved 17′11″ in the 4hrs. 35mins., which,
added to 9°22′, makes the place of ☿ 9°39′11″ ♑. This can
be placed in the proper position in the map.   ♀ may be taken
next : her longitude at noon is 24°21′ ♒, and she is moving at
the rate of 1°15′ per day of 24 hours, which is 3′7½″ per hour, making
the place at 4.35 p.m. 24°35′15″ ♒.   ♂ is in 25°6′ of ♑ moving 46′
per day, his true place at 4.35 p.m. being 25°16′ ♑. The other
planets may be worked out in a similar way, the positions being
as follows : ♃ 3°♐ 51′, ♄ 29°♐ 23′, ♅ 10°♐ 54′ and ♆ 24° ♊ 51′ R.
(R. means that the planet is retrograde).   Under the column headed ☽
Longitude, we find the Moon's place, which it is necessary to calculate very accurately.   At noon the Moon is 21°36′36″ of ♋ and her
rate of motion in the following 24hrs. is 12°10′37″, which is very
nearly 30′26″ per hour.   At 4.35 p.m. the Moon will have moved
2°18′40″, making her place 23°56′16″ ♋.   These planetary positions
may now be filled into the horoscope as follows :

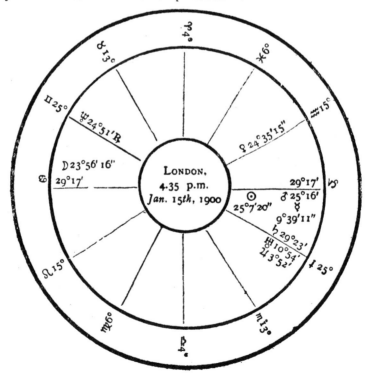

Should the time be before noon, then the interval *between* noon and the time for which the map is to be erected must be deducted from the sidereal time at noon. If a map is required for 9 a.m. then 3 hours, which is the difference between 9 a.m. and noon, must be deducted as follows :

	h.	m.	s.
S. T. at noon, Jan. 15th, 1900 -	19	37	55
Deduct time before noon -	3	0	0
	16	37	55
Deduct correction 3hrs. -	0	0	30
	16	37	25

The map may then be erected for this sidereal time.

Logarithms may be used for calculating the planets' places (see LOGARITHMS), and a uniform rate of 10″ per hour may be used for correction between mean and sidereal time.   (See NATIVITY.)

HOROSCOPES FOR SOUTH LATITUDES

The *Nautical Almanac* and the annual ephemerides now in use among astrologers are calculated for the meridian of Greenwich ; and the following instructions are intended for the use of those who wish to erect foreign horoscopes while using these books.

The rules for calculating foreign horoscopes are naturally classed under two heads. *Firstly*, the student must learn how to find the sidereal time for noon at the place for which he wishes to erect the figure. *Secondly*, he must know how to reckon the places of the planets correctly.

To find the Sidereal Time for Noon at any place.

The sidereal time for noon, as given in the ephemeris, means noon at Greenwich.   Therefore, to find the sidereal time for noon at any other place, a correction has to be made.

Ascertain the longitude of the place in question in degrees and minutes of space, and then turn it into hours and minutes of time by means of the following table.

One degree of space equals four minutes of time.

One minute of space equals four seconds of time.

Having found the longitude in time, the necessary correction has to be made for it. This is done by means of the " Table to reduce Mean to Sidereal Time." For each hour of longitude take 9.86

seconds ; and for each minute of longitude take 0.16 seconds, according to the table of corrections. This amount is to be *subtracted* from the sidereal time for Greenwich noon in the ephemeris if the place is *east* longitude, and is to be *added* if *west*.

Example I.—What is the sidereal time for noon on June 4th, 1897, at New York ?

Longitude of New York	-	-	-	-	75° 0′W.	
Equivalent in time	-	-	-	-	4h. 56m.	
Correction for 4h. 56m.	-	-	-	-		48.64s.
Sidereal time, noon, Greenwich, June 4th	-	4h. 52m. 45s.		
Add correction for west	-	-	-	-		48.64s.
Sidereal time, noon, New York		-	4h. 53m. 33.64s.		

Example II.—What is the sidereal time for noon on June 4th, 1897, at Athens ?

Longitude of Athens	-	-	-	-	23° 42′E.	
Equivalent in time	-	-	-	-	1h. 35m.	
Correction for 1h. 35m.	-	-	-	-		15.61s.
Sidereal time, noon, Greenwich, June 4th	-	4h. 52m. 45s.		
Subtract correction for east	-	-	-		15.61s.
Sidereal time, noon, Athens -	-	-	4h. 52m. 29.39s.		

Having thus found the sidereal time at noon for place in question, proceed to ascertain the sidereal time at the birth of the child (or right ascension of the mid-heaven in time), in the usual way. Add the time of birth if after noon, and subtract the difference between it and noon if before noon ; being careful not to forget the correction for the difference between mean and sidereal time, which is to be taken also from the " Table to reduce Mean to Sidereal Time."

Example III.—Find the sidereal time of birth of a child born at New York, June 4th, 1897, at 10 p.m.

The sidereal time for noon at New York on the day in question has already been found by Example I, therefore we proceed thus :—

	h.	m.	s.
Sidereal time, noon, New York - - -	4	53	33.64
Add time elapsed - - - - -	10	0	0
Also add correction for 10h. - - -		1	38.57
Sidereal time of birth - - -	14	55	12.21

Example IV.—What is the sidereal time of birth of a child born at Athens on June 4th, 1897, at 10 a.m. ?

The sidereal time for noon at Athens on the day in question has already been found by Example II.

	h.	m.	s.
Sidereal time, noon, Athens =	1	52	29.39
Subtract difference before noon -	- 2	0	0
	2	52	29.39
Also subtract correction for 2h. - -	- 0	0	19.71
Sidereal time of birth - - -	2	52	9.68

Taking the decimals as the nearest whole number, the sidereal time of birth in Example III is 14h. 55m. 12s. ; and in Example IV 2h. 52m. 10s.

Having found the sidereal time of birth, the cusps of the midheaven and other houses are written in the figure by means of a table of houses for the latitude of the birthplace ; or they may be worked out by trigonometry.

If the correction for longitude is wholly omitted, the error will never exceed two minutes—the less the longitude the less the error.

TO FIND THE PLANET'S PLACES

In the ephemeris, the places of the planets are given for noon at Greenwich ; and when an astrological figure is erected for some distant place, it is necessary to take the difference of longitude into consideration.

The longitude of the birthplace in time will already have been ascertained as above. Add this to the time of birth if west of Greenwich, but subtract if east. The result will give the time for which the planets' places must be calculated from the ephemeris. They are then inserted in the map in the usual way.

Example V.—A child was born at Dublin at 2 p.m. any day. For what time on that day must the places of the planets be calculated in a Greenwich ephemeris ?

Dublin is 6°17′ W. ; and when turned into time this amounts to 25 minutes. As Dublin is west, this must be added to the time of birth, 2h. 25m. p.m. will be the time for which the positions of the planets must be calculated.

Example VI.—A child was born at New York at 10 p.m. on January 1st in any year.

> Longitude of New York -   -   -   - 74°0'W.
> Equivalent in time   -   -   -   - 4h. 56m.

Add this to the birth time, and the result is 2h. 56m. a.m. on the *next day*, January 2nd.

Example VII.—A child was born at Paris at 9 a.m. any day.

> Longitude of Paris   -   -   -   - 2°21'E
> Equivalent in time   -   -   -   - 9m. 24s.

As Paris is east, subtract this from the time of birth, and (ignoring the seconds because less than half a minute) 8h. 51m. a.m. is the required time for calculating the planets' places.

Example VIII.—A child was born at Athens at 1 a.m. on May 1st any year.

> Longitude of Athens   -   -   -   - 23°41'E.
> Equivalent in time   -   -   -   - 1h. 35m.

As Athens is east, subtract this from the birth time. The required time is then found to be 11h. 25m. on the *previous day*, April 30th.

SOUTH LATITUDES

In the ordinary horoscope for a place north of the equator, the cusp of the ascendant is on the left-hand side of the figure and that of the seventh house on the right. That is to say, if the reader faces due south, the ascendant of the heavens will be on his left, and the stars will set on his right. In the southern hemisphere this will be reversed. He would there stand facing the north (because the Sun is in the north at noon) and the ascendant will be on his right and the descendant on his left. Consequently, in transferring this to paper, that which in a horoscope for north latitude would be the cusp of the seventh is the cusp of the southern ascendant, and the rising sign with its degree and minute are marked there accordingly ; that part which is the northern sixth house being the southern second ; the northern fifth, the southern third ; and so on.

The student may draw the southern horoscope in exactly the same way as the northern, so far as the mere position of the houses is concerned. Make the figure with ascendant on the left as usual. To reverse it, though correct in idea, causes endless confusion to one accustomed to the common position.

HOURS, PLANETARY. Each hour from sunrise to sunset is under the influence of a special Deva, and over each event in every day a lord or ruler presides : over bathing and meditation is Saturn ; over affection and meals is Venus ; over social and moral duties is Jupiter ; over strength and business enterprise is Mars ; over speech and correspondence, Mercury ; and over all physical and mundane things generally is the Moon ; while the Sun is lord over all.

These planetary hours are found by dividing the time between sunrise and sunset into twelve equal portions. The planetary " hour " commencing at dawn is ruled by the planet ruling the day ; for instance, on Saturday, ♄ rules the first " hour " after dawn. The succeeding " hours " are ruled by the other planets taken in the order of their distance from the Sun ; thus, ♄ ♃ ♂ ☉ ♀ ☿ ☽, ♄ ♃ ♂ ☉ ♀ ☿ ☽, and so on. The time intervening between sunset and sunrise is similarly divided into twelve equal " hours," and at sunset the planetary rulership follows on in the above order, the planet ruling the " hour " commencing at sunset on a Saturday being ☿ (as will be seen from what has been said). Following round the circle of twenty-four hours, we find ♂ ruling the last hour before dawn of the next day, giving us the ☉ as ruler of the first hour after dawn on Sunday. Similarly the ☽ rules the first hour after dawn on Monday, ♂ Tuesday, ☿ Wednesday, ♃ Thursday, ♀ Friday, and as aforesaid ♄ Saturday.

A perpetual table of Planetary Hours for all places will be found in *Casting the Horoscope*.

The older European astrologers have all given a twenty-four hours classification of the day, but the one given by Mme H. P. Blavatsky and founded on occult fact divides each day into four quarters as follows :

	Monday	Tuesday	Wednesday	Thursday	Friday	Saturday	Sunday
1	☽	♂	☿	♃	♀	♄	☉
2	☿	♃	♀	♄	☉	☽	♂
3	♀	♄	☉	☽	♂	☿	♃
4	☉	☽	♂	☿	♃	♀	♄

Monday is so called because its first quarter, beginning shortly before sunrise, is ruled by the Moon, which apparently exercises a kind of general rulership over the whole day. Its second quarter, which is strongest at noon, is ruled by Mercury ; its third, strongest at the moment of sunset, by Venus ; and its fourth, midnight, by the Sun. And so on with the other days in order.

This quite obviously corresponds to the division of the zodiac into four triplicities, fire, earth, air, water ; and both can be symbolised in the same way, by the cross inscribed within the circle. The thoughtful reader will not be surprised to learn that exactly the same result can be achieved—so far as the names of the days are concerned that is—by dividing each day into three parts ; and that these parts correspond to the division of the zodiac, into the three quadruplicities described in the previous Chapter.

It will be noticed that in the fourfold classification we have employed the seven " sacred " rulers in the order of their rapidity of motion as seen from the earth, and that we begin with the swiftest, the Moon. In the three-fold classification, we begin with Saturn, the slowest, as follows :

Saturday	Sunday	Monday	Tuesday	Wednesday	Thursday	Friday
♄	☉	☽	♂	☿	♃	♀
♃	♀	♄	☉	☽	♂	☿
♂	☿	♃	♀	♄	☉	☽

The division of the day into three equal parts was used in ancient Egypt.

HOUSE CIRCLE. A convenient term for that great circle of the Heavens which marks the boundary between the area of influence of one house and the next ; the word " cusp " is often used in this sense, but this word (from Lat. *cuspis*, a point) properly applied only, to the point of the ecliptic or zodiac through which such circle passes and it is best to employ the word only in that sense.

Thus, the " House Circle " of the tenth and fourth houses is the meridian, and the " House Circle " of the first and seventh is the horizon.

HOUSE DIVISION. The dividing of the heavens into the twelve mundane houses and the determination of the degree of the zodiac upon each cusp.

The methods of computing the twelve houses which have been adopted from time to time, and some of which are still employed, are as follows :—

1. EQUAL METHOD (*modus equalis*) attributed to Ptolemy. The

Ascendant is determined in the usual manner. The cusps of the houses are then determined by successively adding 30° of the zodiac thereto. The tenth house consequently is in exact zodiacal square to the ascendant, but does not necessarily coincide with the degree of the zodiac then culminating. This may be described as a " rough-and-ready " method. It has been practically abandoned.

The principle of this system is the Trisection of a Quadrant of the Ecliptic, commencing with the Degree Ascending.

2. METHOD PROPOSED BY PORPHYRY. Here the Ascendant and M.C. are determined in the usual way. The arc of the zodiac between them is then divided into three equal parts, giving thus the cusps of XI and XII; similarly, the arc between Ascendant and cusp of fourth house is divided into three parts, thus giving cusps of II and III. This also may be described as a rough-and-ready method which has been practically abandoned.

The principle of this system is the Trisection of the Arc of the Ecliptic intercepted between the Horizon and the Meridian.

3. METHOD ATTRIBUTED TO ALCABITIUS. At a first glance this method may be confused with the " semi-arc system " upon which the ordinary Tables of Houses are based ; but a little thought will show the difference. Here the degree on the Ascendant is determined in the usual way ; the Sidereal Time at which this degree reaches the cusp of the tenth house is next determined, and the difference between it and the Sidereal Time at birth is divided into *three equal parts*, which are successively added to the Sidereal Time at birth, and the respective degrees then found culminating are the cusps of houses XI, XII, I : a precisely similar process followed with regard to the cusp of the fourth house gives us the cusps of III, II, I, *subtraction* being here used in place of addition.

The principle of this system is the Trisection of the Semi-Arcs, diurnal and nocturnal, of the Ascendant.

4. METHOD OF CAMPANUS.

The principle of this system is the Trisection of a Quadrant of the Prime Vertical (which is a great circle passing through the zenith point, and at right angles to the meridian), by great circles mutually intersecting at the North and South points of the horizon : the cusps of the houses being the degrees of the Ecliptic cut by these circles.

5. RATIONAL METHOD ASCRIBED TO REGIOMONTANUS (*modus rationalis*).

The principle of this system is the Trisection of a Quadrant of the Equator, comprised between the horizon and meridian, by great circles mutually intersecting at the North and South Points of the Horizon ; the cusps of the houses being the degrees of the Ecliptic cut by these circles.

6. RATIONAL AND UNIVERSAL METHOD, PROPOSED BY MORINUS. Practically abandoned.

The principle of this system is the Trisection of said Quadrant of the Equator by great circles through the Poles of the Ecliptic.

7. METHOD OF PLACIDUS, COMMONLY KNOWN AS THE " SEMI-ARC SYSTEM." This is the method in common use.

The principle of this system is the Trisection of the Semi-Arc of each degree of the Ecliptic. By successively adding ⅓ S.A. (diurnal) of any degree, to the Sidereal Time of its Ascension, said degree is found upon cusp of XII, XI, X, respectively; similarly, by adding ⅓ S.A. (nocturnal) to Sid. Time of its Descension, said degree is found upon cusp of VI, V, IV. In this way a Table of Houses can be constructed, as shown in Chapter IV.

8. EQUAL DIVISION METHOD, PROPOSED BY ZADKIEL, AN AUSTRALIAN ASTROLOGER. In this method the Equator is divided into twelve equal segments, starting from the meridian, by great circles passing through the poles of the earth.

In principle, it is tantamount to regarding a child as born under the meridian of the birthplace, but at the Equator, instead of at the place of birth.

HOUSES, MUNDANE. The twelve divisions or compartments into which the circle (or more strictly the sphere) of the Heavens is divided, or in other words, the divisions of the celestial sphere formed by trisecting the quadrants formed between the meridian and the horizon. Each of these divisions will therefore consist of 30° of space, as viewed from the place of birth. In order to illustrate plainly to the reader what astrologers mean by the " Houses of Heaven," it is proper for him to bear in mind that there are four Cardinal Points in the mundane circle formed by the rotation of the earth about her own axis ; these are (1) where the Sun rises at Dawn, (2) where he comes to the meridian at midday or Noon, (3) where he sets in the evening at Sunset, and (4) where he comes to the Nadir or lower meridian at midnight or 12 p.m. of the same day.

The first of these, that is, the line (or imaginary line) which is level
with the horizon, when the Sun rises, is the cusp of the astrologer's
First House, or the Eastern Angle, termed the " horoscope " or Ascendant.   The next, or the degree when he is at his highest altitude, which
invariably is in every latitude at noon-day, is the astrologer's *Tenth
House* cusp, Zenith or Mid-heaven, the most powerful angle, and the
house of honour.   Pursuing the same course, the apparent line level
with the horizon when the Sun sets, constitutes the cusp of the *Seventh
House* in the sidereal art, being the third grand angle and setting horizon
or Descendant.   Again, at midnight the Sun arrives at the cusp or line
of the lower heaven, or Nadir, or as astrologers term it the Imum
Cœli and *Fourth House*.

Now at the *equator*, where the Sun is vertical, and all celestial arcs
are measured by rectangles, equal parts of the zodiac pass through the
great circle of the equator in equal times, or in other words, every house
of heaven would contain just *thirty* degrees.   But in every other part
of the globe, the oblique inclination of the earth's axis towards the
plane of her orbit (to which we owe the varying length and shortness of
our days) causes the Sun apparently to rise earlier and set later at one
period of the year than another ; and this causes his semi-diurnal arc,
or the time intervening between sunrise and noon, to be greater or less
as the year advances or decreases.   Therefore, when the time of sun-
rising is obtained, and subtracted from that of noon, it is self-evident
that the difference constitutes *half the day*.   This space of time the
astrologer next turns into degrees and minutes (each hour being
equivalent to fifteen degrees of the equator, and each minute to fifteen
minutes thereof), and divides it into three equal parts, thus constituting
three houses of heaven, namely, the twelfth, eleventh, and tenth.

To take the simplest case.   Suppose a birth to occur at the Equator when 0°♈ is rising, then 0°♑ will be upon the meridian.   If we
divide this quadrant, the cusps of the eleventh and twelfth houses will
be respectively ♑27°54′ and ♒ 27°49′.   By comparing these with the
22°♑ and 18°♒ at New York and the 18°♑ and 13°♒ at London, as
given in the Tables of Houses for those places, we shall have some idea
how the Latitude of Birth-place influences the distribution of the signs
in the horoscope.

The same method is pursued as to the ninth, eighth, and seventh
houses, and on the same principle, with the remaining half of the great

K

diurnal and nocturnal circle, the sixth, fifth, fourth, third, second, and first houses, giving for the result the whole of the Twelve Mundane Houses.

The four chief of these houses, namely, the first, tenth, seventh, and fourth, are termed *Angular Houses* (or angles), as being of the greatest strength and power. The next four are termed *Succedent Houses*, as being of less energy, but still next in sympathetic power ; they are the eleventh, eighth, fifth, and second houses. The weakest of all in influence are the *Cadent Houses*, namely, the twelfth, ninth, sixth, and third houses. It is not without reason that these divisions and classifications are made, as the attentive student will soon discover.

Each of the twelve houses in a nativity has an importance of its own, and is quite distinct in its special influence.

The following is the general nature of each house :—

I. *First House.*—Personality, natural disposition, worldly outlook generally. Physical experiences as obtained through the five senses. The parts of the body denoted are the *head* and *face.*

II. *Second House.*—Finance, monetary prospects. Desires caused by tenth-house influence affecting moral growth. The parts of the body denoted are the *throat* and *ears.*

III. *Third House.*—Relatives and kindred, travelling, intellect derived from education and study, and minor impressions made upon the physical brain. The parts of the body denoted are the *neck, arms* and *shoulders* and the *lungs.*

IV. *Fourth House.*—Hereditary tendencies ; home and domestic life ; parentage, environment, and the general state of things at the close of life. The parts of the body denoted are the *breasts, stomach* and *digestive organs.*

V. *Fifth House.*—Offspring ; generative powers, sensations and pleasurable emotions arising from the senses, worldly enterprise and energy. The parts of the body denoted are the *loins, heart,* and *back.*

VI. *Sixth House.*—Service and attachments arising from the expression of the tenth house, therefore servants and inferiors in social rank. This house also denotes sickness arising from worry and anxiety. It is also the house of phenomenal magic arising from the powers of the southern angle. The parts of the body denoted are the *bowels* and *solar plexus.*

VII.—*Seventh House.*—Unions, marriages, partnerships, individual character and humane tendencies. The parts of the body denoted are the *veins* and *kidneys*.

VIII. *Eighth House.*—Death, all matters pertaining to legacies or affairs connected with death. It is also what is termed an occult house, owing to its relation to the fourth, which denotes the psychic tendencies. The parts of the body denoted are the *secret parts* and the *generative system.*

IX. *Ninth House.*—Higher mentality, scientific, philosophic and religious tendencies. It also denotes long journeys, dreams and the image-making power. The parts of the body denoted are the *thighs* and *hams.*

X. *Tenth House.*—Profession, business ability, fame, honour and material reputation. All worldly activities and moral responsibilities are shown by this house. The parts of the body denoted are the *knees.*

XI. *Eleventh House.*—Friends, acquaintances, hopes, wishes and aspirations. The parts of the body denoted are the *legs* and *ankles.*

XII. *Twelfth House.*—Occult tendencies. In connection with the fourth house shows the psychic thought inheritance from the past and the result as either joy or sorrow. This may be said to be the most critical house of the twelve. The parts of the body denoted are the *feet* and *toes.*

These twelve houses are the concrete centres of force, which, in the advanced person, react upon and so modify the more subjective centres of the signs and planets. The houses represent hereditary conditions, and that which is fixed as fate for the current life. Persons who live in their purely physical conditions, that is habitually think that they are the physical body alone, and those who are generally classed as materialists will respond to the conditions of the twelve houses apart from the signs or planets occupying them. This is in reality the Minor Circle, and its overcoming is the first attempt to escape LIMITA-TION. That is to say, when the influence of the various planets in their respective *houses* begins to wane, the planets manifesting their nature through the various *signs*, the soul may be said to be taking its first steps upon the " path of liberation."

HOUSES, ZODIACAL. The signs which any planet rules, or in which it has most influence, are said to be its " houses " ; for example, ♈ and ♏ are the houses of ♂.

HUMAN SIGNS. These are ♊, ♍, ♒ and the first half of ♐. They are said by Ptolemy to give the native a humane disposition, when either the lord of the geniture or the ascendant is in one, otherwise (says he) he will be brutish and savage. He also says, that the lord of an eclipse (*e.g.*, of the sign in which the eclipse occurs) being in any human sign, its vile effect will fall on mankind.

HUNTING THE MOON. One of the most certain and direct transits is that of Saturn " hunting the Moon," as it is termed, that is, when Saturn is in transit over the Moon's progressed place. Since the progressed Moon takes twenty-eight and Saturn thirty years to complete the circle, this will often last for many years and in some cases for a lifetime. The most unfortunate aspect in a nativity is the affliction of the Moon by Saturn, either by square or opposition, and when the aspect is very close and the progressive Moon is moving slowly, or at the same rate as Saturn, the transit of Saturn goes on for the best part of the life. For the Moon by progressive motion moves through one sign of the zodiac in two and a half years and Saturn's motion by transit is at the same rate, therefore, unless the Moon is moving fast and moving out of the sphere of influence of Saturn, a double affliction is kept up for the best part of the life. This, of course, can only be the case where the Moon is in conjunction, square or opposition with Saturn at birth.

HYLEG. The Hyleg is that point in the horoscope upon which health and life depend, and has to be carefully considered when estimating the probable length of life and the constitutional strength. The Ascendant, Sun, and Moon, have all three to be taken into account when dealing with this subject.

The oldest rules for ascertaining which point is hyleg are those of Ptolemy. According to this system, the hylegiacal places are houses I, VII, IX, X, XI. If the Sun is in one of these places it is always hyleg ; if it is not there and the Moon is, the latter is hyleg ; and if neither is there the cusp of the ascendant is hyleg. There has, however, scarcely been an astrologer who has not suggested some more or less important alteration of these rules. Ptolemy himself would sometimes allow the strongest planet in the horoscope to be hyleg. In our own day " Raphael " has suggested that the Sun is always hyleg with a man and the Moon with a woman. Others have doubted whether one body ever can be hyleg to the entire exclusion of the other two, point-

ing out that it is not uncommon for all three to be afflicted by direction at death ; and they have drawn from this the conclusion that the
hylegiacal office may be shared among the three. Others would allow
the lower half of the twelfth house to be a hylegiacal place, especially
for the Sun.

The student may be safely left to put all theories to the test of
practical experience and draw his own conclusions ; but in the meantime
the following summary would probably obtain the assent of a large
number of astrologers.

1. The Sun, Moon, and Ascendant are three centres upon which
life depends.

2. The Moon governs child-birth and the feminine functions, and
its positions and aspects are therefore far more important in the
horoscope of a woman than in that of a man. It is also alleged to
exercise considerable influence with very young children of both sexes,
probably for the first seven years of life.

3. The centre indicated by the Ptolemaic rule given above is
always important, whether it be exclusively hyleg or not.

It is important to know what length of life is shown in the horoscope, but the ordinary rules will not apply in all cases, and judgment
of a special kind is needed where the horoscope shows a tendency
to study the laws of hygiene and to live a temperate life. Astrology
does not teach fatalism, but the working of natural law. Some horoscopes show long life, others a short duration of life, while the majority
may be said to have a limit up to which they may live. There are no
special rules for showing the limit of life in individual cases, and it is a
matter of judgment as to whether the native will pass through a critical
aspect or not ; but when a train of evil directions is in force lasting over
a very long period, death may be expected when the vitality drops
below the power to recuperate. Many horoscopes show a delicate
state of health in infancy but robust conditions at middle life ; and
others the reverse. It is the astrologer's duty to advise careful and
temperate living, a proper attention to the laws of hygiene, a conservation of energy, and right methods of living, but *never* to predict death.
The approximate time of death may be stated with regard to the
limit of life, but never the actual date. The fact that what we call
death, is but a withdrawal of the life from the physical body into a finer
body and to another plane should show us that we cannot be sure in

many cases as to the actual date of death any more than we can predict the time a person will go to sleep on any particular night. We may discover the time when there will be a liability to serious accidents, to disease, or lowered vitality, but we cannot gauge the actual power behind the personality to turn aside the influence into another channel. In the undeveloped horoscopes we may see fatality more or less clearly, but the difficulty increases when the life becomes more thoroughly self-conscious.

An illustration of this may help students of Astrology to understand the working of a higher law.

An astrologer many years ago publicly predicted the death of Mrs. Annie Besant in her 60th year. Mrs. Besant has passed that critical period, and on asking her opinion about the prediction, instead of ignoring the prediction she showed that love of truth which she possesses by remarking that " she would have passed out at the time predicted had it not been for the help of her Master," who foresaw the usefulness of her life and took upon himself the responsibility of preserving it. Every student of Astrology should endeavour to realise that there is a law of love which does not interfere with natural laws, but transmutes the lower into the higher law ; but only those who know the law and work with it have the power to change the lower into the higher. If death could in *all cases* be predicted with absolute certainty, then it would be useless to hope that effort could be stronger than destiny. There are always circles within circles, and all evolution is an expansion from smaller to larger circles.

ILLUMINATION. That period of the Moon when she may be seen, which is 25 days and about 12 hours.

IMPEDITED. This signifies being afflicted by evil stars. But the Moon is also impedited in the highest degree when in conjunction with the Sun.

IMUM CŒLI. See MEDIUM CŒLI.

INCONJUNCT. The Quincunx aspect (*q.v.*).

INCREASING IN LIGHT. When any planet is leaving the Sun, and is not yet arrived at the opposition ; after which it decreases in light. The former is a good, the latter an evil testimony, especially as regards the Moon.

INCREASING IN MOTION. When any planet moves faster than it did on the preceding day.

INDIVIDUALITY AND PERSONALITY. The *Individuality*, shown by the sign in which the Sun is placed, represents to us the pure mind, or what is termed in Sanskrit, Manas ; it is the human portion, as distinct from the animal—the MAN—and is the permanent, or reincarnating, part of our nature. The *Personality*, represented by the Moon (together with the Ascendant), is what is known in the Eastern Philosophy as Kama-Manas, or the mind linked with desire—generally known as the ANIMAL MAN—and is the fleeting part of our nature, which only exists as a very small ray of the Individuality. The Individuality and Personality together comprise the seven principles or aspects of human consciousness, each one of which is represented by one of the planets.

We may represent these states of consciousness and their governing planets in tabular form :

⊙ Spirit   expressed as Will ♅ ⎫
☿ Spiritual Soul   ,,   ,, Wisdom ☿ ⎬ INDIVIDUALITY
♀ Human Soul   ,,   ,, Love ♀. ⎭

♄ The Bridge or Individualiser.

☽ Personal Mind   expressed through The Brain ☽.
♂ Personal Feelings   ,,   ,,   The Animal Soul.
♃ Physical Cells   ,,   ,,   The Etheric and Dense Body.

⊙ Vitality or life of the body.

Saturn forms the Bridge, or the straight and narrow way, between the Individuality and the Personality. This planet is the divider and separator of the gross from the fine, the impure from the pure, and hence is the great source of sorrow and pain, the chastener, and also the individualiser.

Every Individuality is evolving under the care and guidance of one of the great Beings represented by the planets, and every incarnated Personality is born under the rulership of one of them ; but whereas the Individuality, or permanent soul, remains constantly in touch with the same one of the Seven, normally at least, throughout the whole of its long series of incarnations, the Personal ruler changes from life to life.

INFERIOR PLANETS. Those whose orbits lie within that of the earth, namely Venus and Mercury.

INFORTUNES. Those are ♅, ♄, and ♂ ; also ☿ when he is much afflicted. Some would add to these ♅ also. See MALEFICS.

INTERCEPTED. A sign which is found *between* the cusps of two houses but not on either of them ; *e.g.*, when ♓ rises at Liverpool ♈ is intercepted in the first house, ♉ being upon the cusp of the second. Many students find it difficult to judge the influence of intercepted signs. In a general sense they absorb the whole of the house in which they occur, and at the same time bring into the house a joint influence from the other signs affecting that house. Planets in the intercepted signs have more importance than usual in their action upon the affairs of the house on which they are situated.

JOINED TO. Being in any aspect, but more especially being in conjunction.

JUPITER. The largest orb (except the Sun) in our solar system. He is about 476 million miles from the centre, and takes twelve years in going round the Sun ; his day consists of about ten hours. Jupiter is the next brightest planet to Venus, and is accompanied by nine satellites ; is in course of preparation for its humanity, being at present uninhabited. His symbol is the half-circle over the cross.

Jupiter is the planetary representative of the Roman God of the same name ; Zeus of the Greeks ; Brihaspati or Brahmanhaspati of the Hindus (called also *Guru* by Hindu astrologers) ; the Scandinavian Thor ; Ammon of Egypt ; with other names in other mythologies and religions. Astrologically and mystically it has a great variety of interpretations ; depending upon whether it is employed in the highest spiritual sense (whether cosmic or human), in a lower personal sense, or physically only. By the ancient astrologers it was termed the " greater fortune " and its influence was considered very benign and propitious ; nevertheless, although modern experience entirely confirms this view in a general sense, it is yet certain that by the abuse of a so-called bad aspect the planet can work much evil. See PLANETS.

KALI YUGA. The fourth, the *black* or the Iron Age, our present period, the duration of which is 432,000 years. The last of the ages into which the evolutionary period of man is divided by a series of such ages. It began 3102 years B.C. at the moment of Krishna's death, and the first cycle of 5,000 years ended between the years 1897 and 1898.

KALPA. The period of cosmic activity ; a day of Brahma ; 4,320 million years.

KOSMOS. The Universe, as distinguished from the world, which may mean our globe or earth.

KRONOS. Saturn. The God of Boundless Time and of the Cycles.

LATITUDE, CELESTIAL. The perpendicular distance of any star or planet north or south of the ecliptic. The Sun, of coure, has no latitude.

LATITUDE TERRESTIAL OR GEOGRAPHICAL. The distance of any place north or south of the equator.

LAYA CENTRES. The neutral states between solid, liquid, and gas, governed by the critical planet Saturn. Just as the physical planet Saturn is ringed, so does his influences mark the " ring pass not " between each plane of consciousness.

LEO. The fifth sign of the zodiac. A fixed sign, and the second of the fiery triplicity. Its position on the ecliptic is from 120° to 150°. It is a hot, dry, and positive sign. The Sun appears to enter this sign about the 22nd of July each year.

LIBRA. The seventh sign of the zodiac. A cardinal sign, and the second of the airy triplicity. Its position on the ecliptic is from 180° to 210°. It is a hot, moist, humane, and positive sign. The Sun appears to enter this sign about the 23rd of September each year.

LIGHT OF TIME. The Sun by day and the Moon by night.

LIGHTS. The Sun and Moon.

LOCAL TIME. More correctly *Local Mean Time*. The true mean time at any place, depends upon its distance east or west of Greenwich. The local mean time at any place can readily be found from Greenwich time by *adding* to the latter at the rate of

$$
\left.
\begin{array}{lll}
\text{1 hour for every } 15° \text{ E.} \\
\text{4 min.} \quad ,, \quad ,, \quad 1° ,, \\
\text{4 sec.} \quad ,, \quad ,, \quad 1' ,,
\end{array}
\right\}
\quad
\begin{array}{l}
\text{(or, on the other hand,} \\
\quad \textit{subtracting} \text{ if W.)}
\end{array}
$$

and conversely, if we require to find Greenwich mean time from a given local mean time, we *subtract* when the longitude is East and *add* when it is West.

LOGARITHMS. A series of numbers in arithmetical progression answering to another in geometrical progression, whereby it is possible to perform multiplication by the process of *addition* and division by that of *subtraction*.

Diurnal Proportional Logarithms are the logarithms of the minutes in twenty-four hours or degrees (= 1440), less the logarithm of the minutes in the given time. For instance, the logarithm for 7 hours

14 minutes or 7°14′ = 434m. or 434′ is ·5208, which has been obtained thus,

$$
\begin{array}{ll}
\text{Log.} \quad 1440 & \text{that is } 3\cdot1584 \\
\textit{minus} \text{ log. } 434 & \textit{minus } 2\cdot6375 \\
\hline
& \textit{equals } 0\cdot5209
\end{array}
$$

Consequently these are only to be used when the *daily* (" diurnal ") motion of a planet is in question.   But for this purpose they are invaluable and the student is recommended to use them *always*, except when the time of birth is, in Greenwich Time, 4, 6, 8, or 12 hours from noon ; in which case it is of course simpler to divide the daily motion of the planet by 6, 4, 3 or 2 as the case may be, and add or subtract according as the time of birth is p.m. or a.m. at Greenwich.   The Diurnal Proportional Logarithms are used as follows :—

Rule.   Add the p. log. of the planet's daily motion to the p. log of the time from noon ; the sum will be the p. log. of the planet's motion in the given time.   Find the value of this p. log. by looking in the tables and ADD TO or SUBTRACT FROM the planet's position at noon, according as the time was p.m. or a.m. : if the planet is *retrograde*, subtract for p.m. and add for a.m.   The result will give the planet's place at birth.   By " time " is meant not local time but G.M.T.

Example 1. *What is the longitude of the Moon on April 21st,* 1901, *at* 7.35 *p.m. G.M.T. ?*   The Moon's motion from April 21st to April 22nd, 1901, is 14°27′.   Then say :

$$
\begin{array}{ll}
\text{Prop log. } 14°27′ & .2203 \\
\text{ ,, \quad ,, \quad } 7\text{h. } 35\text{m.} & .5003 \\
\hline
& .7206 = 4°34′
\end{array}
$$

		°	′
☽'s longitude April 21st, noon		7 ♊	12
☽'s motion in 7h. 35m.		4	34
☽'s longitude at 7h. 35m. p.m. G.M.T., April 21st		11 ♊ 46	

LOHITANGA.   The planet Mars.

LONGITUDE, CELESTIAL.   The distance of any body from the First Point of the Zodiac, ♈0°0′0″, measured on the ecliptic, either in degrees and minutes as is done by astronomers, or in signs, degrees and minutes as is done by astrologers.   It should be borne in mind that Celestial

Longitude is of two kinds, geocentric and heliocentric, The former is now very rarely used by astronomers and is only given in the Nautical Almanac for the Sun and Moon, but it is the only kind of longitude referred to by the astrologer, who by that term means nothing more nor less than zodiacal position. Thus if ♂ is in ♈ 3° its longitude (geocentric) is 3°.

LONGITUDE, TERRESTRIAL OR GEOGRAPHICAL. The distance of any place east or west of Greenwich. It is measured by geographers as a rule in degrees, minutes and seconds (° ′ ″) but by astronomers mostly in hours, minutes, and seconds (*h. m. s.*); 1*h.* = 15°, 1 *m.* = 15′, 1*s.* = 15″.

LORDS. Planets which have the most powerful effects in particular signs. Thus, if ♈ ascends in any figure, ♂, who rules that sign, is the lord of the ascendant. The lords or rulers of signs are as follows : ♄, ♒ and ♑ ; ♃, ♓ and ♐ ; ♂, ♈ and ♏ ; ☉, ♌ only ; ♀, ♉ and ♎ ; ☿, ♊ and ♍ ; ☽, ♋ only ; ♅ and ♆ have had no houses accorded them, but are considered strong in ♒ and ♓ respectively. The *odd* signs are the day, and the *even* the night houses of these lords, which have the more powerful rule over one or the other according as it is day or night time that the figure is cast for.

LORDS OF HOUSES. The planet ruling the sign upon the cusp of a house is said to be *lord* of that house. Planets in houses are usually stronger than the rulers or lords of houses and in a general sense should be given preference.

LUMINARIES. The Sun and Moon. These should always be considered as distributors and collectors of influence, and not as actual factors or causes of influence.

LUNATION. The ☌, ☐ or ☍ of the ☉ and ☽; also the length of time in which the ☽ appears to move round the earth ; the time from New Moon to New Moon. The term is most frequently used to signify the position ☽ ☌ ☉ (New Moon). When in square to each other the luminaries are said to be in quadrature, while their conjunction or opposition is referred to as syzygy.

LUNE. The portion of the surface of a sphere which is contained within two great semicircles.

MALEFICS.—Saturn and Mars have been termed " malefic planets," and some would add Uranus and Neptune also. They are the disseminators of what we consider evil throughout the world, and Astrology can throw considerable light upon this so-called evil that abounds, for it is through the individual and personal manifestation of the two great forces in nature known as heat and cold, motion and inertia, that we see the abuse of these two useful states or conditions of matter. The wise astrologer does not recognise evil as a permanent factor in any nativity, but fully understands how the attitude of the mind and feeling may produce the abuse of any special planetary vibration, which will then become vice and misfortune, pain and disease.

If the natures of the two " malefic " planets are carefully studied from a philosophic point of view, their exact value in each nativity will be much more clearly understood.

MARS. The planet next to our earth. It is about 139 million miles from the Sun, has a year of 687 of our days, and a day about 40 minutes longer than our own. He has been known as the god of war and hunting, by the names of Ares and Nimrod ; his mission appears to be to dispel terror and fear. This planet also belongs to our chain of worlds. His symbol is the circle under the cross.

Mars is the planet of focused force, and out-going impulse. Physical heat and motion are more under the direct influence of Mars than any other planet. He governs the sense of taste in its widest application. All the animal propensities, sensations, passions, desires and appetites come under the vibration of Mars, the ruler over the animal nature in man.

It will be seen by the foregoing how Mars will become an evil influence in any nativity where the animal side is uncontrolled. Misfortune and disaster, accident and fever, will be the result of over-excitement, impulse, rashness and over-indulgence in sensation. In fact, to control the animal passions and appetites is to control and guide the vibrations coming from the planet Mars. See PLANETS.

MASCULINE SIGNS. The odd signs ♈, ♊, ♌, ♎ ♐, ♒.

MATUTINE. Appearing in the morning. The planets are called matutine when they rise before the Sun in the morning, until they reach their first station, where they become retrograde. The Moon is matutine until she has passed her first quarter.

MEAN MOTION. The *average* diurnal motion of a planet over its whole revolution. Thus the average or mean daily apparent motion of the Sun is 59′ 8″, but its actual apparent motion varies between 57′ and 61′.

MEAN TIME. The standard of time measurement in use for all civil purposes, and based upon the Sun's mean motion. Owing to the Sun's true irregular motion, sometimes more and sometimes less than 1°, the true astronomical day is not a convenient standard, being sometimes less and sometimes more than 24 h. 4 m. of sidereal time. This discrepancy it is which gives rise to the " Equation of time " found in certain old Ephemerides calculated for " apparent noon." Astronomers therefore adopt as their standard the mean solar day. The mean solar day is simply the *average value* of the varying solar days throughout the entire year, and therefore actually consists of 1/365¼ part of the Equinoctial year—which is the time between two successive passages of the Sun across the equator from S. to N., or in other words its entry into Aries.

MEASURE OF TIME. The time in years, months, and days to which an arc of direction is equivalent. In Ptolemy's method each degree of Right Ascension measures one year of life. This is the simplest and most widely used method, but others have been suggested at different times, and will be found summarised in *The Progressed Horoscope*, pp. 328-332.

MEDIUM CŒLI (*M.C., Mid-Heaven ; Meridian, Upper Meridian*). These terms are all used synonymously for the cusp of the tenth house, and also for the tenth house itself. Etymologically considered, they imply a " lune " or space of say 30° or thereabouts in extent, bisected by the meridian. The use of the word meridian should properly be restricted to its astronomical significance, defined below. The opposite portion of the heavens is denoted by the terms, *I.C., Imum Coeli, Lower Meridian*, which are respectively antithetical to the above.

MERCURY. Mercury performs a revolution round the Sun in 88 days 23¼ hours, which makes the length of his year ; his distance from the Sun is about 36 million miles. He is a small planet, shining with a pale bluish light ; but as he is never more than about 30 degrees from the Sun he is rarely visible to the naked eye. This planet was typically known as Hermes, also as the winged messenger of the gods, by the mythologists, while the Chaldeans called him Nebo ; he has always been the planet of warning. It is interesting to note that according to a certain body of occult teaching this planet is destined to become the future physical home for the majority of our humanity, and also that he belongs to our own chain of worlds. His symbol is the half-circle over the circle over the cross.

MERCURY is known as the "convertible" planet. It is neither positive nor negative, but *both*. It is the planet of the adept, being the planet of adaptation in the widest sense of the word, and takes upon itself the vibrations of all the other planets. It is, in one word, the planet of *Reason*. In the physical world Mercury governs the sense of seeing. It has also a very close relationship with the mind. Mercury accompanying the soul into Hades, represents the silver thread of memory, upon which are strung the beads which represent the personalities of its earth lives. In every nativity Mercury will represent the ego in physical manifestation, the actor, playing the part allotted to him during each separate earthly existence ; and at the close of each life Mercury represents the knowledge gained, as Memory, the cream of which is rendered a permanent possession of the ego as Wisdom. See PLANETS.

MERIDIAN. A great circle of the celestial sphere passing through the Zenith and the Poles, and corresponds to the geographical longitude.

MERIDIAN DISTANCE. The distance, measured on the equator, and expressed in degrees of time, between any celestial point and the upper or lower meridian. It is, in fact, a portion of the semi-arc (*q.v.*) : thus, if a planet is on the cusp of the eleventh house, its meridian distance is one-third of its semi-arc.

MIDHEAVEN. See MEDIUM CŒLI.

MODERATORS. The significators Sun, Moon, Midheaven, Ascendant, and the Part of Fortune. They are so-called, because each is said to have its own mode of operating on the native, according to its nature. Thus the Midheaven operates differently from the Ascendant, the Sun differently from the Moon, and the Part of Fortune differently from them all.

MOON. The Moon is a satellite of the earth, and makes a revolution around it in an elliptical orbit of 29½ days ; she also appears to revolve from one point in the heavens to the same point again in 27 days 7 hours 43 minutes ; she is 240,000 miles from the earth. The Moon is an important body in Astrology, and should be very carefully studied astronomically. The Moon may be called the mother of the earth ; for all life that once existed there, together with its water and atmosphere, has been drawn off by the earth, the Moon being the physical globe in a past chain of worlds connected with our evolution. She has been best known as Luna or Isis ; her symbol is the half-circle or the crescent. The Moon is the collector of aspects and influences, and acts only in accordance with the sign that she is in, having no definite nature of her own ; she is in fact coloured, as it were, by the sign through which she passes. Her office and mission is *to reflect the light*. As she passes out from the Sun she gathers up the influences on her way until she reaches the full ; thence she returns laden with the fruits of experience to the Sun, and once more re-emerges, cleansed for a new experience. See PLANETS.

MOVABLE SIGNS. The Cardinal signs ♈, ♋, ♎, and ♑. Not to be confused with the *Mutable Signs (q.v.)*.

MUNDANE ASPECTS. Distances in the world, measured by the semi-arc wholly independent of the zodiac. Thus the distance of the tenth to the twelfth is always a mundane sextile although their cusps are perhaps not 50° of the zodiac apart.

If a planet at birth is on the cusp of the ascendant, and another on the cusp of the third house, these are in *mundane* sextile aspect, but they will not be in *zodiacal* sextile aspect, unless the cusps of the two houses themselves are in zodiacal sextile, a thing that only happens infrequently in the temperate latitudes. Similarly, any planet which by the Earth's rotation arrives at the cusp of the twelfth, eleventh, tenth, . . . etc., houses will be then in mundane semi-sextile, sextile, or square to the ascendant as the case may be.

MUNDANE ASTROLOGY. The branch of Astrology that deals with the destiny of nations and the world at large, or the study of the effects of Equinoxes, Solstices, New Moons, Eclipses, planetary conjunctions, and similar celestial phenomena, as applied not to separate individuals but to nations and large communities of people.

MUTABLE SIGNS. These are the Signs ♊, ♍, ♐, and ♓, otherwise called Common Signs.

MUTE SIGNS. The signs ♋, ♏, and ♓.

NADIR. That point in the heavens which is directly opposite to the zenith, or, in other words, the cusp of the fourth house.

NATAL ASTROLOGY. The branch of Astrology which deals with the influence of planets and signs upon the lives and characters of human beings.

NATIVITY. Birth, the instant the native draws breath, or rather that when the umbilical cord is constricted, or cut.   In astrological parlance it usually signifies a figure of the heavens for the time of birth.

NATURAL DAY.   The time of a complete revolution of the Earth on its axis ; a Sidereal day.

NEOMENIUM.   The change of the Moon, that is, the time of New Moon.

NEPTUNE.   The most distant planet as yet discovered, who revolves round the Sun at a distance of about 2,746 millions of miles. His year is equal to 165 of our years, and his symbol is the trident.

Neptune has, on the whole, but a faint influence upon our earth and its inhabitants.   The undeveloped psychic who is unable to control the mediumistic tendencies induced from without, and those who are easily obsessed or of very weak will, always subject to changing impressions, will in one sense come under Neptune as will also those who are very highly advanced psychically.   Experience tends to prove that the influence of an afflicted Neptune as a rule is undesirable.   There is a possibility of there being such a thing as a lost personality, metaphorically speaking, and such may be in some peculiar manner under this influence.   Depravity and exceptional immorality seem to be under the influence of Neptune, but many years must elapse before sufficient tabulation is made to warrant a reliable opinion concerning Neptune's vibrations.   See PLANETS.

NOCTURNAL ARC.   See SEMI-ARC.

NODES.   The point where a planet crosses the ecliptic from south latitude into north latitude is called its north node, and where it crosses into the south latitude its south node.   The term applies, of course, to all the planets equally, but is chiefly used in reference to the nodes of the Moon.   The Moon's north node is called the Dragon's Head (q.v.), and marked ☊ ; the south node is called the Dragon's Tail, and marked ☋.   Their motion is retrograde, about 3′ per day. (3.1770935′ per day.)

NORTHERN SIGNS. These are the first six signs, namely ♈, ♉, ♊, ♋, ♌, ♍. They are also called " commanding " signs, because planets, in them, are said to command, and those in the opposite signs to obey.

OBEYING SIGNS.   The Southern signs.   See also *Northern Signs.*

OBLIQUE ASCENSION.   A part of the equator which rises obliquely in an oblique sphere.   If a star be not on the equator, it will, when it rises, form an angle with that part of the equator which is rising at the same time ; this is called its *Ascensional Difference* (*A.D.*), which later *added to* its right ascension (*R.A.*) if it have South Declination, but *subtracted therefrom* if it have North Declination, gives its Oblique Ascension (*O.A.*).   For places in the Southern Hemisphere this latter rule must be reversed, " add " being read instead of " subtract " and *vice versa*.

OPPOSITION.   When two planets are 180° distant, or just half the distance of the zodiac apart, which places them in a diametrical relation.   This is considered an aspect of perfect hatred, or, on the other hand, of perfect balance.   Probably the balance is only reached when the opposition is partile (*q.v.*), and it may well be that the hatred engendered by an incomplete opposition is due to the disharmony arising out of the incompleteness of this balance, rather than to the opposition aspect itself.

Esoterically the opposition denotes the ending or finishing of fate, or Karma, and is of the nature of Uranus and the Sun.

ORBS.   The word is used to describe the distance from a partile or exact aspect at which a planet may operate before it quite loses its effects.   In ancient times it was taught that each planet had an " orb " or " sphere " of influence which extended beyond its own body out into space in all directions ; in fact, it might be termed the " aura " of the planet ; and that the influences or " rays " of the planets were mingled as soon as the peripheries of these " orbs " came into contact— or into aspecting distance, as the case might be.   The latest researches in scientific Astrology seem to be approaching an actual physical explanation of this statement, and there can be little doubt that it is the true basis of the " orbs " employed by astrologers, and will thus explain why orbs should differ for each planet, as well as for every aspect.   Experience can be the only real guide in deciding how many degrees of " approach " and " departure " may be allowed before and after any aspect becomes technically complete, and the following hints must be accepted as such, and not taken as hard and fast rules.

For conjunction or opposition allow 12° when the Sun aspects the Moon, about 10° when either luminary aspects a planet, and about 8° for planets aspecting each other.

L

For square and trine about 8° all round may be allowed. For sextile about 7°. For semi-square and sesquiquadrate 4°. For semi-sextile and quincunx 2°. For the parallel of declination 1°.

These are the outside limits. In all cases the closer an aspect is, the stronger it is, and *vice versa*. An aspect that is only just within orbs is very weak. In some cases two planets that are widely apart by aspect may be brought closer together by a third planet ; for instance, if the Sun is at 0°♈ and the Moon at 10°♎ the aspect is a wide opposition and not very important ; but if Mars were 5°♋ it would not only be in square to both but would render the opposition worse than it otherwise would be.

ORIENTAL AND OCCIDENTAL. The two words literally mean *rising* and *falling*, and in a general sense planets in the left-hand half of the map (*i.e.*, in the space occupied by houses X, XI, XII, I, II, III) are said to be oriental or rising, those in the opposite half (houses IV, V, VI, VII, VIII, IX) occidental or failing. [Latin : *orior, oriori*, to become visible, appear, arise ; *occido, occidere*, to fall, fall down, die or perish.] The ascendant relates directly to the native, the Self ; and planets in or near the ascendant bear upon character and upon actions that arise out of character. The descendant, on the other hand, relates to persons and things in the outer world, with their bearing upon the native ; the line of the meridian combines the two. We may therefore say that planets in the eastern half of the map, and especially those in the ascendant, tend to create fresh karma, and represent destiny that is the natural outcome of character and which is avoidable if character can be controlled. Planets in the western half of the map represent rather the fulfilling or working out of a previously made destiny, the re-action of the environment upon the native, which is less avoidable or modifiable than the former.

In regard to the Sun, he is said to be oriental in houses XII, XI, X, or VI, V, IV, and occidental when in the opposite houses ; the reason being that when the Sun has reached the seventh house cusp he is then *becoming visible* in the opposite hemisphere of the world, and when he has passed the fourth house cusp he has culminated and is therefore setting in that hemisphere, or *falling down*. Similarly with the Moon also.

A planet is said to be oriental of the Sun when it rises before, and occidental of the Sun when it sets after, that luminary.

PARALLELS. In the *zodiac*, these are equal distances from the equator, or having the same declination ; whether one is North and the other South, or both North or both South, makes no difference (Par. Dec.).   The student should pay very careful attention to the declination of the planets, for the zodiacal parallel is of more importance than any other aspect.   The effect of this position is similar to that of a close conjunction, but even more powerful.

In the *world*, they are equal distances from the meridian—or horizon—in proportion to the semi-arcs of the planets which form them (Par. mund.).

Rapt parallels are parallels formed by the motion of the Earth on its axis, whereby both bodies are *rapt* or carried away by the same until they come to equal distances from the meridian.

PARS FORTUNAE.   See PART OF FORTUNE.

PARTILE.   An aspect is partile when it falls in the same degree and minute, both with respect to longitude and latitude.   Thus Jupiter would be in partile conjunction of Mars, if they were both in 3°4' of Aries and if at the same time both had 0°57' N. Lat.   This will seldom happen, though a few minutes will make little difference, and any difference in latitude may for the most part be ignored.

PART OF FORTUNE (*Pars Fortunae.* Symbol ⊕). A sensitive point in the horoscope.   It is held by many that the " Part of Fortune " indicates inherited wealth, property accruing, or worldly fortune in a general sense.   This point is found as follows :   Add the longitude of the Ascendant to that of the Moon and subtract that of the Sun, adding the circle of 360° if necessary : the operation is best performed by expressing the longitude in signs, degrees and minutes.   For instance : Suppose ☉ ♒ 18° 4', ☽ ♑ 26° 4', Asc. ♊ 20° 29' ; then say

	Signs	Degrees	Minutes
Asc.	2	20	29
+☽	9	26	4
	12	16	33
—☉	10	18	4
PART OF FORTUNE	1	28	29 *i.e.* ⊕ in ♉ 28°29'

It is advisable to reflect upon the metaphysical significance of this so-called "imaginary" point : the old rule is worded "As the ☽

is to the ☉ so is the ☉ to the ascendant." That is, the Part of Fortune stands in the same relationship to the ascendant as the Moon does to the Sun. Now we know that the Moon supplies the *vehicle* for an expression of the Solar life : similarly, then, we should regard the " Pars Fortunae " as indicating the *pabulum* for the sustenance of that general synthesis of the personal life controlled by the ascendant. Hence the reason for allotting to the Part of Fortune chief control of the pecuniary well-being of the native is readily seen. This point of the horoscope is a matter greatly neglected by many modern writers, which is regrettable.

PASSIVE QUALITIES. Moisture and dryness.

PASSIVE STARS. The Sun and the Moon are termed passive, taking their " colouring " as it were, entirely from the signs they are in or the planets they are in strongest aspect with.

PEREGRINE. A term used in Horary Astrology to describe a planet posited in a sign where it has no essential dignity of any kind. It is reckoned a debility of five degrees. In questions of theft, a peregrine planet in an angle, or in the second house, is the thief. No planet, however, is reckoned peregrine if it be in mutual reception with another.

PERIGEE. See APOGEE.

PERIHELION. See APHELIM.

PHASE. A term used by some writers for *Decanate (q.v.).*

PISCES. The twelfth sign of the zodiac Amutable sign, and the third of the watery triplicity. Its position on the ecliptic is from 330° to 360°. It is a cold, moist, double-bodied, and negative sign. The Sun appears to enter this sign about the 20th of February each year.

PLANETARY SPIRITS. Primarily, the rulers or governors of the planets. As our earth has its hierarchy of terrestrial planetary spirits, from the highest to the lowest plane, so has every other heavenly body. In Occultism, however, the term " planetary spirit " is generally applied only to the seven highest hierarchies corresponding to the Christian archangels. These have all passed through a stage of evolution corresponding to the humanity of earth on other worlds, in long past cycles. Our earth, being as yet only in its fourth round, is far too young to have produced high planetary spirits. The highest planetary spirit ruling over any globe is in reality the " personal God " of that planet and far more truly its " over-ruling providence " than the self-contradictory Infinite Personal Deity of modern churchianity.

PLANETS. Seven planets are employed in astrology, namely Mercury ☿, Venus ♀, Mars ♂, Jupiter ♃, Saturn ♄, Uranus ♅, and Neptune ♆, and to these are added the Sun ☉, and the Moon ☽, which, though not planets, are usually treated as such for convenience. Details of these bodies will be found under the appropriate headings.

According to occult teaching there are ten schemes of evolution in our Solar System, of which, however, only seven have physical globes, these being presided over by the seven Planetary Logoi. Each scheme consists of a chain of seven globes, and each chain passes through seven incarnations. In the first and seventh incarnations of any chain there are no planets lower than the Mental plane ; in the second and sixth the lowest planet of the chain is Astral ; in the third and fifth there is one physical planet ; and in the fourth, three are physical. During each incarnation the life wave passes seven times round the chain, each complete circuit being termed a Round. The stage of evolution reached by each of the seven schemes that have physical globes is as follows :—

(1) *Vulcan Scheme.* Vulcan is a planet, not yet discovered by astronomers, that revolves in an orbit between the Sun and Mercury. It is the only physical representation of its scheme, which is in its third incarnation.

(2) *Venus Scheme.* This has only one physical planet, Venus, and is in the seventh round of its fifth incarnation.

(3) *Earth Scheme.* This is in the fourth round of its fourth incarnation, and has three physical planets, namely Mars, the Earth, and Mercury. The life wave in its fourth round has left Mars and will pass to Mercury after its period of activity upon the earth is finished.

(4) *Jupiter Scheme.* This is in the second round of its third incarnation, and Jupiter is the only physical planet.

(3) *Saturn Scheme.* This also has only one physical planet, Saturn, and is in an early round of its third incarnation.

(6) *Uranus Scheme.* Uranus is the only physical planet, and the chain is fairly well advanced, being probably in the fifth incarnation.

(7) *Neptune Scheme.* This scheme is in the same stage of evolution as the earth scheme, being in its fourth incarnation. There are

therefore three physical planets, namely Neptune and two other planets, not yet discovered by astronomers, whose orbits lie beyond.

In addition to the astrological details of each planet given under its own heading, the following practical notes will be found of service.

THE SUN, *in the outer world*, signifies the King, Emperor, President or chieftain, as the head of the nation ; princes, the nobility, all dignitaries and important personages in city or county, and representatives of the King or the nation, such as Viceroys ; anyone who is exalted in position, superiors in general, down to the employer and the husband as head of the household. It represents these not as private persons but only in respect of their relative position or rank. It signifies the places in which such persons carry on their characteristic activities, such as palaces, official residences, large or grand edifices, perhaps theatres ; bankers, minters, money ; gold and goldsmiths, diamonds, the colour orange. In some lists ruby, carbuncle, and other stones are included ; also pewterers, braziers, coppersmiths ; but these are doubtful, or are only to be taken as representative of ornament, luxury, and display in general. It governs sunlight and all vital and other forces that proceed from the Sun and flow through the solar system, enabling life and all activities to be carried on.

In consciousness, it signifies power, the sense of dignity, authority, grandeur, pride, ostentation, ambition, ardour, generosity, will, and it vitalises desire as well as wisdom.

In body, it rules the heart and circulation, arteries, eyes, spinal cord, and the vital force.

THE MOON, *in the outer world*, signifies mothers and women generally, female occupations and those who follow them, such as maidservants, nurses, midwives ; in the State, the Queen and women of title, also the common people ; water and liquids in general, and persons who follow occupations connected with these, sailors, fishermen, brewers, publicans, ships, harbours, places and houses near water, travellers, vehicles, baths, food ; colours violet and silvery white ; metal silver, moonstone, opals, and milk-white stones.

In consciousness, it signifies sensation, instincts, impulses ; feelings belonging to home and domestic life ; ideas that are not abstract but are applied to concrete purposes and practical ends ; cautiousness, economy, receptivity, imagination, impressionability, changeableness, some kinds of psychic faculty and mediumship.

In body, it signifies in a general sense the substance of the body as distinguished from the vitality flowing through it ; the stomach and digestion, bladder, breasts, womb, child-bearing, the female functions, the nervous system in part, especially the cerebellum, the base of the brain, and lower ganglia ; the eyes ; the etheric double of the body.

MERCURY, *in the outer world*, signifies schools, colleges, and all places where teaching and learning go on, scientific and literary institutions, printing-works, publishing offices, and all who are occupied at these places ; writers, editors, authors, speakers, teachers, professors, men of science, thinkers, lawyers, booksellers, books, post-offices, messengers. It has some general significance in connection with merchants of all sorts, in so far as they require to exercise skill and intelligence ; also in connection with servants, employees, skilled workers and artificers. Colour yellow, metal quicksilver, topaz.

In consciousness, it signifies thought, understanding, reason, intelligence, intellect ; the abstract kinds of these rather than the concrete, knowledge for its own sake apart from any practical application or from any question of right or wrong ; cunning, craft, subtlety ; speech and memory. Its highest application seems to be what is called " pure reason."

In body, it governs the brain and nervous system, the tongue and organs of speech, hands as instruments of intelligence.

VENUS, *in the outer world*, signifies all beautiful objects and anything that is prized for its beauty, ornaments, things of luxury and pleasure, jewels, toys, fine clothes, articles of adornment, pictures, flowers ; dancing, singing, acting, in so far as these express beauty or pleasure apart from skill or intelligence ; all persons who follow occupations dealing with these ; all places where these things belong, and where such occupations are carried on ; sweethearts, wives, the home and household as embodying affection ; sapphire, copper, colour indigo.

In consciousness, it signifies the emotions and affections, especially love and those arising out of love ; the æsthetic sense, appreciation of beauty, elegance, good taste, comfort, and pleasure.

In body, it governs throat, kidneys, and to some extent the generative system. It has an indirect influence upon features, complexion, hair, etc., but only in so far as those express beauty.

MARS, *in the outer world*, signifies soldiers, surgeons, chemists, butchers, barbers, carpenters, blacksmiths, gunners, engineers, machinists ; iron, steel, cutlery, weapons of war, sharp tools, fires, slaughter houses, mortuaries, brick and lime kilns ; colour red, ruby, bloodstone, and red jewels ; athletics and sports in so far as they express courage, enterprise strength and dexterity.

In consciousness, it signifies courage, bravery, enterprise, positiveness, self-reliance, dignity, desire, passion, impulse, combativeness, anger.

In body, it governs the head externally, the nose and smell, the generative system in part, the gall bladder, fevers, high temperature, infectious disease, eruptions, burns, scalds, surgical operations, bloodshed, sharp pains.

JUPITER, *in the outer world*, signifies occupations, persons, and places associated with religion and law, churches, chapels, priests, ministers, judges, magistrates, courts of justice, universities, students, public functions and assemblies of a state or official character : it has some rule over charitable and philanthropic movements and institutions, hospitals, health resorts, physicians, social gatherings, theatres, clothes, clothiers, grocers ; metal, tin, colours blue and purple, jewels turquoise and amethyst.

In consciousness, it signifies a combination of feeling and thought, giving benevolence, good nature, sociability, hopefulness, love of beauty, order, harmony, devotion. It also governs those things in the outer world that express these qualities ; health as physical harmony, law as social harmony, religion as spiritual harmony ; and not as channels of intellect or means of making money.

In body, it governs feet, thighs, liver, blood, muscles, growth, and to some extent digestion.

SATURN, *in the outer world*, signifies the ultimate uncombined atomic condition of matters ; also the state of matter called " earth," and those whose occupations are concerned with it, agriculturists, builders, brickmakers, miners, potters, gardeners, sextons, plumbers, dyers, chimney-sweepers, shepherds, hostlers ; ascetics of every description, whether religious or not, monks, hermits, misers, and those who fast or starve ; policemen, scavengers, workers employed by municipalities or the State ; and such places as mountainous, hilly, or open country, especially rocky and uncultivated, caves, ruins ;

also it is said corpses, graves, and churchyards ; metal lead, colour green.

In consciousness, it signifies, the concrete mind tending to separation, isolation, and the emphasis of the personality ; the sense of " self " is strong ; emotion is held in check by thought and will. The will is stronger than with any other planet except Uranus, and perhaps Mars at times ; but where Mars is passional and impulsive, Saturn is slow, cold, and deliberate. There are self-control, patience, steadfastness, reserve, gravity, austerity, chastity, prudence, thoughtfulness, and much practical ability.

In body, it governs bones, teeth, the spleen ; diseases produced by cold, rheumatism, falls, accidents, melancholia.

URANUS, *in the outer world*, governs those who have power and authority over others, whether on a large or small scale, from King, Parliament and Prime Minister downwards ; the chief, the ruler, the wielder of authority ; inventors, discoverers, pioneers, antiquarians, electricians, railways ; occulists, mesmerists, physical researchers, and new and uncommon occupations. Metal perhaps uranium and radium ; colour uncertain, possibly a blue or violet with an admixture of orange.

In consciousness, it governs Will, in the highest sense of deliberate, free, and conscious choice and action ; love of freedom, independence, the sense of power and authority, positiveness, self-reliance, dislike of control, originality. It gives these qualities equally to thought, feelings and action, so that persons born under this planet break new ground, suggest new ideas, depart from established customs, are often careless of conventional morality, and start new occupations. It is the freedom or newness that belongs to Uranus, rather than the actual ideas, discoveries, or occupations. Its highest application seems to be the perfected Adept, the Manu.

In body, its rule is not known for certain, but it seems to have some influence over the brain and nervous system ; possibly the ears and hearing, and the teeth.

NEPTUNE, *in the outer world*, signifies democratic and popular movements, mobs, the common people ; mystics, dreamers, visionaries, psychics, mediums ; perhaps hospitals and charities.

In consciousness, it relates to feeling, desire, emotion, imagination, æsthetics, psychic faculty, and intuition.

In body, its rulership is not known, but its general influence resembles that of the Moon in some respects, and may relate to similar parts of the body.

PLATIC.   Wide.   An aspect that is not exact, but is within orbs.

POLARITIES.   The soli-lunar combinations formed by blending the influences of the Sun and Moon in the various signs.   The Sun is the positive, primary, and life-giving element, and the Moon the negative or secondary and formative element.   So that when the nature of the sign is thoroughly understood, it can easily be seen on the one hand, how far the life side, represented by the Sun, influences the *character* ; and on the other, how far the form side, represented by the Moon, affects the *personality* ;   the blending of these two being the Polarity.

POLAR ELEVATION.   This term, often abbreviated into simply " pole," has caused much confusion.   At the Equator, the Pole Star will lie exactly on the horizon.   As we ascend northwards towards the Pole, it can easily be seen that the Pole Star will rise above the horizon and ascend higher and higher in the heavens.   Consequently the height of the pole above the horizon, as viewed from any place, if measured in degrees will be equal to the geographical latitude of that place.   It is this polar elevation that is usually meant when the " pole of the ascendant " is spoken of.   The " pole " of the XII, II, XI, and III houses is a certain fraction of the geographical latitude.   So that to say, for instance, that the pole of the twelfth or second house in the latitude of London (51°30′N.) is 40°51′, means really that *the degree on the cusp of the twelfth house* at London is the same as that *on the ascendant* in a place having latitude 40°51′N. WHEN *the R.A.M.C. is* 30° *less*—or, if the second house is concerned, 30° *more*—and it can therefore be calculated in the same way.

POLE.   See POLAR ELEVATION.

POLE OF THE ASCENDANT or HOROSCOPE.   The geographical latitude of the place for which the figure is cast.   See POLAR ELEVATION.

PONDERABLE or PONDEROUS PLANETS.   These are Neptune, Uranus, Saturn, Jupiter, and Mars, and are so called because they move more slowly than the rest.

POSITED.   Situated in any place.

PRECESSION OF THE EQUINOXES.   This term, which is often abbreviated to *Precession*, refers to the gradual advance of the equinoctial point, or vernal equinox, namely the first degree of Aries, due to the pole of the equator revolving round the pole of the ecliptic. Its effect is to cause the signs of the zodiac to pass backwards through the constellations at the rate of about 50¼″ per annum.

The Twelve Constellations form the zodiac of the whole solar system, the horoscope in which its fate from beginning to end is written. And just as the rotation of the earth makes the signs rise and set, a new sign being on the ascendant every two hours, on an average ; so, as the result of precession, the far greater circle of the constellations passes, across the earth's ascendant, the equinoctial point, the beginning of the zodiac. In this way the great day of precession, comprising over 25,000 of our years, comes to correspond with one of our days, because during that period all the twelve constellations rise and set once.

At present the constellation Pisces is on the ascendant of the earth's horoscope, and it has been there for many centuries past, the vernal equinox having entered that constellation soon after the dawn of the Christian era. The effect it has had upon the world in general and upon western civilization in particular has been only too evident. The twelfth house and constellation correspond to the sign Pisces. This is the house of imprisonment, bondage, grief, loss and treachery ; and since the world came under the influence of this constellation, these evils have been manifest enough in history. Its record has been one of darkness, ignorance and bigotry ; for the formalism and external ritual of the priest has taken the place that should be occupied by the spiritual illumination of the prophet.

PREDICTIVE ASTROLOGY. The branch of Astrology that deals with "Directions," or the methods by which future influences are ascertained. The consideration of this branch opens up the whole question of Fate *versus* Freewill, and it at once determines the difference between the "exoteric" and the "esoteric" astrologer. The former is a confirmed fatalist, who believes himself for ever under the bane of Destiny, with his whole life mapped out before him—a life over which he himself has no control whatever. For him there is no re-embodiment of the soul, no continuity of existence, no real meaning of purpose in life. A cruel or a kind fate, as the case may be, has forced him into existence, and has imposed upon him his present environment, and until he is released therefrom by the same capricious power he must abide by its decree ; nor can he alter the terms of his bond by one iota.

The " esoteric " astrologer has no such creed. His faith is based upon the belief that *as a man sows, so he must reap* ; his motto is " MAN KNOW THYSELF " ; and he knows that man may become master of his destiny, being himself in essence inseparable from the Divine Ruler of that universe in which he is manifesting. It is from this latter stand-point that all " directions " should be made, and all its rules be based upon the idea that " THE STARS CONDITION, THEY DO NOT COMPEL."

PRENATAL EPOCH. A point of time, occurring about nine months before birth, known to the ancient astrologers as the moment of conception, but actually not coinciding with conception. The Moon and the Ascendant occupy a definite relation to each other during the successive months of gestation up to the time of birth, so that the Moon's place or its opposition on the day of the Epoch becomes either the Ascendant or Descendant at birth.

This relation was originally known as the " Trutine of Hermes," and a general outline of its use in correcting the birth-time will be found under the heading RECTIFICATION.

PRIMARY DIRECTIONS. By motion of the *Primum Mobile (q.v.)* planets are gradually carried round the earth, past the cusps of the houses and are in turn brought into various mundane aspects (*q.v.*) one with another. The calculation of these aspects and their times of formation, is termed " directing," and the number of degrees and minutes of right ascension (*q.v.*) passing over the meridian between the moment of birth and that when the aspect is complete is termed the Arc of Direction, each *degree* being equivalent to one year of the native's life. (For more detailed information see Section D of *The Progressed Horoscope*.) See also DIRECTIONS.

PRIME VERTICAL. A great circle passing through the zenith and nadir of any place, and also through the east and west points.

PRIMUM MOBILE. The first mover, the 10th sphere of the ancients. It was supposed to be beyond the sphere of the fixed stars, which was their 9th sphere, and by a motion of its own to whirl itself and all the subordinate spheres round the Earth once every 24 hours.

PRINCIPAL PLACES. The five places in which the luminaries are said to have the most beneficial effects in a nativity, namely the hyle-giacal places or the first, eleventh, tenth, ninth, and seventh houses.

PROFECTIONS. Equal and regular progressions of the Sun and other significators in the Zodiac, allowing to each profection the whole circle and one sign over ; as, if the Sun in the first year be in 30 degrees of Aries, the next year it will be in 30 degrees of Taurus ; and so on. Briefly we proceed as follows : Number the years from birth to the one for which the profectional directions are desired to be taken, and for every year add one sign to each of the signs containing the Hyleg, the Sun, the Moon, the Ascendant, and the Meridian at birth. The lord of the sign so deduced from the place of the Hyleg is the chronocrator for that year. Note that the computation is made from the degree of the sign holding the Hyleg, therefore the term may include portions of two signs. Thus if it be required to find the annual chronocrator for the twenty-seventh year, the Hyleg at birth being in 2°♎13', we see that from 2° ♎13' to 2°♏13' would be the ruling period for the first year, and from 2°♏13' to 2°♐13' that for the ensuing year, so that for the twenty-seventh year a progression through the various signs of the zodiac would have been completed twice before arrival was made again at the point required, *viz.*, 2°♐13' to 2°♑13', the lords of which signs are the actual chronocrators for the year.

Having determined this point, the monthly profection may be acquired therefrom in this manner : Allow twenty-eight days for the month, and for every month after natal month add one sign, counting from the sign of the year. To the days may be also apportioned their rulers, if desired, by allowing a sign for every two days and eight hours after birth, still keeping to the month of twenty-eight days, and counting from the day of the month on which the birth occurred.

Judgment is arrived at by a judicious combination of the several elements as they stand. The annual sign and its rulers will exhibit the general influence for the year, and the monthly places the equivalent monthly influences. Notice, however, is to be paid to the representation of these places in the radix, both as regards sign and planet and their position by this progressed motion in regard to the ascendant, M.C., etc. ; also what planets, if any, are at the time of profection passing by transit through such signs ruling the year or month.

That these profections have a value seems pretty evident, and Raphael has somewhere said that he is inclined to discredit the usual forms of directing in favour of them, believing that everything runs in cycles. There is no doubt an element of truth in this, but all we can say in the present state of our knowledge is that their principal use would appear to be in supplying media for primaries and secondaries to function in.

PROGRESSED HOROSCOPE.   A horoscope erected for as many days after birth as the native is years of age, and from which directions are calculated. See DIRECTIONS.

PROHIBITION.   A Horary term similar to *Frustration* (*q.v.*).   It indicates the state of two planets that are significators of some event, or the bringing of some business to an issue or conclusion, and are applying to each other by conjunction ; but before such conjunction can be formed, a third planet, by means of a swifter motion, interposes his body and destroys the expected conjunction by forming an aspect himself ; and this indicates that the matter under contemplation will be greatly retarded, or utterly prevented.

PROMITTOR.   That which promises to fulfil some event.   Thus Saturn and Mars are anarctic promittors and promise to destroy the life of the Native when the Hyleg is directed to them.   Jupiter and Venus are promittors of good, when directions to them are fulfilled. In Horary questions the planet signifying the event is the promittor ; thus, in a question of marriage, the lord of the seventh house is the promittor.

QUADRANTS.   The four quarters of heaven.   In the circle of the twelve houses the two oriental quadrants are from the first house cusp to the tenth, and from the seventh to the fourth ; and the two occidental are the opposite, namely, from the fourth to the first, and from the tenth to the seventh.   In the zodiac the oriental quarters are from the beginning of Aries to the beginning of Cancer, and from the beginning of Libra to the beginning of Capricorn.   The opposite are the Occidental Quadrants.

QUADRATE.   The Square aspect (□) of 90°.

QUADRATURE.   See under LUNATION.

QUADRUPEDAL.   The *four-footed signs*, ♈, ♉, ♌, ♐, and ♑, all of which represent quadrupeds.   Those born when they ascend were said by the ancient astrologers to have the qualities of such animals, as being bold as the lion, lustful as the goat, etc.

QUADRUPLICITY or QUALITY.   These terms are very important because they give a direct clue to the meaning of the horoscope as a whole and so form a basis for synthesis ; they have stood the test of

many years' practical work and are to be relied upon. Originally the
word quality was used, because they are only an adaptation of the
Hindu gunas ; Rajas, the active movable quality ; Tamas, the fixed,
stable quality ; and Sattva, the balancing, harmonising, rhythmical
quality. More recently, the word Quadruplicity has been used, as it
bears an obvious analogy with Triplicity. Each Triplicity contains
three signs arranged in accordance with the so-called elements or states
of matter ; three airy, ♒, ♊, ♎ ; three fiery, ♌, ♐, ♈ ; three watery,
♏, ♓, ♋ ; and three earthy, ♉, ♍, ♑ ; and they divide the circle
into four parts, the cross in the circle. Each Quadruplicity contains
four signs arranged in accordance with the gunas or modes of motion
in matter ; four Cardinal, active, movable, or rajasic, ♈, ♋, ♎, ♑ ;
four fixed, unchanging, or tamasic, ♉, ♌, ♏, ♒ ; and four rhythmical,
mutable, or Sattvic, ♊, ♍, ♐, ♓, intermediate in nature between the
other two. They divide the circle into three parts, the triangle in the
circle.

The Cardinal signs govern the head as a centre of consciousness in
the same manner as the angles. They divide the circle of the zodiac
into four quarters, answering to the four quadrants of the horoscope.
Their chief characteristic is activity, which shows out in any depart-
ment of life to which it may be directed, physical, emotional or intellectual. In each of these directions they are signs of external contact,
bringing the native into continual touch with the outer world, and
vice versa, directing constant impacts from the environment upon the
native. They bring the greatest amount of outward experience ;
they are the most diffuse and the least concentrated. In a way their
influence may be regarded as continually passing from angle to angle
or from cardinal point to cardinal point, across the four fields of their
unceasing motion.

The Fixed signs are associated with the heart and desire. They
contain the same amount of motion as the former signs, but tend to
gather it into a fixed centre, and so make less outward show. Inertia
and stability characterise them. They bring experiences evolving out
of themselves, repetitions of the same conditions taking place over and
over again until turned outward by the movable signs or modified and
harmonised by the common.

The mutable or common signs are associated in the animal body
with limbs, lungs, and bowels. Just as vibratory motion passes from

one point to another and back again, linking together the two extremes of its motion, so these signs stand for everything whether in the body or in consciousness that is intermediate between the head or intellect and the heart or will. They correspond to cadent houses, which stand for means of communication, servants, agents, journeys, and for other matters in which the idea of an influence uniting two extremes can be plainly discerned. They are dual in nature and fluctuating in character as are the men that are born of them.

These three qualities, operating through three groups of signs, correspond to the three phases of man's own being : will in motion, or action ; feeling, emotion, passion, intuition, or instinct ; and thought or reason.

QUARTILE. The Square aspect (□) of 90°.

QUERENT. In Horary astrology the querent is he or she who enquires or asks the question, and desires the result of any event. The querent is always represented by the first house and its lord.

QUESITED. In Horary astrology the quesited is the person or thing enquired about.

QUINCUNX. An aspect of 5 signs or 150°, its symbol being ⚹, considered as an inconjunct position by Ptolemy, or one that had no influence. The quincunx is variable and of the nature of Mercury. It is humane and selective, and is disturbing only when in aspect with Saturn or Uranus ; but being an indifferent aspect, it partakes more closely of the nature of the aspected planet than is usually the case. It assimilates two contrary influences, such as earth and fire, or air and water, and such elements do not readily combine. The influences of the planets in aspect are modified considerably by the quincunx, or even partly neutralised, so as to produce an attitude of mind similar to that known as " sitting on the fence," an indecisive non-committal frame of mind which tends to hold things in abeyance or to put them off to a more fitting occasion.

QUINTILE. A weak aspect of 72° of a mildly benefic nature.

RADICAL. 1. Pertaining to the radix, or horoscope of birth.

2. A term used in Horary astrology to indicate that a figure is fit to be judged, and likely to give a correct answer.

Radix. Root. The horoscope of birth.

RAHU. The Sanskrit name for the *Dragon's Head* (*q.v.*) or the Moon's North node. (See NODE.)

In Hindu mythology Rahu is a *Daitya* (demon) whose lower parts were like a dragon's tail. He made himself immortal by robbing the gods of some *Amrita*—the elixir of divine life—for which they were churning the ocean of milk. Unable to deprive him of his immortality, Vishnu exiled him from the earth and made of him the constellation Draco, his head being called Rahu and his tail Ketu—astronomically, the ascending and descending nodes. With the latter appendage he has ever since waged a destructive war on the denouncers of his robbery, the sun and the moon, and (during the eclipses) is said to swallow them. Of course the fable has a mystic and occult meaning.

RAPT MOTION (Lat. *raptus*, carried away). The apparent diurnal motion of the Heavens, occasioned by the real diurnal motion of the earth. It was called rapt, or forcibly carried away, because the stars were supposed to be forcibly carried round by the motion of the *Primum Mobile* (*q.v.*). See PARALLELS.

RAYS. In the common acceptation of the word, a ray is a beam of light emanating from a star or luminous body; but, in astrology it signifies a beam of influence or sympathy, which accompanies such ray, and is supposed only to proceed from a *planet*. Thus, the doctrine that the fixed stars emit no rays does not mean that they emit no light, but that a fixed star has no distinct influence by aspect, but only operates with a planet when joined to it, *i.e.*, within from 5° to 2° of its body, according to the magnitude of the fixed stars.

RECEPTION. When two planets are each in the house of the other, as for example Jupiter in Leo, and the Sun in Sagittarius, they are said to be in mutual reception, and this gives strength and good fortune and lessens the seriousness of any bad aspect between them. Some would extend this to include reception by exaltation, as with the Sun in Libra and Saturn in Aries; and others would attach a similar importance to planets aspecting one another from their own houses, as Mars in Aries square Moon in Cancer, which may give much strength, although of a martial and impulsive kind. A planet in house or exaltation shows that its characteristics are strong and well developed in the person.

RECTIFICATION. The method of bringing a nativity to its true time, since it is supposed that the inaccuracy of a clock or watch, or the mistake of those whose business it is to observe them, may cause an error in the time of birth, which requires to be rectified. The

M

term is also often applied to the determination of a quite unknown birth-time from events that have transpired in the native's life, day and place of birth only being stated. There are two chief methods of rectification : (1) by important events that have occurred during the life, and (2) by the relation of the Moon to the Horizon at birth. These methods will now be outlined.

1. *Rectification by Events*.   This depends on the motion of the heavens after birth, whereby the places of the planets are carried toward the " angles " of the figure, or towards aspects thereof, or towards aspects of the places of other planets.

Since *some* such aspect can be calculated for every year and nearly every month of life, and since in certain cases it is a matter of very delicate astrological judgment to fit the given event to the precise aspect indicative thereof, the student is recommended to restrict his investigation entirely to *transit of the angles*, and to avoid aspects in this connection altogether.

The student will have learned in his study of directions that the R.A.M.C. is 1° or 4m. more each day at the same hour, which is termed the " diurnal acceleration of the meridian." If, therefore, a planet be within 1° of culmination at the actual moment of birth, that particular point of the zodiac will be just culminating at the exact hour and minute of birth on the following day.   Now it is found that the events of life are in harmony with the movements of the planets after birth, each *day* foreshadowing the events of the corresponding *year* of life.   In the case supposed the influence exerted by the planet would thus culminate about a year after birth, after which its power would gradually wane. The house or houses ruled by the planet at or about the time of birth should be considered, and, since the M.C. is significant of either the father, or the external environment in general, as opposed to the purely *domestic* environment, it should not be difficult to see whether or not the given event corresponds with the transit of the planet in question.

In practice, the method may be worked thus : Turn to the Table of Houses and find therein the approximate degree culminating, *i.e.*, in the cusp of the tenth house at the estimated time of birth. Run the eye down the table and see if during the life of the native—taking 1° of the M.C. for each year of life—the degree occupied at birth by any planet has arrived at the M.C., descendant, I.C., or ascendant. If not, it will be advisable to abandon this method of rectification entirely ; but if, on the contrary, this has happened, a very little perspicacity will generally enable one to see if the given event coincides in nature with what might be expected in consideration of (1) *the nature of the planet,* and (2) *the house ruled by it.*

This method, indeed, may be often employed with success when the birth-time of the native is entirely unknown.   Equipped with a photograph and a few of the leading events of life, the careful investigator may with a little trouble ascertain the approximate moment of birth in this way, and it can then be confirmed and rectified by the method now to be described.

It should be remembered that the influence of a planet (and its corresponding house) when coming to the

Ascendant   -   *commences,* and thenceonward increases

Midheaven   -   *culminates,* and thenceonward decreases

Descendant -   *is broken,* and thenceonward wanes

Nadir   -   -   *disappears,* or " dies "

A little questioning of the native, where possible, often elucidates something of considerable interest not thought of at the time of setting down events on paper, and is invariably of great assistance when trying to determine a doubtful ascendant.

2. *Rectification by the Relation of the Moon to the Horizon.* This method has been used from very early times and is generally known as the " Trutine of Hermes."

The account here given is adapted from an article in *The Astrologers Magazine* for 1794.   The author quotes Sir Christopher Heydon.

" The rule of Hermes teaches, by the Moon's place in the nativity, to come to the true time of conception[1] ; for her place in the nativity was the true ascendant in the generation ; and her place at the conception, or the opposite, is the true ascendant, or the opposite, of the nativity ; which being (as I can speak of my own experience in divers genitures, besides the confirmation of the learned ever since Hermes' time) found true, is alone sufficient to strike all those barkers against Astrology dumb.   I know that some say they have sometimes failed in the practice of this rule, but then they neither [*sic*] consider the true rule, taking the degree of her true motion in the Zodiac for her place, when, as in truth, her place considered with latitude, is truly understood in the rule,

---

[1] *Note.*—There would seem to be some doubt as to whether this epoch is necessarily identical with conception proper.

and the degree co-ascending therewith." The last part of this paragraph should be noted by all who wish to make any deep study of this subject.

It may be added that the figure for " conception " obtained in this way is by many thought to be the horoscope of the Astral Body and environment in the same way that the nativity is of the Physical Body and environment.

We will limit ourselves here to a general outline of the process which will be sufficiently exact for all but exceptional cases.

First it is necessary to find the day of " conception " or as we will call it the Epoch, since it may not be coincident with conception in a physiological sense.

GENERAL RULE.

1. The *Horizon, i.e.,* the Ascendant or Descendant, at birth is the Moon's Place at Epoch, and the *Moon's Place* at birth is the Horizon at Epoch.

Distance of ☽ from Horizon. Ascendant if below earth. Descendant if above.	☽ increasing and below *or* decreasing and above.	☽ decreasing and below *or* increasing and above.
Degrees.	*Days.*	*Days.*
0	273 + 0	273 — 15
12	1	14
24	2	13
36	3	12
48	4	11
60	5	10
72	6	9
84	7	8
96	8	7
108	9	6
120	10	5
132	11	4
144	12	3
156	13	2
168	14	1
180	15	0

2. When the Moon at birth is *increasing in light, i.e.*, passing from ☌ ☉ to ☍ ☉, consider the *Ascendant*, and make the Moon's Place at Birth *rise* at the Epoch. Conversely, when *decreasing* consider the *Descendant* (cusp of seventh house), and make the Moon's Place at Birth *set* at Epoch.

The number of days between epoch and birth is given in the accompanying table. The " degrees " are strictly speaking the number of degrees of *Oblique Ascension* intervening between the Moon and the horizon to which by the rotation of the earth it is next proceeding, *i.e.*, the ascendant if below the earth and the descendant if above ; but they may be taken for practical purposes as *degrees of the Zodiac*. Thus if for example the Sun is in ♋ 5° and the Moon is in ♐ 16° and the ascendant is ♌ 16°, look under 120° and in the column headed " ☽ increasing and below," and the answer will be 273 + 10, *i.e.*, 283 days ; ☽'s place Asc. at epoch.

The day having been thus determined, it will be found that the Moon was then in the sign ascending at birth, or descending as the case may be, and near the exact degree ; or if not, such day will be very near and must be taken instead.

To find the *exact degree* occupied by the Moon at epoch, turn to the Tables of Houses and note the sidereal time when the Moon's place at birth or the opposite point ascends ; find the difference between this amount and the S.T. at noon on day of epoch, and the result determines the time a.m. or p.m. of the moment of epoch, for which the Moon's place can be calculated in the ordinary way. This degree when found is then the ascendant or descendant of the nativity.

The above may be taken as a concise statement of the general law governing the large majority of cases, but there are certain exceptional births, such as seven months' children, etc., where this general rule will not apply. Should the reader find that the rectification necessary appears excessive in any particular case, he will do well to consider it one of the exceptions spoken of and revert to method (1).

We will conclude with an example, showing the method of working.

ILLUSTRATION.

Male, born in London, 7/8/'60, 5.50 to 6.10 a.m. What was the true time of birth?

At the estimated time of birth, say 6.10 a.m. we find (1) the ascendant ♍ 1°13′, (2) longitude of ☽ ♈ 15°31′, the latter (3) *decreasing* in light and (4) *above* horizon, (5) the estimate R.A.M.C. being 3h. 15m.

  Now since ♍1°13′ ascends, ♓ 1°13′ will be on the cusp of the seventh house, and therefore the ☽ will be *above* the earth and proceeding, by the earth's rotation (which is the factor concerned, and not the ☽'s motion in the zodiac), to the descendant or western horizon. The distance from this latter, ♓ 1°13′ to ♈15°31′, is about 44°, and we therefore look in the table under 48°, the nearest thereto, and in column marked ☽ decreasing and above. This shows the period to be 273 days (or ten lunar months) *plus* 4, *i.e.*, 277 days, which must be counted backwards from the date of birth, August 7th, 1860, bringing us to November 4th, 1859.

  A simple and ready method of finding the date, without the tedium of counting days, is to turn back to early portion of given year, or to previous year, when the Sun was in square to its radical place, *i.e.*, 90° farther on in the Zodiac : within two or three days of this date the ☽ will be found in the same sign and degree as at birth. Consider the latter date as 273 days before birth, and count + days *backward* and — days *forward* from this date to find the day of epoch. For instance in this case ☉ at birth is in ♌ 15°, and is in ♏15° on November 8th, 1859, the ☽ being in ♈15°, its radical place, on the same day ; counting then four days back brings us to November 4th, the day of epoch required.

  To find the exact degree of ☽ at epoch, and hence of descendant at birth, we proceed thus :

	h.	m.	s.
R.A.M.C. noon 41/1/′59 - - - -	14	52	49
R.A.M.C. ♎ 15°31′ rising at London - -	7	28	5
Time before noon, in sidereal h.m.s. - -	7	24	44
Less correction to mean time - - -		1	14
Time before noon, in mean h.m.s. - -	7	23	30
I.e., G.M.T. of Epoch, a.m., 4/11/′59 -	4	36	30
☽'s place noon 4/11/′59 - - - -	♓	1°	14′
,, ,, ,, 3/11/′59 - - - -	♋	19	25
☽'s motion in 24 hours - - - -		11	49

P. log. 11°49′	-	-	-	-	-	3077
P. log. 7h. 23m. 30s.	-	-	-	-		5115
P. log. ☽'s motion in 7h. 23m. 30s.	-	-				8192

$$=3°38′$$

		°	′
☽'s place, noon, 4/11/'59 -	-	-	-	♓ 1 14
Less ☽'s motion in 7h. 23m. 30s.	-	-	3 38
☽'s place at epoch		♒ 27 36

This gives us the descendant at birth, and as the opposite point is consequently rising, the true time of birth can now be found.

	h.	m.	s.
R.A.M.C. noon, 7/8/'60 - - - -	9	4	55
R.A.M.C., — 27°36′ rising at London- -	2	55	27
Time before noon, in sidereal h.m.s. - -	6	9	28
Less correction to mean time - - -		1	2
Mean time before noon - - - -	6	8	26
I.e., G.M.T. of Birth, a.m. - - -	5	51	34

We thus find that birth occurred at eight and a half minutes to six in the morning.

Other illustrations in abundance will be found scattered through the pages of *Modern Astrology*, Old Series, especially in volumes XI, XII, XIII, and XIV.

N.B.—When the Moon is found *very near* the horizon at birth, its declination and latitude need to be considered, as it may be that it has really passed below the horizon while the ecliptic degree occupied is as yet above ; and *vice versa.*

REFRANATION. When two planets are applying to an aspect, but before the aspect can be completed one of them turns retrograde, which in practice is found to be fatal to the success of the question.

It is a term used in Horary astrology.

RETROGRADE. The *apparent* motion of a planet backwards in the Zodiac, due to the motion of the earth in its orbit. The Sun and Moon are never retrograde, but all the others are at various times. This was once considered a sign of weakness and misfortune, but it is doubtful whether there is any truth in the idea. Astrologers are much divided about it. The retrograde conjunctive of Venus and Mercury with the Sun seem to be very strong, but whether they carry with them any significance of bad luck it is not easy to determine ; it has not been proved that they do.

RETROGRADE APPLICATION. When both planets are retrograde and more contrary to the order of the signs of the zodiac, but apply to the aspect or conjunction of each other.

REVOLUTION (*Solar Revolution* ; *Solar Return* ; *Birthday Map*). A map drawn for the time when the Sun returns to the exact degree, minute and second of longitude that it held at birth. It illustrates in a general manner the fate and fortune for the coming year of life. An alternative method used by some is to find out the hour and minute when the R.A. of the M.C. is the same as it was at birth on that day when the Sun is nearest to the longitude it held at birth (which will generally be the birthday or within a day of it), and then to calculate a map for this time ; the cusps of the houses of such a map will be the same as at birth. The first method is equivalent to using the Sun's position as the exact time-measurer for the birthday anniversary ; the second method is equivalent to maintaining that the Sun's position only indicates the day, and that the hour and minute are determined by the return of the cusp of the ascendant to the position it occupied at birth. Whichever method is adopted—and often there is not much difference between them—the planetary positions must be considered in their bearing upon the horoscope of birth, especially benefic and malefic transits. The birthday information given in the almanacs is practically useless because it is not related to the birth map. The whole subject deserves more careful examination than it has yet received, and the question of the progressed birthday at the rate of a day for a year needs investigation.

RIGHT ASCENSION (abbreviated *R.A.*). The arc of the equator reckoned from the beginning of Aries and ending at that point which rises with any planet or part of the ecliptic in a right sphere. In other words, the distance of a planet from the first point of Aries measured along the equator.

RIGHT DESCENSION. The arc of the equator which descends with any star or point of the ecliptic. It is really an unmeaning term, for the whole is *Right Ascension* from the first point of Aries, again including the whole circle of 360°.

RISING SIGN. The sign of the zodiac occupying the eastern horizon Ascendant, or cusp of the first house at the moment for which a horoscope is cast. The effect of each sign upon personal appearance, character, and fortune is as follows :—

♈ ARIES.—Middle stature or rather above it ; spare body ; long face and neck ; head broad at temples, narrow at chin ; bushy eyebrows ; sharp sight ; eyes grey to greyish-brown ; rough or wiry hair, dark to sandy ; sandy whiskers ; ruddy complexion ; sometimes going bald at temples. Motive temperament. *Characteristics* :— courage, energy, impulse, ambition, pride, combativeness, activity, ardour. *Fortune* :—the native is well able to stand alone, decide for himself, carve out his own way in life. His luck, good or bad, will be largely of his own bringing about ; for he is enterprising, adventurous, and pioneering.

♉ TAURUS.—Stature middle to short, inclining to plumpness ; square face and square build of body; short, strong neck; forehead, nose, lips, cheeks, and mouth all full ; heavy jaw ; dark eyes and hair, the latter sometimes curling ; often stoops ; round and prominent eyes; hands plump, short, and broad. *Characteristics* :—constant, persevering, conservative, obstinate ; sociable, affectionate ; when provoked, unreasonable, prejudiced, jealous ; good practical ability ; sometimes slow and indolent ; bad temper when aroused. *Fortune* :—suited for a life of practical work in the world, business, farming, management of property, managership, politics, etc.

♊ GEMINI.—Tall, slender, erect figure ; long face, nose, and chin ; arms and fingers long ; dark hair ; pale or sanguine complexion ; hazel eyes ; quick and active walk. Mental temperament. *Characteristics* :—quick at learning ; fond of reading and writing ; can receive a good education ; inclination for music, drawing, dancing, languages ; manual dexterity ; good disposition, Sometimes shy and retiring. *Fortune* :—Gemini corresponds to the third house, and any or all matters governed by that house may become active in the life, being sources of profit or loss, according to aspect.

♋ CANCER. Average height ; round face ; full cheeks ; sometimes double chin ; grey or light blue eyes ; pale complexion ; vital or vitalmotive temperament ; tendency to stoutness ; sometimes a heavy or awkward gait ; short nose, sometimes prominent at tip. *Characteristics* :—changeable ; fond of novelty and travelling ; sympathetic, and attached to relatives and the home life ; careful with money ; desirous of possessions ; prudent. *Fortune* :—benefits through parents (generally mother) and the home, also through house or land property ; some suitability for public life. Psychic or occult tendencies are sometimes shown.

♌ Leo.—Tall ; large bones and muscles ; broad shoulders ; hair light and sometimes thin ; head full and round ; grey eyes ; florid complexion ; upright walk ; square build of body in middle age. Motive-vital temperament. *Characteristics* :—self-confident, ambitious, proud, fond of power and distinction, generous, candid, honourable, warm-hearted, impulsive, faithful. *Fortune* :—largely depends upon position of Sun. Benefit through positions of responsibility and distinction ; through social life ; through art, drama, amusements, children ; through appointments, superiors.

♍ Virgo.—Height, average or over ; face and forehead round ; dark hair, eyes, and complexion ; moderately plump ; well formed ; mental-motive temperament. *Characteristics* :—good mental abilities, ingenious, active, mind, apt at learning, sympathetic, quiet, retiring, methodical, critical. *Fortune* :—are most fortunate when content to work with others, as servant, partner, or associate in some way, and not independently. Inclination to medicine and drugs. Adaptability to many occupations, either business or professional.

♎ Libra.—Tall, well-formed body, slender in youth, but tending to stoutness in middle age ; hair smooth, brown to black ; eyes blue or brown ; round face ; good complexion ; features regular, often good-looking. Mental-vital temperament. *Characteristics* :—cheerful, genial, fond of company and amusements ; good-natured, humane ; affectionate, but changeable. Good mental abilities, but tending more in the direction of art, music, poetry, painting, etc., than learning or scholarship ; good powers of perception and observation. *Fortune* :— the native's career is greatly influenced by other people, through friendship, companionship, association, partnership. Marriage is probable.

♏ Scorpio.—Average height ; hair, thick and dark, sometimes curling or waving ; prominent brows ; aquiline or Jewish type of nose and profile ; often square type of face and build of body ; tendency to stoutness. Motive-vital temperament. *Characteristics* :—self-reliance courage, energy, endurance, determination, obstinacy, strong likes and dislikes, dignity, critical turn of mind. Angry and revengeful when provoked. *Fortune* :—good, practical executive ability, working out through the position of Mars, or through the rising planet, if any. There is adaptability for medicine, surgery, chemistry, or as soldier, sailor, engineer, worker in metals, brewer, butcher, or for practical scientific research, Inclination for mysticism or occultism. Money by legacy or partnership. Very often a death occurs in the family or environment shortly before birth or in early life.

♐ SAGITTARIUS.—Tall, slender, well-formed ; hair brown or chestnut ; eyes blue or hazel ; oval face ; fresh complexion ; inclining to baldness near temples ; often stooping. Motive-mental temperament. *Characteristics* :—generous, good-hearted, cheerful, charitable, impulsive, active, enterprising, humane, just, truthful, candid. *Fortune* :—inclination to travelling, voyaging, out-door sports and exercises ; sometimes to religion, philosophy, law, learning, and to association with people and pursuits concerned with these things.

♑ CAPRICORN.—Stature average to short ; sometimes bony and thin ; long or prominent nose ; profile hatchet-faced ; thin neck, long chin ; dark hair, usually not plentiful ; thin beard. Motive or motive-mental temperament. *Characteristics* :—self-possessed and self-controlled, patient, persistent, persevering, steady, just, economical, reserved, subtle ; disposition serious, cold, sometimes despondent. *Fortune* :—suited for public life, public appointments, business, politics ; generally possess practical business ability and tact, sometimes much ambition, love of power or wealth and ability to gain it. Inheritance from parents probable. More fortunate in middle or old age than in youth.

♒ AQUARIUS.—Middle stature, strong, well-formed ; square build ; tendency to stoutness ; good complexion ; sometimes good-looking ; face longish and fleshy ; hair generally dark but sometimes light. *Characteristics* :—good intellectual and practical abilities ; good disposition ; patient and self-controlled, quiet, humane, constant and persevering ; fixed opinions, not easily altered ; ingenious, original, intuitive, fond of knowledge, artistic. Sometimes inclined to occult matters. Good judge of human nature. *Fortune* :—suited for public work, responsible positions, appointments, posts held under local authorities or superiors. Benefit through marriage, friendship, acquaintances, popularity, social position. In some cases a parent dies early.

♓ PISCES.—Stature middle to short ; fleshy person and face ; pale complexion ; full eyes ; tendency to double chin ; small and short limbs ; hair plentiful, dark ; vital temperament. *Characteristics* :— easy-going, good-natured, indolent, uncertain, changeful, emotional, charitable, affectionate ; sometimes diffident and reserved or secretive. *Fortune* :—benefit through religious or philanthropic and humanitarian movements ; domesticated and home-loving ; inclined to alms-giving, works of charity, religion, nursing, helping the poor or sick, and may themselves benefit in these ways in some cases. Taste for music, romantic and imaginative work, novel writing. Good and faithful servants under superiors.

RUMINANT SIGNS. Signs that ruminate, or chew the cud ; Aries, Taurus, and Capricorn. It is well not to give medicine during the Moon's transit through these signs.

SAGITTARIUS. The ninth sign of the zodiac. A mutable sign, and the third of the fiery triplicity. Its position on the ecliptic is from 240° to 270°. It is a hot, dry, and positive sign. The Sun appears to enter the sign about the 22nd of November each year.

SATELLITIUM. A group of planets together in one sign or house.

SATURN. The next planet beyond Jupiter. He is 872 million miles from the Sun and takes nearly thirty years to perform one revolution in his orbit. The length of his day is over ten hours ; he is surrounded by three rings, and has ten Moons. Saturn was the son of Uranus, and was known as Chronos. His symbol is the half-circle under the cross.

The nature and influence of this planet is cold and binding, exactly opposite to that of the fiery Mars. Saturn governs the sense of hearing, a negative or receptive sense. The listener suggests patience, forbearing, silence and caution. The planetary vibration of Saturn restricts limits, crystallises and binds everything; holding, restraining, fashion-, ing and solidifying all that comes under its sphere of influence. · Saturn is, figuratively speaking, the *urn* that holds the *Sat*. This Sanskrit word *Sat* signifies " that one ever-present reality in the infinite world ; the divine essence which *is*, but cannot be said to exist." In this sense Saturn governs the encircling limit of the consciousness, the " ring pass not " for each individual in manifestation. Saturn, as ruler of the personal ego, is the planet of fate, for it represents the personal will, the lower brain-mind, and is practically the ego in manifestation in the physical world, and also the next world to it, which is concerned with the state of the consciousness immediately after death. The highest states signified by the vibrations of Saturn in the physical world are physical purity and justice, which produce the virtues of chastity, economy, thrift, industry, perseverance, prudence, veneration, and love of truth. When the vibrations of Saturn are perverted through the personality, miserliness, meanness, envy, covetousness, and extreme selfishness result. See PLANETS.

SCORPIO. The eighth sign of the zodiac. A fixed sign, and the second of the watery triplicity. Its position on the ecliptic is from 210° to 240°. It is a cold, moist, and negative sign. The Sun appears to enter this sign about the 22nd of October each year.

SECONDARY DIRECTIONS. The directions formed by the motion of the planets on successive days after birth, each day being reckoned as a year, by which new aspects are formed by the planets and luminaries to their birth positions, and also among themselves. See DIRECTIONS.

SEMI-ARC. Half a diurnal or nocturnal arc. Half the arc measured in degrees and minutes of Right Ascension, passing over the meridian during the time a planet (supposed to remain fixed in the zodiac) remains above the horizon from the time of its rising until that of its setting, is called its semi-diurnal arc, or semi-arc diurnal. The half of the arc it would, in like circumstances, form under the Earth from its setting until its rising, is called its semi-arc nocturnal. Thus, the Sun's semi-arc, either diurnal or nocturnal, when in ♈0° or ♎0°, is *six hours* or 90°, all over the globe ; at other seasons one is greater or less than the other, according to the time of the year and the latitude of the place, the greatest discrepancy occurring where the latitude, either N. or S., is high and when the Sun is in ♋0° or ♑0°.

The semi-nocturnal arc is the difference between the semi-diurnal arc and 180° ; and the semi-diurnal arc of any degree is the seminocturnal arc of the opposite degree.

SEMI-DECILE. A very weak aspect of 18°, believed to be slightly good.

SEMI-SEXTILE. A weakly benefic aspect of 30°, and of the nature of Mars, which, however, is often more important than it seems ; for it brings two neighbouring signs into active relation. Semi-sextile aspects are worthy of especial notice in some nativities, because they are natural but contrasting, and bring into action two forces which may be somewhat contrary in nature, such as fire and earth, or earth and air, or air and water ; and yet include the positive and negative influences. Symbol ⋎.

SEMI-SQUARE. A weak malefic aspect of 45°. Symbol ∠.

SEPARATION. When an aspect is past, the planets are said to be separating from that aspect. Observe, that in a nativity the influence of any aspect to the significators is *more* powerful if it be a few (4 or 5) degrees past, than if it be not yet formed, but in Horary Astrology it is *less* so, showing that the influence is passing away, since application is the sign whereby events are denoted to take place, separation denoting what has already passed or taken place, whether good or evil.

SESQUIQUADRATE. A malefic aspect of 135° similar and of equal strength to the semi-square. Symbol ⬚.

SEVEN PRINCIPLES OF MAN. See INDIVIDUALITY AND PERSONALITY.

SEXTILE. A benefic aspect of 60° of the nature of the Moon and Neptune. The sextile aspect is more combining in its nature than any other, in the sense that the influences of the planets forming the aspect are mutually blended. As a vibratory aspect it is more or less colour- less and depends chiefly upon the planets and signs between which it occurs. It is often more potent and favourable than the trine, as it seems to blend two influences of a more or less like nature such as fire and air, or earth and water. In this respect the trine may be said to denote negative goodness, while the sextile is *positively* good ; or, in other words, there is more activity and change shown by the sextile than by the trine. The trine may be likened to the reward of the past, while the sextile contains the potentiality of the future. Symbol ✶.

SIDEREAL TIME. The Sidereal Time at any moment is the angular distance expressed in hours, minutes, and seconds of the First Point of Aries or Vernal Equinox from the meridian at any place. It is the same thing as the Right Ascension of the Meridian (R.A.M.C.), which is merely the same angular distance expressed in *degrees and minutes*. The Sidereal time is that shown by an astronomical clock which indi- cates twenty-four hours in 23h. 56m. 4·0906s. of ordinary clock or " mean solar " time. The S.T. at Noon is always shown in the Ephe- meris. It increases by about four minutes per day, and counts straight on from 0h. 0m. 0s. to 24h. 0m. 0s., in which respect it differs from ordinary clock time which is distinguished by *a.m.* or *p.m.*

SIGNIFICATOR. The planet or luminary representing a person or event. Thus the lord of the ascendant is the native's significator and the lord of the seventh is the significator of his partner, the lord of the second of his wealth, of the eighth, of his partner's wealth, and so on. The term is also applied to the five " moderators," namely, the Sun, the Moon, the Ascendant, the Midheaven, and the Part of Fortune.

SIGNS OF LONG ASCENSION. These are, in the Northern Hemisphere, ♌, ♍, ♎, ♏, ♐, ♑, so called because they take longer time in ascending than others. See SIGNS OF SHORT ASCENSION.

SIGNS OF SHORT ASCENSION. In the Northern hemisphere these are (♑), ♒, ♓, ♈, ♉, ♊. For places in the Southern Hemisphere these terms " long " and " short " must be reversed.

SIGNS OF THE ZODIAC. The twelve equal divisions into which the ecliptic is divided. They are Aries ♈, Taurus ♉, Gemini ♊, Cancer ♋, Leo ♌, Virgo ♍, Libra ♎, Scorpio ♏, Sagittarius ♐, Capricorn ♑, Aquarius ♒, and Pisces ♓. For further particulars see under these headings.

SIGNS OF VOICE. These are ♊, ♍, ♎, ♒, and the first part of ♐, because, it is said, if any of them ascend, and Mercury be strong, the native will be a good orator.

SINISTER AND DEXTER. Aspects cast to the left and right respectively according to the order of the signs. Thus a slow planet in Aries will cast a sinister sextile to a more rapid planet in Gemini, while the latter casts a dexter aspect to the former. Similarly, the Moon's first quarter is a sinister, her last a dexter aspect.

SLOW OF COURSE. A planet moving slower than its mean motion. In Horary astrology it is considered a great debility.

SOUTHERN SIGNS. The signs ♎, ♏, ♐, ♑, ♒, and ♓, so called because they are to the south of the equator. See NORTHERN SIGNS.

SPECULUM. A table appended to a horoscope giving a variety of particulars necessary both for deciding the exact mundane aspects and positions of the heavenly bodies in the houses and for computing primary directions. Different practitioners adopt different forms of speculum, giving more or less detail, but it is necessary in all cases to include Latitude, Declination, Right Ascension, Meridian Distance, and Semi-arc.

SQUARE. A strong malefic aspect of 90° of the nature of Saturn.

The Square is the most critical and conflicting of aspects. It never fails to give an attitude which is disturbed, prejudiced or adverse to the conditions or circumstances accompanying it. It is also, like Saturn, a *separative* aspect, usually affecting the moral tone of the nativity. It is known as the angle of pain and sorrow, bringing remorse and a perturbed state of mind and feeling with worry, anxiety and despondency. Illnesses produced by the square aspect are often slow and lingering, but when acute they are never so quickly over as the opposition. Every condition or event arising out of this aspect is critical and turns the tide of fortune one way or another definitely with more or less permanent results. Symbol ⧠.

STANDARD TIME. Time based upon a certain definite meridian that is adopted by law or usage as the time meridian for a more or less wide extent of country, in place of the various meridians upon which local mean time is based. Its advantage is, that neighbouring places then keep exactly the same time instead of differing by a few minutes or seconds according to their differences of longitude, a matter of especial importance in connection with the operation of railroads and telegraphs or the transaction of any business wherein contracts involve any definite time limits.

In the selection of standard time meridians it is of course desirable not to have them so far apart, as to cause any very marked variation from true local mean time at any point, and the plan usually adopted is to have them exactly one hour of time, or 15 degrees of longitude, apart. It is also desirable, for the sake of international convenience and harmony, to base them upon the prime meridian that is in most common use throughout the world, namely that of Greenwich, England.

STAR OF THE INDIVIDUALITY. The six-pointed star formed by the triangles of the fiery and airy signs.

STAR OF THE PERSONALITY. The six-pointed star formed by the triangles of the earthy and watery signs.

STATIONARY. When a planet is in its *station* and appears to stand still. The Sun and Moon are never stationary. See RETROGRADE.

STATIONS. Those parts in the orbit of a planet where it becomes either retrograde or direct, so-called because it remains for a while there stationary before it changes its course (see RETROGRADE). The first station is where it becomes retrograde ; the second station is after it has passed its perigee and where from retrogradation it becomes direct.

STRONG SIGNS. The signs Leo, Scorpio, and Aquarius because they are said to give strong athletic bodies.

SUCCEDENT. The houses that follow or succeed the angles. These houses are next in power to the angles, and are the second, fifth, eighth, and eleventh. They correspond to the Fixed signs.

SUN. The central body of our solar system, round which all the planets revolve. The Sun, we are taught by those who are seeking the Path of Wisdom, is the body of *God*, the *Logos* of the solar system, through which He gives His Love, Light, and Life. In astrologic study the Sun gives to every living organism its *Prāna*, or life and heat, and stands in each nativity as the symbol of vitality and activity, mind and intellect, love and feeling. In one word it represents the centre of each separate individual character as the sun total of himself, by absorbing into himself as much of the influence of the solar rays and the planetary vibrations as possible during his previous physical mani- festations. The permanent and vital conditions of each life are denoted by the Sun. See PLANETS.

SUPERIOR PLANETS. Those whose orbits lie outside that of the earth, namely Mars, Jupiter, Saturn, Uranus, and Neptune.

SWIFT IN MOTION. When a planet is faster than its mean motion. It is reckoned a fortunate testimony in Horary astrology.

SYMBOLS. All astrological symbols are formed by the various combinations of three primary symbols, namely the Circle, the Semi- circle, and the Cross.

The *Circle* denotes Spirit, life, consciousness and expansion, and has been the universal symbol for the Supreme Intelligence in all ages and among all nations.

The *Semicircle* represents the Soul in man, that which is neither wholly spiritual nor wholly material, but partakes of the nature of both and is the connecting link between the spirit and the physical body.

The *Cross* divides the circle into the four primary quarters of East, West, North, and South, and represents all definiteness of form or limitation, such as the Body in man, birth, life periods of varying lengths, death or change of form and the moulding of forms that are coming into manifestation.

According to the arrangement of these symbols, the nature of the planets' influence is revealed. Thus if the Circle is under the Cross, spirit is represented as limited by matter, the Cross being the symbol

N

of restriction and bondage in matter ; while if the circle is over the Cross, spirit is represented as practically free from the denseness and limitation of matter—not wholly free, but comparatively disentangled.

⊙ THE SUN is the symbol of the essence of Life, the circle alone.

☽ THE MOON is the semi-circle alone, symbolising Soul, instinct, and vaporous, volatile and constantly changing matter.

☿ MERCURY, semi-circle over circle over cross, represents the complete union of the three symbols in one, denoting perfectibility.

♀ VENUS is the symbol of Spirit triumphant over matter, circle over cross. It represents beauty, grace, refinement, and all that expresses the *human* state.

♂ MARS, really the cross over the circle, ♂, is the symbol of spirit constrained by matter. It represents strength, force, physical energy and the animal in man—the animal-man state.

♃ JUPITER, the semicircle rising over the cross, is the symbol of soul liberating itself from matter. It represents mercy, expansion, and sympathy.

♄ SATURN, the cross over the semicircle, is the symbol of the soul bound by the form ; it represents justice, restraint, and definiteness.

♅ URANUS symbolises the unity of the three symbols on a higher grade than Mercury, of which it is the higher octave. It represents will, or the control and abnegation of desire.

♆ NEPTUNE symbolises diversity, or the Many as against the One. It represents submission to authority, divine or otherwise.

SYNODICAL LUNATION. This is the return of the progressed Moon, after birth, to the same distance from the progressed Sun as that which, at birth, the radical Moon was from the radical Sun. This takes place once every 29½ days or thereabouts. Each such lunation or month is considered to measure to one year of life, and a map of the heavens for the moment of the exact return of the Moon to this position, when compared with the horoscope of birth, is treated as symbolical of the influences prevailing in the life at that time.

SYNTHESIS. The art of blending together the separate influences in a nativity, and of giving a summary of the main features of the character. The ability to synthesise a nativity is the crown of the student's knowledge on natal astrology for it leads, by the intuition required to do this effectually, to those abstract methods of pure synthesis which will finally reveal the true purpose of every horoscope.

Students should practise the art of synthesis by giving a short synthesis at the end of every delineation on the following lines :

NAPOLEON. Elements :—
$$\begin{cases} \text{Fire} & 2 \\ \text{Earth} & 4 \\ \text{Air} & — \\ \text{Water} & 3 \end{cases} \begin{matrix} \text{Cardinal} & 3 \\ \text{Fixed} & 4 \\ \text{Common} & 2 \end{matrix}$$

Fixed—Earth

Planets well placed and distributed.

Main features :—Libra rises, second decanate. Venus ruling planet in Cancer, near the M.C., placed in the ninth house ; ♀ ⚹ ♆ ⚹ ♅ ⚹ △ ♃, seven planets above the earth. Jupiter rising next in Scorpio.

Personality :—Tenacious, yet amiable and very perceptive, great magnetic attraction, quietly critical, a keen judge of human nature, and an abnormal ambition.

Summary of horoscope :—Determined and persistent. Love of power, excellent organising ability, some genius ♂ △ ♅, combined with practical and consistent methods.

SYZYGY. The New and Full Moon : also the conjunction or opposition of any two planets. It is often loosely used as a common term for familiarities or aspects of every description.

TABLES OF HOUSES. Tables showing the signs and degrees of the zodiac upon the cusps of the mundane houses for every degree of Right Ascension, or for every four minutes (approximately) of Sidereal Time. These Tables vary with the latitude of the place for which the horoscope is erected, but do not appreciably change over a period of many years. Sets of Tables for latitudes from 0° to 60° are published by Raphael, and a *Table of Ascendants* for all places from 0° to 70° of north or south latitude, which may be used as a Table of Houses for all places within that limit, forms part of *Casting the Horoscope*, to be obtained from " Modern Astrology " Office, price 15s. net.

TAURUS. The second sign of the zodiac. A fixed sign, and the first of the earthy triplicity. Its position on the ecliptic is from 30° to 60°. It is a cold, dry, and negative sign. The Sun appears to enter this sign about the 20th of April each year.

The *constellation* Taurus is a most mysterious constellation of the zodiac, one connected with all the " first-born " solar gods. Taurus is under the asterisk A, which is its figure in the Hebrew Alphabet, that of Aleph ; and therefore that constellation is called the " one," the " First," after the said letter.   Hence, the " first-born," to all of whom it was made sacred.   The *Bull* is the symbol of force and pro-creative power—the Logos.   Hence, also, the horns on the head of Isis, the female aspect of Osiris and Horus.   Ancient mystics saw the ansated cross, in the horns of Taurus (the upper portion of the Hebrew Aleph) pushing away the Dragon, and Christians connected the sign and constellation with Christ.   St. Augustine calls it " the great City of God," and the Egyptians called it the "interpreter of the divine voice," the *Apis-Pacis* of Hermothis.—See ZODIAC.

TERMINUS VITAE.   The end of life ; the fatal direction or direc-tions that cause death.

TERMS.   These are certain degrees in a sign, supposed to possess the power of altering the nature of a planet to that of the planet in the term of which it is posited.   These " terms " are largely disregarded by modern students, who seem to consider them fanciful inventions to account for effects now ascribed to the influence of formerly unknown planets.   But it is probable that the ancient traditions from which they are derived are based on a higher knowledge than we now possess, and students will do well at least to make themselves familiar with the various " terms," " faces," etc.

The terms of the planets are as follows :—

TERMS.

Sign.					
♈	♃6	♀14	☿21	♂26	♄30
♉	♀8	☿15	♃22	♄26	♂ 30
♊	☿7	♃14	♀21	♄25	♂30
♋	♂6	♃13	☿20	♀27	♄30
♌	♄6	☿13	♀19	♃25	♂30
♍	☿7	♀13	♃18	♄24	♂30
♎	♄6	♀11	♃19	☿24	♂30
♏	♂6	♃14	♀21	☿27	♄30
♐	♃8	♀14	☿19	♄25	♂30
♑	♀6	☿12	♃19	♂25	♄30
♒	♄6	☿12	♀20	♃25	♂30
♓	♀8	♃14	☿20	♂26	♄30

Interpret thus ; ♃ rules 1°♈ to 6°♈, ♀ 7°♈ to 14°♈, ☿ 15°♈ to 21°♈, and so on.

TESTIMONY.   Having aspect or dignity, etc. ; or being in any way in operation in the figure as regards the question asked.

TRANSIT.   (1) When a planet passes over the zodiacal degree occupying any influential point of a horoscope such as the M.C., ascendant, Sun's place, etc., it is said to transit that point by " ephemeral motion."   (2) When by progressed motion at the rate of a day for a year, the planet comes to any such place it is said to transit the M.C., Asc., etc., by " directional motion."   Thus, in the horoscope of King George V, whereas the ☽ will transit the M.C. by " ephemeral motion " once in every month, by " directional motion " this will occur once in every twenty-eight years only, the first such transit occurring in the seventh year of life.

TRANSLATION OF LIGHT.   The conveying of the influence of one planet to another by means of a third planet which separates from the first and applies to the second.   Thus, suppose Saturn to be in 20°♈, Jupiter in 13°♈, and Mars in 14°♈.   Here Mars separates from a conjunction with Jupiter, and translates the light and the nature of that planet to Saturn, to whom he next applies.   It is considered a very powerful testimony in Horary astrology and denotes that the matter of the question will be perfected by the assistance of a third person, who is described by the translating planet.

TRIGON.   See TRIPLICITY.

TRIGONOCRATORS.   Rulers of trigons.   The Sun and Jupiter rule the fiery ; Venus and the Moon the earthy ; Saturn and Mercury the Airy ; and Mars alone the watery, though modern astrologers have united Venus and the Moon with him, the former by day and the latter by night.

TRIGONOMETRICAL FORMULÆ.   The following formulæ are all that are necessary in astrological practice, either for the computation of primary directions or for the construction of Tables of Houses.

Note.—The first formulæ are used in the case of the ☉, or of any heavenly body without latitude, or of the degree on the cusp of the M.C., or of any degree in the ecliptic taken without latitude.

FORMULA I.

To convert Longitude into Right Ascension, without Latitude.

+Log. *cosine* of obliquity of ecliptic (23°27′)

+Log. *tangent* long. from ♈ or ♎   (or log. *cotangent* long. from ♋ or ♑)

= Log. *tangent* R.A. from ♈ or ♎   (or log. *cotangent* R.A. from ♋ or ♑).

    If in ♈, ♉ or ♊, the answer will be the R.A. required. If in ♋, ♌ or ♍, add to 90°. If in ♎, ♏ or ♐, add to 180°. If in ♑, ♒ or ♓ add to 270°.

FORMULA II.

To convert Right Ascension into Longitude, without Latitude.

Log. *cosine* of obliquity of ecliptic (23°27′)

+Log. *cotangent* R.A. from ♈ or ♎.   (or log. *tangent* R.A. from ♋ or ♑)

= Log. *cotangent* long. from ♈ or ♎ (or log. *tangent* long. from ♋ or ♉).

    R.A. of 0° ♈ = 0°; of 0° ♋ = 90°; of 0° ♎ = 180°; of 0°♑ = 270°.

FORMULA III.

Longitude being given, to find Declination, without Latitude.

Log. *sine* of obliquity of ecliptic (23°27′).

+Log. *sine* longitude from ♈ or ♎ (or log. *cosine* from ♋ or ♑)

= Log. *sine* declination.

FORMULA IV.

To find Ascensional Difference.

Log. *tangent* declination

+Log. *tangent* latitude of birthplace

= Log. *sine* ascensional difference.

FORMULA V.

To find Oblique Ascension.

With N. declination, R.A.Ascensional – Difference = ˙Obl. Asc.**

With S. declination, R.A.+Ascensional Difference = Obl. Asc.**

To find the oblique ascension of the cusp of a house :—

R.A. of M.C.+ 30°= oblique ascension of cusp of 11th.

,,	,, + 60°=	,,	,,	,, ,, ,, 12th.
,,	,, + 90°=	,,	,,	,, ,, ,, 1st.
,,	,, +120°=	,,	,,	,, ,, ,, 2nd.
,,	,, +150°=	,,	,,	,, ,, ,, 3rd.

FORMULA VI.

To find semi-Arc.

For diurnal** semi-arc with N.declination,90°+Ascensional Difference.

,,	,,	,,	,, S.	,,	90°–	,,	,,
For nocturnal**	,,	,, N.	,,	90°–	,,	,,
,,	,,	,,	,, S.	,,	90°+	,,	,,

Either semi-arc substracted from 180° will give the other semi-arc.

FORMULA VII.

Oblique Ascension being given, to find the degree of longitude on the cusp of any house.

PART 1. Log. *cosine* oblique ascension from ♈ or ♎ (or log. *sine* oblique ascension from ♋ or ♑)

+Log. *cotangent* pole of the house

=Log. *cotangent* first angle.   Call this *A*.

The pole of the ascendant is the latitude of the birthplace. The Midheaven has no pole. The poles of the other houses are given at end of book, and by formula VII (*a*).

** This is, of course, for places in the northern latitudes. For places in the southern latitudes these rules must be reversed ; also in northern latitude above 66°33′.

PART 2.   If oblique ascension be less than 90° or more than 270°, A
+ obliquity of ecliptic (23°27') = B.**

If oblique ascension be more than 90° and less than 270°, the
difference between 23°27' and A = B.**

PART 3.   Log. *cosine* B (arithmetical complement)
+Log. *cosine* A

+Log. *tangent* oblique ascension from ♈ or ♎ (or log.
cotangent oblique ascension from ♋ or ♑)

=Log. *tangent* longitude from ♈ or ♎ (or log. *cotangent*
longitude from ♋ or ♑).

NOTE.—If B. exceed 90°, take log. *sine* (arithm. complement) of its
excess.   The longitude will fall the reverse way from the point from
which the oblique ascension is taken.

When the R.A. or M.C. is exactly 0° (or 360°) or 180° :—Log. *sine*
obliquity of ecliptic + log. *tangent* latitude of birthplace = log. *cotangent* ascending degree from nearest equinox.

FORMULA VII. (a)[1]

To find the Pole of any House.

(i)   Log. *tangent* of obliquity of ecliptic (23°27')
+Log. *tangent* latitude of birthplace
=Log. *sine* X.   Take ⅓ X, ⅔ S.

(ii)   Log. *sine* ⅓ X.
+Log. *cotangent* obliquity of ecliptic (23°27')
=Log. *tangent* Pole of Eleventh and Third Houses (which
have each the same Pole).

(iii)   Log. *sine* ⅔ X
+Log. *cotangent* obliquity of ecliptic (23°27')
=Log. *tangent* Pole of Twelfth and Second House (which
have each the same Pole).

**This is, of course, for places in the northern latitudes.   For places in the
southern latitudes these rules must be reversed ;   also in northern latitudes above
66°33'.

[1] This is the usual formula, based upon the point of extreme declination
23°27', and by it have been calculated the Poles or "polar elevation of House
Cusp" given at foot of the Table of Ascendants.   Mr. J. G. Dalton of Boston
has recommended the use of a point of about 18¼° declination, and has published
a table of poles so calculated.   The difference is quite trifling, except in very high
latitudes.

FORMULA VIII.

R.A. and Declination being given, to find Longitude and Latitude.

PART 1.   Log. *sine* R.A. from ♈ or ♎ (or log. *cosine* R.A. from ♋ or ♑)

    +Log. *cotangent* declination

    =Log. *tangent* angle A.

PART 2.   R.A. and declination same name (if R.A. is less than 180°, call it *North* : if more, call it *South*), A + obliquity of ecliptic (23°27′) = B.

    But if R.A., and declination be of different names, the difference between A and 23°27′ = B.

PART 3.   For Longitude :—

    Log. *sine* A (*arithm. complement*)

    +Log. *sine* B

    +Log. *tangent* R.A. from ♈ or ♎ (or log. *cotangent* R.A. from ♋ or ♑)

    =Log. *tangent* longitude from ♈ or ♎ (or log. *cotangent* longitude from ♋ or ♑).

PART 4.   For Latitude :—

    Log. *cosine* A (*arithm. complement*)

    +Log. *cosine* B

    +Log. *sine* declination

    =Log. *sine* latitude.

NOTE.—If B exceed 90°, use the *cosine* of its excess in Part 3 and its *sine* in Part 4. The latitude will then be of contrary name to the declination.

FORMULA IX.

Longitude, Latitude, and Declination being given, to find R.A.

    Log. *cosine* declination (arithmetical complement)

    +Log. *cosine* latitude

    +Log. *cosine* long. from ♈ or ♎ (or *sine* longitude from ♋ or ♑)

    =Log. *cosine* R.A. from ♈ or ♎ (or *sine* longitude from ♋ or ♑).

TRINE. A strong benefic aspect of 120°, of the nature of Venus. It blends the influence of the planets in aspect harmoniously. If formed between Saturn and Mars, the extremes and contrasts of these planets are modified and made to act more after the nature of Venus than either Mars or Saturn. It harmonises the bodies, or vehicles, represented by the signs occupied by the planets.

Through watery signs it influences the astral or emotional body, and through fiery signs the mental body. In this respect it is a fortunate aspect, for it establishes harmony between the influences without and the attitude of mind within, so that its nature is without friction, antagonism, or harshness, and is peaceful, forgiving, and charitable. This aspect does much to improve an otherwise adverse nativity. When occurring between the luminaries it is more fortunate than any favourable aspects to the benefics alone, especially if one of the benefic planets joins in the triangle. See SEXTILE.

TRIPLICITY. The zodiac is divided into four groups of signs, each termed a Triplicity or trigon. They are the Fiery Triplicity, consisting of the signs Aries, Leo, and Sagittarius ; the Earthy Triplicity, of Taurus, Virgo, and Capricorn ; the Airy Triplicity, of Gemini, Libra, and Aquarius ; and the Watery Triplicity, of Cancer, Scorpio, and Pisces.

The four triplicities govern the four Hindu castes. They are also the indicators of the force, active and energetic, represented by the fiery signs ; the quality of solidity and stability denoted by the earthy signs ; powers of extension and expansion indicated by the airy signs : and finally the plasticity and mobility shown by the watery signs.

In themselves the triplicities are perfect triangles, but are never broken up or separated like the qualities.

The fiery, watery, earthy, and airy triplicities are always harmonious in themselves, but are not harmonious when opposed to triplicities of a diverse character such as the fiery and watery, or the fiery and earthy triplicities ; water quenching fire, and earth smothering it. The triplicities effect everyone, more or less, according to the preponderance of planets in them ; and when blended with the quadruplicities, form the final synthesis of every nativity. For all practical purposes, the earthy signs represent the physical body ; the watery signs the astral, or body of feeling ; the fiery the mental body or body of mind and intellect ; the airy signs the body of pure reason, the higher and most refined part of human nature.

THE FIERY TRIPLICITY is the symbol of SEPARATENESS. Air commingles with and interpenetrates all substances ; fire burns and disintegrates, allowing the finer particles to escape and mingle with the air : thus fire is a separator, and air a unifier. The airy triplicity symbolises the higher mind and the fiery triplicity the lover.

The EARTHY TRIPLICITY is the symbol of the DENSE body of man ; it represents the concretions, excretions, and the residue of the other planes. It is the plane of action, conservation of energy, and con-centrated forces.

The AIRY TRIPLICITY is the symbol of UNITY. It is the unifying triad, and when this trinity is operating in unison with a favourable quality, true harmony is the result ; but when the planets are all located in one of the airy signs and not well distributed, there is danger of stagnation or " peace at any price," and a submission to that which should be striven against and overcome.

The WATERY TRIPLICITY is the symbol of the PSYCHIC MAN. It is the fluidic, impermanent and changeable triad, in which sensations, feelings and emotions are ever coming and going like the waves on the ocean. It represents the lower, mortal and perishable man, and as such its centre is the fixed-water sign Scorpio. See also QUADRU-PLICITY.

TROPICAL SIGNS. These are Cancer and Capricorn, and are so-called because they limit the course of the Sun, which, after arriving at their first points, seems to turn, thenceforward diminishing in declination ; defining midsummer by the turn he makes in Cancer, and mid-winter by that which he makes in Capricorn.

TRUTINE OF HERMES. See RECTIFICATION.

UNDER THE SUNBEAMS. A term applied to a planet when less than 17° from the Sun. In Horary astrology it is reckoned an evil testimony, though not quite so serious a one as Combustion and indica-tive of fear, trouble and oppression. See COMBUST and CAZIMI.

UNFORTUNATE SIGNS. The even and negative signs Taurus, Cancer, Virgo, Scorpio, Capricorn, and Pisces. The natives of these signs, and especially of Capricorn, were said by the ancient astrologers to be unfortunate in the general tendency of the events of their lives.

URANUS. The next planet beyond Saturn, commonly called *Herschel*, after his re-discoverer. His distance from the Sun is about 1,754 million miles ; he revolves round the solar orb once in 84 of our years, and is accompanied by four satellites. The planet URANUS has less influence at the present day than any other planet except Neptune. It is the planet of the coming race, for its vibrations will then be more important than to-day. It is thought by the author to represent the fully individualised Ego, and as such is the houseless wanderer half-way between earth and heaven. Its vibrations are different from those of any other planet, governing all things that are not bound by convention or limited entirely to the form side of things to such an extent as to make the form more important than the life. It appears to govern all things that are original, eccentric, and free to act apart from any conventional groove or accepted custom. It has been found to exercise the greatest influence for good over advanced thinkers —those who act independently, and from within more than from without. It seems to have little or no effect upon those who are bound or limited by opinion or custom, and to come fully under its influence the limitations of Saturn must have been passed and the form side of life conquered more or less. No definite or precise rules can be laid down with regard to Uranus ; the most elaborate plans and calculations may be upset in an instant of time by the vibrations of this planet. Sudden and unexpected events will occur, and act in an almost un-knowable manner, which makes it impossible to judge accurately exactly what will happen under his vibrations. It is now certain that the ancients knew of the planet Uranus, but only those who were as far removed from the ordinary humanity as the poles came under its influence, and that for an occult and esoteric reason that cannot be explained at present.

In the outer world of human activities Uranus appears now to be exercising more sway. Electrical and mechanical enterprises and inventions of all kinds, railways, educational " short cuts," index systems, the comparative study of religions, etc., etc., are all more or less under his direct influence and illustrate his peculiar mission—to cause man to seek by the destruction of a *lesser* form the added life and intelligence dwelling in the higher form of which that lesser form was an integral though separated part ; in short, regeneration as distinguished from generation. See PLANETS.

VENUS. The most distant of the inferior planets from the Sun. Venus is nearly sixty-seven million miles from the centre, and makes one annual revolution in 224 days 17 hours, the length of this planet's day almost coinciding with our own. She is the bright evening star often seen about sunset, though at certain times during the year (when she rises before the Sun) she is the Morning Star. Venus was known to the Greeks as Aphrodite, and to the Latins as Lucifer when the morning star and Vesper when the evening star. Her symbol is a circle surmounting the cross. Venus preserves, nourishes, rebuilds, and all who come fully under the influence of this planet are capable of living purely and appreciating beauty and goodness to the full. She is the planet of creation, ever tending to act through the Soul and not the senses. The love shown by Venus always sanctifies and makes for harmony through conjugality, friendship and soul union. The vibrations of Venus directly affect the higher part of the nature through the human soul and the higher mind. In the physical world Venus presides over the sense of touch, which sense is not related to one special part of the body, but the whole. All the distinctly human and refining qualities come under the influence of Venus, the whole of the tendencies of this planet's vibration being to centralise and draw in from the objective world the experience necessary to awaken the inner and more subjective centres of consciousness. Venus is on the side of Will and the Immortal Trinity, and all vibrations that are assimilated are made permanent soul possessions.

In some mysterious manner a ray from Venus touched the life of the animal on its first separation from the group soul. The " Sons of Mind " who came from the planet Venus gave to infant humanity its first germ of that true mind which is in its essence immortal, and through this the period of man's evolution was considerably shortened, for by receiving this divine spark the seed of the human soul was implanted in the animal man, who would otherwise have spent countless ages in acquiring that which these beneficent beings through their love and compassion gave to humanity. See PLANETS.

VERNAL EQUINOX. See EQUINOXES.

VERTICAL. Directly overhead. See PRIME VERTICAL.

VESPERTINE. The reverse of *Matutine* (*q.v.*), that is when a planet sets in the evening after the Sun. The Moon is vespertine after she has passed her first quarter.

VIA COMBUSTA. The combust way. This is the last 15 degrees of Libra and the first 15 degrees of Scorpio. It was considered by the ancient astrologers to be particularly unfortunate, especially to the Moon who was said to suffer there as much as during an eclipse. According to a few authors the Via Combusta is the last half of Libra and the whole of Capricorn.

VIOLENT SIGNS. The signs Aries, Libra, Scorpio, Capricorn, and Aquarius, which are the houses or exaltations of the malefic planets. Those signs or parts of signs are also called violent in which lie violent fixed stars.

VIRGO. The sixth sign of the zodiac. A mutable sign, and the second of the earthy triplicity. Its position on the ecliptic is from 150° to 180°. It is a cold, dry and negative sign. The Sun appears to enter this sign about the 23rd of August each year.

VOID OF COURSE. Forming no aspect in the sign the planet then is. That is, when a planet passes out of the sign it occupies without encountering the aspect of any planet. It is an important consideration in Horary astrology, and when the Moon is void of course it denotes in general no success in the matter of the question.

WATERY SIGNS. The signs Cancer, Scorpio, and Pisces, which form the watery triplicity.

WHOLE SIGNS. Gemini, Libra, and Aquarius, which were said by the ancient astrologers to cause those born under them to be strong, robust, and not so liable to accidents as the natives of other signs.

YUGA. A 1,000th part of a Kalpa. An age of the world of which there are four, and the series of which proceed in succession during the manvantaric cycle. Each Yuga is preceded by a period called in the *Puranas* Sandhya, twilight, or transition period, and is followed by another period of like duration called Sandhyansa, "portion of twilight." Each is equal to one-tenth of the Yuga. The group of four Yugas is first computed by the *divine* years or "years of the gods"— each such year being equal to 350 years of mortal men. Thus we have in divine years :

1. Krita or Satya Yuga.	-	-	-		4,000	
Sandhya	-	-	-	-	-	400	
Sandhyansa	-	-	-	-	-	400	
					——	4,800
2. Treta Yuga	-	-	-	-	-	3,000	
Sandhya	-	-	-	-	-	300	
Sandhyansa	-	-	-	-	-	300	
					——	3,600
3. Dwapara Yuga -	-	-	-	-	2,000	
Sandhya	-	-	-	-	-	200	
Sandhyansa	-	-	-	-	-	200	
					——	2,400
4. Kali Yuga	-	-	-	-	-	1,000	
Sandhya	-	-	-	-	-	100	
Sandhyansa	-	-	-	-	-	100	
					——	1,200
						12,000

This rendered in years of mortals equals :

4,800 × 360 -	-	-	-	-	1,728,000
3,600 × 360 -	-	-	-	-	1,296,000
2,400 × 360 -	-	-	-	-	864,000
1,200 × 360 -	-	-	-	-	432,000
		Total			4,320,000

The above is called a Mahayuga or Manvantara; 2,000 such Mahayugas, or a period of 8,640,000,000 years, made a kalpa : the latter being only a " day and a night," or twenty-four hours, of Brahma. Thus an " age of Brahma," or one hundred of his *divine* years, must equal 311,040,000,000,000 of our mortal years. The old Mazdeans or Magi (the modern Prasis) had the same calculation, though the Orientalists do not seem to perceive it, for even the Parsi mobeds themselves have forgotten it. But their " Sovereign time of the Long Period " (*Zervan Daregho Hvadata*) lasts 12,000 years, and these are the 12,000 *divine* years of a Mahayuga as shown above, whereas the *Zervan Akarana* (Limitless Time), mentioned by Zarathustra, is the *Kala*, out of space and time, of Parabrahm.

ZENITH. The point directly over the head, through which pass the Prime Vertical (*q.v.*), and Meridian Circles. Every place has its own zenith, and the nearer the planet are to that zenith, the more powerful is their operation. The term is sometimes loosely applied to the cusp of the tenth house, which, strictly speaking, is only the point of the zodiac (ecliptic) through which the meridian circle passes, but no planet can ever be in the *zenith* except in latitudes not exceeding about 25°. Mathematically, the zenith is the pole of the horizon.

ZODIAC (from the word *zodion*, a diminutive of *zoon*, animal). This word is used in a dual meaning ; it may refer to the fixed and intellectual Zodiac, or to the movable and natural Zodiac. " In astronomy," says Science, "it is an imaginary belt in the heavens sixteen or eighteen degrees broad, through the middle of which passes the sun's path (the ecliptic)." It contains the twelve constellations which constitute the twelve signs of the Zodiac, and from which they are named. The fixed and intellectual, or astrological Zodiac proper, however, is an imaginary circle passing round the earth in the plane of the ecliptic, its first point being called Aries, o degrees ; (this is measured from the point where the ecliptic and equatorial circles intersect). It is divided into twelve equal parts called " Signs of the Zodiac," each containing thirty degrees of space, and on it is measured the longitude of celestial bodies.

The movable or natural Zodiac is a succession of *constellations* forming a belt of forty-seven degrees in width, lying north and south of the plane of the ecliptic. These must not be confused with the *signs*. The constellations are groups of fixed stars, the twelve central groups being called by the same names as the twelve signs, although they do not cover the same area of the heavens. The procession of the Equinoxes, caused by the " motion " of the Sun through space, makes the constellations appear to move forward against the order of the signs at the rate of 50⅓ seconds per year. A simple calculation will show that at this rate the constellation Taurus (Heb. *Aleph*) was in the first sign of the zodiac at the beginning of the Kali Yuga, and consequently the Equinoctial point fell therein. At this time, also, Leo was in the summer solstice, Scorpio in the autumnal equinox, and Aquarius in the winter solstice ; and these facts form the astronomical key to half the religious mysteries of the world—the Christian scheme included. The Hindus and some other oriental nations work by these constellations, but the western astrologer always calculates in terms of the signs, and when he speaks of " the zodiac " he always means the ecliptic or Sun's path. In the Tetrabiblos of Claudius Ptolemy, (Ashmand's translation, published 1822, 1896) we read on page 32 : " The beginning of the whole zodiacal circle . . . is . . . the sign Aries which commences at the Vernal Equinox," and the translator goes on to say :—" This shows the futility of the objection raised against Astrology, that the signs have changed and are changing places. It is clear from this sentence that Ptolemy ascribes to the 30 degrees after the vernal equinox, that influence which he has herein mentioned to belong to Aries ; to the next 30 degrees, the influence herein said to belong to Taurus ; and so of the rest of the Zodiac . . . Ptolemy himself seems to have foreseen this groundless objection of the moderns, and has written, in the 25th chapter of this book, what ought completely to have prevented it."

The Zodiac was known in India and Egypt for incalculable ages, and the knowledge of the sages (magi) of these countries, with regard to the occult influence of the stars and heavenly bodies on our earth, was far greater than profane astronomy can ever hope to reach to. If, even now, when most of the secrets of the Asuramayas and the Zoroasters are lost, it is still amply shown that horoscopes and judiciary astrology are far from being based on fiction, and if such men as Kepler and even Sir Isaac Newton believed that stars and constellations influenced the destiny of our globe and its humanities, it requires no great stretch of faith to believe that men who were initiated into all the mysteries of nature, as well as into astronomy and astrology, knew precisely in what way nations and mankind, whole races as well as individuals, would be affected by the so-called " signs of the Zodiac."

ZODIACAL ASPECTS. Aspects measured along the zodiac in degrees of longitude, so called to distinguish them from Mundane Aspects (*q.v.*). The term has also been applied in primary directing to refer to zodiacal directions without latitude.

THE END

O

Complete List of Topics, sorted by page number.

Better books make better astrologers.
Here are some of our other titles:

AstroAmerica's Daily Ephemeris, 2010-2020
AstroAmerica's Daily Ephemeris, 2000-2020
  - both for Midnight. Compiled & formatted by David R. Roell

Al Biruni
The Book of Instructions in the Elements of the Art of Astrology, *1029*
  AD, translated by R. Ramsay Wright

David Anrias
Man and the Zodiac

Derek Appleby
Horary Astrology: The Art of Astrological Divination

E.H. Bailey
The Prenatal Epoch

Joseph Blagrave
Astrological Practice of Physick

C.E.O. Carter
The Astrology of Accidents
An Encyclopaedia of Psychological Astrology
Essays on the Foundations of Astrology
The Principles of Astrology, *Intermediate no. 1*
Some Principles of Horoscopic Delineation, *Intermediate no. 2*
Symbolic Directions in Modern Astrology
The Zodiac and the Soul

Charubel & Sepharial
Degrees of the Zodiac Symbolized, *1898*

H.L. Cornell
Encyclopaedia of Medical Astrology

Nicholas Culpeper
Astrological Judgement of Diseases from the Decumbiture of the Sick,
  1655, and, **Urinalia,** *1658*

Dorotheus of Sidon
Carmen Astrologicum, *c. 50 AD, translated by David Pingree*

Nicholas deVore
Encyclopedia of Astrology

Firmicus Maternus
Ancient Astrology Theory & Practice: Matheseos Libri VIII,
c. 350 AD, translated by Jean Rhys Bram

Margaret Hone
The Modern Text-Book of Astrology

Alan Leo
The Progressed Horoscope, *1905*
The Key to Your Own Nativity, *1910*

William Lilly
Christian Astrology, books 1 & 2, *1647*
   The Introduction to Astrology, Resolution of all manner of questions.
Christian Astrology, book 3, *1647*
   Easie and plaine method teaching how to judge upon nativities.

Jean-Baptiste Morin
The Cabal of the Twelve Houses Astrological
   translated by George Wharton, edited by D.R. Roell

Claudius Ptolemy
Tetrabiblos, *c. 140 AD, translated by J.M. Ashmand*

Vivian Robson
Astrology and Sex
Electional Astrology
Fixed Stars & Constellations in Astrology
A Beginner's Guide to Practical Astrology
A Student's Text-Book of Astrology, Vivian Robson Memorial Edition

Diana Roche
The Sabian Symbols, A Screen of Prophecy

Richard Saunders
The Astrological Judgement and Practice of Physick, *1677*

Sepharial
The Manual of Astrology, the Standard Work
Primary Directions, a definitive study
Sepharial On Money. *For the first time in one volume, complete texts:*
   • **Law of Values**
   • **Silver Key**
   • **Arcana, or Stock and Share Key** — *first time in print!*

James Wilson, Esq.
Dictionary of Astrology

H.S. Green, Raphael & C.E.O. Carter
Mundane Astrology: *3 Books, complete in one volume.*

_____

If not available from your local bookseller, order directly from:
The Astrology Center of America
207 Victory Lane
Bel Air, MD 21014

on the web at:
http://www.astroamerica.com

Lightning Source UK Ltd.
Milton Keynes UK
UKHW01f0806240718
326193UK00005B/149/P

9 781933 303420